ISSUES IN POLITICAL THEORY

Political Theory has undergone a remarkable development in recent years. From a state in which it was once declared dead, it has come to occupy a central place in the study of Politics. Both political ideas and the wide-ranging arguments to which they give rise are now treated in a rigorous, analytical fashion, and political theorists have contributed to disciplines as diverse as economics, sociology and law. These developments have made the subject more challenging and exciting, but they have also added to the difficulties of students and others coming to the subject for the first time. Much of the burgeoning literature in specialist books and journals is readily intelligible only to those who are already well-versed in the subject.

Issues in Political Theory is a series conceived in response to this situation. It consists of a number of detailed and comprehensive studies of issues central to Political Theory which take account of the latest developments in scholarly debate. While making original contributions to the subject, books in the series are written especially for those who are new to Political Theory. Each volume aims to introduce its readers to the intricacies of a fundamental political issue and to help them find their way through the detailed, and often complicated, argument that issue has attracted.

PETER JONES
ALBERT WEALE

ISSUES IN POLITICAL THEORY

Series editors: PETER JONES and ALBERT WEALE

Published

Christopher J. Berry: **Human Nature**
Tom Campbell: **Justice**
Michael Lessnoff: **Social Contract**
Richard Lindley: **Autonomy**
Susan Mendus: **Toleration and the Limits of Liberalism**
Andrew Reeve: **Property**

Forthcoming

David Beetham: **Legitimacy**
Tim Gray: **Freedom**
John Horton: **Political Obligation**
Peter Jones: **Rights**
Raymond Plant: **Equality**
Hillel Steiner: **Utilitarianism**

Justice

Tom Campbell

HUMANITIES PRESS INTERNATIONAL, INC.
ATLANTIC HIGHLANDS, NJ

First published in 1988 in the United States of America by
Humanities Press International, Inc.,
Atlantic Highlands, NJ 07716

© Tom Campbell 1988
Reprinted 1990

Library of Congress Cataloging-in-Publication Data

Campbell, Tom, 1938–
   Justice / Tom Campbell.
      p.   cm. —— (Issues in political theory)
   Bibliography: p.
   Includes index.
   ISBN 0–391–03593–2.   ISBN 0–391–03594–0 (pbk.)
   1. Justice.   I. Title.   II. Series.
   JC578.C42 1988   88–12816
                                     CIP

Printed in Hong Kong

To Tara, who listens patiently

Contents

Justice

Justice

1 What Justice is About

Arguments about justice and injustice feature centrally in current political debates concerning law, social policy and economic organisation. Inequalities of income, employment opportunities and property ownership, deprivations which arise from unemployment, disablement and old age, uncompensated injuries sustained through accident or as a result of the criminal behaviour of others and the sufferings of the victims of state repression — all these, and much more, are routinely denounced as not simply wrong, but wrong because they are unjust. It is with the conflicting ideas of justice which emerge in argument about such contentious political issues that this book is concerned. What is justice? Why is it important? How does it relate to other political values?

The extensive variety and internal complexity of the ideas which are associated with the notion of justice make many different analyses of justice seem — at least initially — equally plausible. Thus there is some basis for the belief that it is the sense of *in*justice or grievance that is at the core of our ideas about justice and explain its powerful emotive force. Justice is normally the language of complaint, and sometimes of revenge. It is in resented deprivation and the consciousness of having been wronged that much justice talk is rooted. Justice is often, therefore, analysed as a negative virtue whose demands can be met simply by doing nothing beyond correcting the wrongs inflicted on others. However, most worked-out views as to what constitutes injustice involve at least an outline image of justice in a positive sense which goes beyond putting right the wrongs that have been done and include an impression of just human relationships. There are positive as well as negative notions of justice.

Again the idea of injustice is closely associated with reactions

1

to the disappointment of existing expectations. Hence justice, at least in its negative expressions, can have strong conservative implications in that it seeks to sustain the *status quo* in society against destructive and disorderly intrusions. Justice is often taken to mean keeping within the rules of established social relationships. However reformist political programmes, which highlight novel grievances or extend traditional expectations to other social groups, can also appeal to the community's sense of justice and injustice. Established social rules are not immune to the critique of injustice. There are reformist as well as conservative notions of justice.

Other analyses are founded on the fact that justice is a standard ingredient of the language of legitimacy. Political regimes use their role in furthering the cause of justice as a central basis for the justification of their right to rule, while the perpetration and protection of injustice by governments is a common justification for civil disobedience and political revolution. In this context justice often represents the minimal requirements for the vindication of political power. Nevertheless justice can also be used to express perfectionist ideals about the best forms of human relationships in the most utopian of societies. There are maximalist as well as minimalist notions of justice.

Further, the relevance of justice is not confined to narrowly political matters. Families, friendship groups and voluntary associations as well as courts and governments can be just and unjust. It is a matter for investigation whether justice in the small group has any bearing on justice in the state, as it is whether justice in the law is the same sort of thing as justice in the society as a whole, but justice has significant applications in all these areas. There are social as well as political notions of justice.

Behind and beyond these distinctions, justice takes on different guises in different political ideologies. There are, for a start, free-market libertarian, welfare liberal and socialist notions of justice, which differ in form as well as in content. Such political divergencies often underlie the juxtaposed ideas of justice as negative or positive, conservative or reformist, minimalist or maximalist. Conceptual analysis of key political concepts cannot be entirely insulated from ideological disagreement.

Any account of justice must be able to take account of the immense variety and complexity of its applications and seek to uncover such unity as may underlie its different political mani-festations. In the absence of the naive belief that there is a 'true' meaning of 'justice', we must proceed by elucidating the actual deployment of the language of justice in all its variety to the point where stipulative choices have to be made in order to arrive at a clear and coherent set of conceptual distinctions which point up to the nature of the political questions which are at issue. There may be no one correct analysis of justice but there are certainly more or less useful ones.

In this chapter I sketch some of the essential conceptual distinctions relating to the idea of justice and open up issues to which a theory of justice must be addressed. This rather dry and abstract analysis prepares the way for the more concrete treatment of theories and their applications in the remainder of the book.

Levels of analysis

Due to the prominence of justice in modern political thought, the philosophical literature on justice is vast and its growth exponen-tial. Even if confined, as it often is, to a purely distributive role the ramifications of principles of justice are endless. Moreover both the content of these principles and also the very concept of justice itself are ideological battlegrounds which exhibit some of the most basic differences in moral and political outlook. It is therefore a considerable undertaking to provide, as this book sets out to do, an overview of current theories of justice and their implications for contemporary policy issues. Indeed, because the concept of justice is so prevalent, and so contested, there is little prospect of presenting any reasonably specific analysis of justice which will find general acceptance, let alone of securing a neutral view of the detailed substantive content of the various competing ideals of justice.

In these circumstances it is tempting to fall back on the technique of outlining an exceedingly vague and catch-all analysis which captures all the varied uses of justice as the term is actually used and then to move rapidly on and distinguish the varying conceptions of justice which embody the differing and competing moral views which coexist within the catch-all umbrella concept. The *concept* is then taken to provide the 'meaning' of justice, while the *conceptions* enunciate the evaluative criteria variously deployed to determine that certain types of situation are just or unjust. Thus the concept of justice may be analysed as a set of principles for assessing social and political institutions, while conceptions of justice represent differing views on the proper content of these principles.

Rawls, for instance, sees justice as a set of principles for 'assigning rights and duties in the basic institutions of society' and defining 'the appropriate distribution of the benefits and burdens of social co-operation' (1971, p.4). In this context, the concept of justice means 'a proper balance between competing claims', while a conception of justice is 'a set of related principles for identifying the relevant considerations which determine this balance' (p.10).

Alternatively, since Rawls's starting-point does not take in all the uses to which the language of justice has been put, we might, in preference, adopt the more traditional approach according to which the concept of justice is defined as 'giving to each his [or her] due', with rival conceptions of justice indicating what is to count as a person's due in accordance with differing moral outlooks. Thus Miller (1976) holds that 'the just state of affairs is that in which each individual has exactly those benefits and burdens which are due to him' (p.20) and goes on to say that 'the important questions about justice emerge when we try to settle what a person's "due" actually means' (p.24).

According to either view, it may be assumed that analyses of the concept of justice tell us what justice is all about in a detached and philosophical manner, while analyses of the differing conceptions of justice state what justice is in concrete terms and so enter the disputed arena of contentious political debate. Utilising the concept/conceptions distinction is a common and to some extent an illuminating and unavoidable strategy, but it has certain drawbacks, which, as we shall see, are exacerbated by current assumptions about the primacy of justice as a political value.

In the first place the concept/conceptions distinction tends to become disengaged from the actual uses of the language of justice in the debates from which the conventional analyses take their initial material and impetus. This is particularly so at the 'concept' level which often fails to capture the distinctive content of the consciousness of justice in contrast to other ideals, such as humanity or the pursuit of happiness. Indeed any analysis which sets out to capture the full range of uses to which the language of justice is put may turn out to be unmanageably open-ended. This characteristic of over-extendedness, which tends to be the fate of all political terms with essentially favourable emotive connotations, is a common and unfortunate result of the deployment of the concept/conceptions distinction.

In order to clarify the nature of political disagreements, it is helpful to develop a set of concepts which are as distinct and precise as possible. It is therefore important, when analysing the concept of justice, not to cast its net too wide, so that justice becomes indistinguishable from the sum of social and political values. This can be done without ignoring the full range of justice discourse as it is applied in different spheres, provided that, in each sphere, we distinguish broad or loose uses from those which seek to use 'justice' in its particular connotations. Here it is best to follow Aristotle in Book V of his *Nicomachean Ethics* where, having distinguished between justice as the 'complete virtue' and justice as 'a part of virtue', he goes on to concentrate on the latter.

Further, the concept/conceptions distinction can be misleading if based on the assumption that there is a clear line of demarcation between a morally neutral, if highly general, concept of justice on the one hand and specific conceptions which embody substantive moral interpretations of the general concept on the other hand. This strategy does not allow for the possibility that the concept of justice itself represents a distinguishable moral point of view which puts limitations on what can reasonably count as a conception of justice. For instance, serious consideration has to be given to the possibility that justice is an inherently legalistic concept which cannot function usefully outside a legal or quasi-legal context.

There is, however, a danger of arriving at a restrictive analysis of the concept of justice which excludes rival political or philosophical views on an arbitrary basis. Nevertheless the avoidance of excessive generality in the pursuit of a relatively value-neutral concept of justice as a partial political virtue may be achieved by paying close attention to the uses of the language of justice which do enable us to pick out those instances where 'justice' is used in a sense which is clearly intended to distinguish it from other values. We must be aware, however, that the linguistic usages to which we appeal in order to establish a very specific concept of justice may be tendentious or dated, reflecting the experience and bias of the philosopher rather than the alleged neutrality of ordinary and typical discourse. Analyses of the concept of justice which dictate its specific meaning may often be no more than devices for putting one set of values beyond the scope of critical evaluation.

For these reasons I adopt in this book a two-level analysis of theories of justice. At the first level, those who are generally regarded amongst English-speaking philosophers as important and original theorists of justice in recent times are presented in their own terms and in accordance with their own assumptions about the meaning and scope of justice. None have been excluded on the grounds that their theories are not really about justice but about something else which is mistakenly called justice, although such brutal treatment might have philosophical justification in some cases. At a second level, however, the theories presented are subjected to criticism from the point of view of a particular and controversial analysis of justice as a specific rather than an all-encompassing social and political value.

The specific analysis I have adopted at the second level is the meritorian analysis according to which there is an essential connection between justice and desert, first in the broad sense that justice in all its aspects has to do with treating persons equally as responsible agents, and second in a narrower sense that such treatment normally entails dealing with people in accordance with their deserts. Using the concept/conception distinction, the meritorian analysis is that the concept of justice is treatment in accordance with desert, while differing conceptions of justice have to do with what counts as desert. This develops into the general contention that a just state of affairs is one which accurately reflects the equal worth and unequal worthiness of responsible agents.

The primacy of justice

The apparently traditionalist analysis of justice in terms of desert is rendered unexpectedly open in its implications when it is dissociated from the common assumption that justice is necessarily the prime social value, even if only in matters of distribution. When conjoined with the premise that justice is the prime value of sound social institutions, conceptions of justice become antagonists for ideological supremacy in a manner which distorts rather than clarifies the distinctiveness of justice-relevant considerations. If justice is defined as the priority political value, then whatever is adopted as a political priority automatically becomes dignified with the title of justice. On the other hand, if we take the view that the moral significance of justice in relation to other values is external to its analysis, and remains a matter for independent moral assessment — so that justice is not axiomatically given any special privileges in the competition for political primacy — then we can adopt a more dispassionate approach to the question of what justice is about. From this ideologically unpressured position it is plausible to say that the idea of justice as desert appears to capture most accurately the import of the language of justice in its distinctive uses.

However, to deny the political primacy of justice runs counter to the consensus of most contemporary theorists of justice. Justice is generally held to be second only to economic prosperity as the prime value of contemporary social and political organisation. The popularity of justice as a political concept is reflected in Rawls's view that 'justice is the first virtue of social institutions, as truth is of systems of thought' (1971, p.3). In other words, whatever the other moral values a society may seek to realise, it must first achieve justice. Although this position has been vigorously disputed by some recent theorists, notably Sandel (1982), it is generally held that, at least in distributive matters, 'justice is a very important, perhaps the most important virtue displayed by a society' (Sadurski, 1985, p.12). Few take the line — which is nevertheless canvassed in this book — that not only is justice merely one distributive consideration amongst others, but it is a factor which is not necessarily of the highest moral significance in politics. In general, however, justice is held to be the central and commanding concept of current mainstream normative political philosophy.

The priority of justice has become so much a common philosophical premiss that it has for many theorists the feel of an analytic truth, but this is clearly a mistake. If 'justice' is *defined* as the overall standard of social rightness, then logically no other value can stand prior to justice since all relevant values are subsumed under its umbrella. But if justice is anything less than the sum or proper balance of all social values, its priority cannot simply be assumed, even in distributive matters. Judgements of priority are substantive moral opinions and the priority of justice as a particular value, once brought into the light of day, may be open to serious doubt. It is possible arbitrarily to define justice as the prime social value and then to go on and fill in its content with whatsoever is thought to be morally most important in social distribution, and perhaps also in the aggregation of benefits and burdens. But this dogmatic approach has the effect of undermining our efforts at conceptual clarification by removing the constraints imposed by the informal logic of the language of justice in actual political debate, thereby rendering dangerously misleading any subsequent appeals to our 'intuitions' about what we think is 'just' or 'unjust', for such intuitions are rooted in our operative rather than in our stipulative normative concepts. If, instead, we keep an open mind about the primacy of justice, it is possible to take a more relaxed and philosophical approach to the conceptual analysis of justice, for we will not, in arriving at this analysis, be committing ourselves at the same time to any particular political priorities.

Spheres of justice

The non-prioritising meritorian analysis of justice sketched above is intended to provide a manageable standpoint for relating and criticising theories of justice and does not serve as the philosophical conclusion of this book, the main aims of which are the identification of the issues to which justice has relevance and the provision of a survey of central competing theories of justice illustrated by reference to practical political disagreements.

Apart from the first and the last, each chapter outlines a particular approach to justice (conceptual and substantive), discusses in some detail one or more exemplars of that approach (for example, Rawls or Ackerman) and goes on to consider its application to an area of political dispute (such as criminal justice or discrimination). These areas of dispute have not been selected primarily because they bring out the strengths or weaknesses of the approach in question but rather because they help to illustrate its distinctive features. No theory can be adequately tested by considering its application in any one area. Indeed it may well appear to the reader that there is something in the view that different approaches to justice are more at home in some practical spheres than in others, so that it may be a mistake to seek an overall theory of justice which has an equal force in all spheres.

The idea that there are different spheres of justice which ought to be kept distinct has recently been persuasively argued by Michael Walzer (1983). Walzer's thesis is that justice has to do with the distribution of goods and that different considerations apply according to the type of goods in question, so that it is wrong to look for one criterion (or set of criteria) which covers the distribution of such disparate goals as social security, money, offices, work, leisure, education, love, religion and political power. He argues that the tendency to erect a comprehensive and unitary set of principles of justice reinforces the politically and morally unfortunate practice of cumulating the inequalities which may arise legitimately in the distribution of particular species of good. Through the encouragement of the assumption that the good reasons for having inequalities in one sphere are also good reasons for inequalities in all spheres, the resultant distributions of wealth, political power and educational opportunity, for example, tend to coalesce around the same individuals and groups. This produces the phenomenon of 'dominance' in which some people are at the beck and call of others in all significant aspects of life. Such dominance is an evil which can be avoided by making the different spheres autonomous so that there will be in each society a variety of distinct inequalities in different spheres, a state of affairs which he describes as 'complex' equality.

Notwithstanding the attractions of this thesis it is a part of the second (critical) level of presentation adopted here that a theory of justice should be able to identify common features which explain how we are able to speak of justice and injustice in such diverse spheres as taxation, liability in tort and equality of opportunity in education. Indeed it can be seen as a major weakness of much contemporary philosophy of justice that it has so little to contribute to our understanding of the relationship between justice in the three principal spheres in which current issues of justice arise: law, welfare and remuneration for work. In particular, although many analyses of social justice do at least seek to bring together considerations of justice in the welfare and employment spheres, they are often at a loss to explain how justice in these areas relates to justice in the administration of law, thus fostering the conceptually and politically unhappy idea that legal justice and social justice are quite distinct phenomena.

Walzer's undoubted insights can be accommodated by allowing that the specification of what counts as just may well vary from sphere to sphere — so that, for instance, a just distribution of political offices need not be on the same basis as a just distribution of educational facilities — while leaving for further consideration whether or not there are common assumptions behind the specific criteria of justice used and what degree of overlap there is between the determinants of justice in each sphere. Walzer overstates his case with his implausible contention that there are distinct 'social meanings' associated with each type of social good which contain their own autonomous distributive considerations, so that, for instance, 'need' is relevant to the provision of health care but not to the distribution of political authority. This contention, which is convincing in some contexts but is of dubious generality, is highly dependent on the priority assumption which we have questioned, namely that whatever are the prime grounds for distribution in a sphere are considerations of 'justice', so that all decisively good reasons for particular social arrangements are misleadingly deemed to be requirements of justice.

Thus Walzer's particular case against desert as the general criterion of justice is that there are sometimes other morally acceptable grounds for distributing such goods as political office, or sexual love (ibid., pp.23–5). This ignores the possibility that these other grounds relate to moral justification of the allocations in question which have nothing to do with justice in its distinctive sense. Thus we may rightly select people for political office for reasons other than doing justice to the rival political candidates for office. In general, Walzer's efforts to erect boundaries between different spheres appears to be motivated more by his desire to have a conceptual basis for resisting 'dominance' than by a concern for justice as such. Injustice is a particular evil which needs explication independently of the distinct problem of the tyranny which results from cumulative injustices.

Walzer's contribution illustrates the difficulties which can arise from combining a generalised concept of justice with the working assumption of the primacy of justice. It also demonstrates the problems of distinguishing between approaches to justice on a consistent basis. Different theorists address themselves to rather different issues. Some concentrate on the general analysis of the idea of justice and its role in political debate and decision-making, others are more taken up with the specific criteria of justice — that is, the nature of the standards that are used in determining the justice or injustice of social arrangements and choices. Still others are primarily interested in the epistemological question of how we can make rational decisions about what criteria of justice to adopt and how to apply them in practice.

Despite these divergent emphases, and the other difficulties to which I have drawn attention, I assume that, ideally, every theory of justice should seek to establish an outline of the overall concept of justice, clarify the meaning and application of certain preferred criteria or conceptions of justice and give some indication of how we are to go about assessing the acceptability and significance of such criteria. In the context of a particular theoretical approach, each subsequent chapter raises questions about the conceptual analysis of justice, considers the normative criteria of justice employed and examines the preferred methodology for settling disputes about what is just and unjust. The intention is to help the reader to grasp the central features of each theoretical approach to justice and gain some appreciation of its practical import. This scheme of presentation is designed to encourage comparisons between theories, even where they differ radically in their emphases. At the same time some general criticisms of each theory will be offered in terms of its conceptual plausibility, its substantive moral content and its epistemological foundations.

Justice and distribution

The illustrative analyses of the concept of justice which have been mentioned so far presuppose that justice, in all its aspects, has to do with states of affairs which involve persons, or at least sentient beings. Justice does not arise in our treatment of inanimate things, and possibly not in our treatment of animals. Thus

Raphael contends that 'justice and injustice, impartiality and partiality, arise only in our treatment of human beings' (1970, p.177). Precisely what it is about persons that makes them appropriate subjects for justice is unclear. It may be their capacity for feeling pleasure and pain; it may be their possession of reason and/or their capacity for making choices and acting accordingly. It is part of a theory of justice to identify the characteristics of human beings which are logically presupposed by these conceptual limitations on the applicability of justice.

A useful starting point here is the influential analysis of justice provided by Hume (1739). For Hume justice is a conventional device for preserving social order by settling disputes between individuals who are making incompatible claims on relatively abundant but nevertheless scarce resources. This means, in Hume's case, that justice is primarily concerned with a system of property, but his view can be more generally stated in terms of the thesis that justice has to do with the distribution of benefits and burdens, and in particular the distribution of scarce resources. Thus injustice may be regarded as a feature of situations in which one person or group of persons wrongly receives less or more than other persons or groups. This makes justice essentially a matter of contested unfavourable comparisons concerning the allocation of desirable and undesirable objects and experiences in a society or group.

If we accept this view, we can then proceed to distinguish different types of justice according to the nature of the valued and disvalued things whose distribution is in question, whether they be economic (economic justice), political (political justice), educational (educational justice) or punitive (criminal justice), and then consider the nature of the 'justicising' (that is 'just-making') factors in each sphere of distributive concern.

This distributional definition of justice may be considered unduly restrictive in its exclusion of all aggregative import. For instance, although Rawls takes a basically distributive view of justice — at least in so far as what he calls 'social justice' is concerned — he argues that justice also requires the maximising of benefits so long as everyone is advantaged. Others take a similar line, either in a weaker form, to the effect that maximising benefits is not in itself unjust, or, in a stronger form, according to which justice positively requires maximisation of benefits, always provided that certain distributive considerations are also taken into account.

The move to incorporate aggregation into the domain of justice can be seen as an example of the tendency to broaden the concept of justice so that it may take in all socially desirable objectives. Rawls himself, as we shall see, is somewhat cavalier with respect to the distinctive meaning of justice, and it is unsurprising therefore that the *prima facie* moral desirability of maximising goods and minimising evils should be brought into his overall scheme of justice. It is regrettable that this over-inclusive approach weakens a contrast which is one of the fixed points of most analyses of justice, namely the qualitative difference between justice and the principle of utility (that is, the principle that it is always right to maximise goods and minimise evils). One of the standard objections to utilitarianism is that it leads to distributions which are substantively unjust. This fixed-point contrast between justice and utility is greatly weakened when aggregative considerations are introduced into the concept of justice. Rawls's line is not, however, fatal to the contrast between utility and justice, since the essence of utilitarianism is the claim that utility is the *sole* moral criterion, both of aggregation and distribution, and any view which limits the role of utility is, to that extent, non-utilitarian. Nevertheless to include aggregative considerations within justice does undermine a conceptually fundamental distinction which clarifies the moral point at issue in many areas of political disagreement. On the other hand, the exclusion of aggregation from justice may have the — perhaps unfortunate — consequence that it then becomes an analytical and not just a moral truth that there can be no acceptable purely utilitarian theory of justice.

It is more difficult to deal with the contention that justice is not always comparative, as the distributive analysis seems to imply that it must be. The argument here is that, while most types of justice are to do with whether a person A has more or less than person(s) B (or C), it is at least sometimes the case that A had too much or too little of some benefit or burden, irrespective of how A stands in comparison to B (or C). Thus it may be said to be unjust that an innocent man is starving, or is being punished, whether or not any other innocent persons are in the same plight, or, again, that we can know that it is just to reward bravery or to praise saints, without entering into comparisons between the individuals concerned.

Thus Feinberg (1973) argues that 'when our task is to do non-comparative justice (as we might call it) to each of a large number of individuals, we do not compare them with each other, but rather compare each in turn with an objective standard and judge each "on his own merits" ' (p.98). In other words, justice may involve direct reference to standards of treatment without requiring us to compare the situations of different people.

Something here will depend, in the case of benefits, on whether they are scarce and in demand, and, in the case of burdens, on whether these have to be carried by somebody or could be eliminated altogether. Where there is competition for scarce benefits or to escape burdens which must fall on somebody, comparisons are inevitably involved. In the case of avoidable evils, such as punishment, there is a distinct problem about whether or not to inflict the burden at all and here it makes sense to think about the justice of punishing one person without entering into comparisons with others. In the case of plentiful benefits, when bestowing a benefit on one person does not preclude bestowing them on others, we may still raise the question of whether or not to benefit certain individuals, irrespective of the way others are treated.

Sadurski (1985) argues that, even in these apparently non-comparative cases, there is an element of comparison involved, since what counts as benefit or burden is inevitably defined relative to normal treatment and expectations (p.17). Thus what counts as a deprivation can only be determined by comparing human situations, just as what counts as bravery can only be determined by comparing different people's behaviour in dangerous situations. Nevertheless, given that any distinction involves this sort of comparison, there is a clear difference between those cases of justice judgements which involve direct comparisons between individuals or groups, where the injustice is primarily to do with the fact that A gets more or less than B, and those which involve comparisons only at some prior conceptual level at which the terms involved acquire their meanings.

The issue as to whether or not all judgements of justice are comparative in the first and direct sense cannot be determined conceptually for it raises moral questions about whether the selected criteria of justice have moral relevance in non-comparative situations. Thus, if desert is the selected criterion of justice it is conceptually proper to say that justice is relevant only to the particular distributions of rewards and punishments, the whole system of having rewards and punishments being justified on grounds other than those of justice, perhaps by utilitarian reasons, such as providing incentives for good behaviour. But it is also conceptually proper to believe that it is intrinsically desirable that desert be rewarded and ill desert punished, so that it may be right to punish a thief if he is the only thief that can be caught. On the former view justice is always comparative, on the latter view it need not be so. It would seem, therefore, that we have to allow for the possibility that the distributions with which justice are concerned are sometimes to do with the propriety of what particular individuals receive, a matter which is, in important ways, independent of the comparison of one person's treatment with that accorded to others.

A more radical dispute about justice and distribution concerns the claim that it is fundamentally misleading to link justice to any distributive goal whatsoever. Thus Hayek (1976, pp.62–100) denies that the distribution of benefits and burdens is the consequence of a distributive process, and argues that the whole notion of social or distributive justice is therefore meaningless. No person or group, he contends, has made a general distribution of wealth or any other desirable or undesirable thing. It is therefore mistaken to speak of a distribution as being unjust, for only the actions of persons can be unjust. This, in turn, means that it is nonsense to speak of *re*distribution, since there never was in the first place any distribution which could serve as the basis for a revised distribution. He then goes on to argue that the attempt to impose patterns is inherently destructive of liberty. Thus, in a society where there is a free market in commodities, so that the overall outcome of economic activity is not the product of conscious choice but the unintended consequence of the innumerable discrete choices of individuals, there can be no use for the idea of redistributive justice and the attempt to impose a distribution is destructive of the freedom of the individual within that society.

Hayek's approach fails to make the important distinction between states of affairs which are consciously and deliberately brought about and those which *can* be intentionally altered, whatever their origin. There is an uncontroversial and choice-neutral sense of 'distribution' in which it refers simply to the quantity of any given variable belonging to a number of distinct individual entities or persons. And, where there is any possibility of a distribution which affects human welfare being changed by human action, then there may be reason to assess that state of affairs in terms of justice and injustice, or indeed in terms of balancing one liberty against another, so that appropriate remedial action may be attempted. Whether or not the original distribution is the intended result of human action is immaterial, unless we wish to go on and raise the separate question of who, if anyone, is responsible for its occurrence. Hayek is not, of course, unaware of this distinction. His position is rather that, in a liberal society, no one has the duty to promote any particular distribution, if only because this cannot be done without constant interference with individual liberty to an extent which would destroy the free market. This is an ideological position which gives priority to certain forms of liberty over justice and does not in itself render the idea of distributive justice meaningless in situations capable of being changed by political intervention. Furthermore it some-times makes perfect sense to speak of situations as just or unjust when it is not within anyone's power even to change them. Value judgements do not always have to be directed at action in each instance of their use. They may also be used to assess the desirability of unalterable situations. Certainly it is possible to hold the pessimistic view that, in an imperfect world, justice is an ideal norm which is capable only of very limited implementation.

Nevertheless the idea that justice is essentially concerned with sustaining a particular pattern of distribution in desired goods and undesired ills does seem too constricting in so far as it ignores those theories which regard justice as having to do with acting in accordance with one's rights or entitlements, a view which we shall look at further in the next chapter. Thus Nozick (1974, Part II), argues that a person's possessions or 'holdings' are just if they are the result of legitimate actions, that is, actions which are in accordance with rules of ownership, transfer and the rectification of illegitimate transfers, whatever the distributive pattern which results. Without dropping the term 'distributive justice', Nozick favours what he calls an 'historical' rather than an 'end-state' approach to justice in which justice is a matter of how people came to possess their holdings, rather than a matter of measuring holdings against some characteristics of the holders — such as their needs or their moral merits — which would enable us to think in terms of a particular pattern as the end-state of the distributive process in which holdings are matched with the present characteristics of the individuals concerned.

It is relatively easy to brush aside as overly dogmatic the refusal to countenance the possibility of end-state views of justice which Nozick, like Hayek, rejects for what appear to be primarily ideological reasons. It is certainly possible for societies to strive to attain patterned distributions, even if they are largely unsuccessful and sometimes coercive in the pursuit of their chosen goals. It is less easy to rule out historical or entitlement theories as possible theories of justice on the grounds that they do not directly relate to distribution as a preconceived objective. However there is no formal difficulty here since distributions, considered simply as patterns, may be characterised by variables which incorporate reference to past events, as when the relevant distributive characteristics are such historical facts as the occurrence of a promise or the receipt of a gift. Indeed this approach overlaps with some standard specifications of patterned end-states, particularly those which draw on the relative deserts of the holders of goods. To distribute according to merit and demerit is an inherently backward-looking exercise. Distributive definitions of justice require only that existing patterns may be altered in the direction establishing favoured patterns and need make no demand that these patterns be ahistorical in their variables.

Defending the view that justice in all its manifestations has to do with questions of distribution does not mean that it is not often useful to distinguish something called 'distributive justice' from other types of justice, even although these other types have an essential connection with distributive matters. Thus, in Book V of the *Nicomachean Ethics*, Aristotle makes an important distinction between 'distributive justice' and 'corrective justice'. Distributive justice, in this narrow sense, refers to the distribution of benefits to social groups while commutative justice concerns punishments, compensation for injuries and unfair exchange. In recent times this distinction has been developed into a contrast between 'social justice' which has to do with 'the distribution of benefits and burdens throughout a society' and 'legal justice' which concerns 'punishment of wrongdoing and the compensation of injury through the creation and enforcement of a public set of rules' (Miller, 1976, p.22).

This distinction is, as we shall see, highly misleading as a general account of the relationship between law and justice, if only because law is a key instrument in the determination of the overall distribution of benefits and burdens in a society. But it is often useful to give separate attention to those distributive issues which arise in situations where one individual has wronged or harmed another, and these tend to be dealt with by specific areas of law. The general characteristic of these situations is that some corrective procedure is in order, perhaps because of a specific demerit of an offending individual (as in the area of criminal law), or because of specific harm caused through the fault of another person which calls for compensation or redress (the law of tort or delict), or because of some unfairness or other impropriety which has arisen in the processes of exchange or other voluntary argeements in society (the law of contract). All these situations presuppose a specific interaction between individuals and the demand that something like the *status quo*, as it existed before that interaction, be restored. This is a limited matter of seeing justice done either between individuals or to individuals, and, perhaps for this reason, 'it seems proper to call this a form of individual, not of social justice' (Honore, 1970, p.65).

However, in practice, every type of justice has to involve some process of abstraction whereby distributions are looked at in the light of specific considerations rather than from an entirely comprehensive point of view which takes in every consideration relevant to a just distribution. Nevertheless it is a reasonable, if somewhat rough, generalisation to say that justice sometimes involves settling disputes arising from the merits or demerits of individual actions and sometimes involves considering wider questions about the general situations of individuals and groups, and that the former cases are more readily seen as requiring restoration of the *status quo* than the latter situations, in which there is unlikely to have been any pre-existing acceptable *status quo* to restore. We may therefore think in approximate terms of a distinction between individual, or commutative justice, on the one hand and social or distributive justice on the other, although it is important to note that there is also a more specific sense of 'commutative justice' which covers only issues of fairness which arise in transactions. It may well be that commutative justice — in the broader, Aristotelian sense — relates more to the distribution of burdens and social justice more to the distribution of benefits. But this does not undermine the contention that in both cases issues of distribution are at stake. Nor does it establish that law is peculiarly a device for attaining individual, or commutative, rather than social, or distributive justice.

Further complexities in the relationship between justice and various branches of law will be considered later, but it should be noted that to speak of commutative justice in relation to the main areas of private law does not imply that justice is or ought to be the sole determinant of the content of these laws. This may or may not be the case. All that the notion of commutative justice requires is that there be authorised standards of right and wrong conduct which enable us to say when an existing *status quo* has been upset and must therefore be restored. There is no necessary implication, for instance, that breaking a contract is an unjust act, only that it is a wrong act and one therefore which, as a matter of justice, calls for rectificatory action.

With all these reservations, it remains illuminating to say that justice has to do with the distribution amongst persons of benefits and burdens, these being loosely defined so as to cover any desirable or undesirable thing or experience. We can then move on to ask whether simply any morally relevant distributive consideration is to be considered as an element in justice or whether only some types of moral consideration are justicising — that is, just-making — factors.

Due deserts

At the first, permissive, level of analysis, perhaps the most promising further specification of the concept of justice is that it is the embodiment of the ancient principle, discussed in Book I of Plato's *Republic*, and given its classic formulation in the *Institutes* of Justinian, that 'justice is the set and constant purpose to give every man his due'.

For some theorists this formula has the advantage of flexibility in that it leaves entirely open what is to count as a person's due, and it also has the advantage of capturing the idea that justice is a requirement rather than an optional extra. Other things being equal people ought — as a matter of right, not of grace and favour — to receive that which is due to them. Indeed much social regulation may be regarded as being directed to ensuring that people receive their dues through specifying the mutual obligations of members of a society or group and determining the remedies for correcting injustices which arise through failures to act in accordance with these obligations. Thus the formula 'to each according to his or her due' appears to take in both the forcefulness and legalism of justice discourse.

However we have seen that the moral priority of justice cannot be taken for granted, so that the extent of the imperative force of 'due' should not be exaggerated. There are in life many minor injustices whose rectification may be very much an optional extra. Certainly it is not the case that justice by definition requires legal expression and protection. Justice features as a standard for judging distributions within families, educational establishments and economic units, in ways which are by and large outside the ambit of the law. Thus, although the use of legal mechanisms to ensure that people receive that which is their due is for some theorists a paradigm of what justice is about, it must be a mistake to give such a restrictive interpretation of 'due' in this context.

A more serious difficulty with this starting-point is that, if we focus on the specific meaning of justice, the formula 'to each his or her due' appears too broad. For, given that it is possible to count almost anything as a person's 'due', it allows for justice to take in discriminatory distributions in accordance with social class, race, sex or many other properties whose distributive use is in general the antithesis of justice. This objection may reflect no more than a misunderstanding of the nature of the analysis of the concept of justice which, it should be remembered, is intended to indicate the general scope of controversies about what is just, rather than to establish how these controversies ought to be resolved in terms of particular conceptions of justice. If it is said to be unjust to allocate goods according to race, class, or birth, then this may be taken as presupposing the thesis that justice (as opposed to liberty or efficiency for instance) has to do with the determination of what is due to persons. A concept of justice aims to distinguish the just from the non-just, not to take a view on what is just as distinct from unjust.

However this response ignores the possibility that justice concerns a limited range of morally relevant distributive criteria. Moreover it seems highly likely that this is so, since there are morally significant criteria, such as maximising happiness, which have distributive implications but are clearly not criteria of justice. Economic necessity may require that extraordinarily high salaries be paid to a few people with essential skills, or that bribes be given to those who have it in their power to inflict serious social harm through their control of vital natural resources. The question of whether or not it is right to distribute goods for such reasons is largely a matter of utility rather than justice and is conceptually different from such issues as what is a fair rate for the job, or to what extent punishment is just.

Such reflections generate suggestions for limiting the range of possible criteria for justice. For instance, Miller (1976, p.20) includes only those which refer to 'personal characteristics and circumstances'. On this basis he goes on to identify three independent 'interpretations of justice which may be summarized in the three principles: to each according to his rights; to each according to his deserts; to each according to his needs' (p.27). This does seem to emphasise that justice has to do with the individual's treatment. However, unless these three types of consideration can be given some further illuminating theoretical connection, it appears a rather arbitrary list of relevant personal characteristics and circumstances, particularly as the criterion of need features centrally in other moral concepts, such as beneficence or humanity.

Another, more limited, suggestion, which is applied only to what he calls 'social justice' is made by Honore (1970) who puts forward two propositions about justice. First, 'all men considered merely as men and apart from their conduct or choice have a claim to an equal share in all those things, here called advantages, which are generally desired and are in fact conducive to well-being'. The second proposition is that 'there are a limited number of principles of discrimination and that the claim of men to an equal share in all advantages can fairly be modified, restricted or limited by only two main factors. These are the choice of the claimant or the citizen on the one hand and his conduct on the other' (p.63).

Honore's two propositions have the advantage that they explain why justice is contrasted, not only with utility, but also with distributions which are the outcome of good luck or ill fortune. Honore's account does, however, seem to call for some explanation as to why it is that principles of justice should be limited in the way he suggests. This explanation may involve putting the matter more positively and attempting to identify the common factor lying behind 'choice' and 'conduct' as criteria for just distributions. One way of doing this is to show the relevance of choice and conduct to assessments of moral worthiness, thus presenting Honore's definition of justice as a meritorian analysis which gives precedence to Miller's principle of desert over his alternative principles of rights and needs. This would mean that all forms of justice have to do with requiting people in terms of their personal responsibility as moral agents. From the point of view of justice, what counts is due deserts.

This suggestion appears to take us from the first level of analysis, in which an open approach is taken to the conceptual legitimacy of competing theories of justice, into an analysis of the idea of justice more suited to the second level of analysis, in which the competing criteria of justice are assessed. It may be, however, that such a change of levels is required if we are to identify the limits of what can count as a criterion of justice without returning to the questionable assumption that every distributive criterion which we consider morally important is thereby a criterion of justice. Moreover, to make 'due deserts' the criterion of justice, as opposed to non-justice, leaves open precisely what is to count as 'desert', and the differences which emerge in giving substance to the concept of desert can be used to identify the different ways of distinguishing justice from injustice. In the words of a recent commentator, 'While everyone agrees that justice, almost by definition, is giving people what they deserve, there appears to be little agreement concerning what it is that people deserve' (Sterba, 1986, p.1). It is not unreasonable, therefore, to use the notion of desert in the analysis of the very concept of justice.

Legal and social justice

Although Honore's analysis of social justice can be used to bring out, through the ideas of desert and individual responsibility, underlying features of social justice which indicate its affinity with legal justice, we have noted that Honore himself maintains a distinction between what he calls 'social' and 'individual' justice, which indicates that he goes along with the standard view that the two are importantly distinct. Indeed most modern theories of justice have little to say about justice in law despite the fact that justice might appear to be *the* legal virtue. The distribution of the benefits and burdens of social co-operation is thought to be one type of concern, the attribution of liability and punishment quite another, hence the sharp distinction between social or distributive justice, on the one hand, and individual or legal justice, on the other.

In so far as they have something to contribute to the integration of so-called social and legal justice, contemporary theorists of justice tend to deploy the distinction between formal and material justice, equating the former with law and the latter with morality or politics. Law, it is said, has to do with the fair and accurate application of rules, that is, in the terminology of Perelman (1963, p.11), with 'abstract' as opposed to the 'concrete' justice which concerns the content of such rules. The same basic distinction is given a number of different labels in the literature. Sidgwick (1901, p.273) contrasts the 'customary' justice, which upholds established conventions, with 'ideal' justice, which has to do with 'an ideal system of rules of distribution which ought to exist, but perhaps has never existed'. Here I shall use the terms 'formal' justice for treatment in accordance with existing authoritative rules and 'material' (or sometimes 'substantive') justice for those criteria of justice which are pertinent to the assessment of the rules themselves.

Formal justice often seems to have an almost arbitrary connection with material justice, and is usually treated as a side issue to be mentioned briefly before proceeding to the substantive moral issues, which are roughly equated with the sphere of social justice. This separation in turn neatly coincides with the sharp line drawn by legal positivists between what the law is and what the law ought to be. Legal theory is then taken to be about the identification of which rules are to count as valid laws and the idea of 'natural justice' is taken to refer only to certain technical matters of procedure which have no significant connection with the justice of the rules' content (see Hart, 1961, pp.202ff). It is then up to moral and political philosophers to argue about the justice of the content of rules and whether these should be founded on merit, need or some other criterion.

This division of labour leaves unexplained the close historical and conceptual ties between law and justice. If legal justice is purely formal and therefore no more than an accurate implementation of legal rules, then it would appear that there is no closer link between law and justice than there is between justice and rule-governed bureaucratic administration. A purely formal sense of justice would seem to have insufficient moral import to explain the association of law and justice and the strength of feeling to which legal injustices give rise.

It may be, however, that a closer analysis of the ideas associated with formal justice, particularly its relation to the principles conformity to which is known as the 'rule of law' will uncover a more profound conceptual connection between the formal and the material aspects of justice discourse and so help to undermine the sharp distinction that is so often drawn between legal and social justice.

Exploration of these issues calls for a more detailed consideration of the idea and significance of formal justice. If formal justice is defined simply as the accurate implementation of pre-existing rules, then it is inseparable from having institutionalised rules at all, of whatever sort, for rules state what is to be done whenever certain conditions pertain so that accurate rule implementation is inseparable from the idea of having rule-governed activities. The significance of formal justice then becomes a matter of the significance of the rules themselves. If the rule is justified, then it follows that its application is justified, and this is so — at least *prima facie* — in every instance to which the rule has application. In the case of some rules (such as the rule of the road, or other complex sets of rules relating to closely interacting co-operative behaviour) something close to complete conformity may be required to achieve their purposes, and consistent rule-following is then of particular instrumental importance. In other cases, such as rules prohibiting homicide, which do not have a similar 'threshold' effect, the value of the rule is realised in every conformity to it, so that its significance in each instance is not directly dependent on the rule being consistently and generally adhered to in other instances. However, with both types of rule, the moral significance of formal justice is derivative from the content of the rules in question and the objectives which they have been designed to achieve.

These examples suggest that the consistent application of rules is not a matter of justice, formal or otherwise, unless the rules are rules of justice. Certainly we do not speak of formal justice in connection with the application of every type of rule. Maladministration of the rules of a game is not generally described as unjust (although here the associated concept of fairness may apply) and it is certainly not 'unjust', although it may be inefficient, to be inconsistent in the use of the rules of language or computer programming. We might, therefore, define formal justice more restrictively as the consistent application of the rules of justice. This would have the advantage of a clear connection between justice in its formal and material aspects.

However, the reduction of formal to material justice in this way does not account for all the assumptions made about formal justice. The idea of formal justice is often applied to the application of any rules which have a bearing on the locations of benefits and burdens, whether or not these arise from considerations of justice in the substantive sense. Thus in the case of an arbitrary rule that redheads in the workforce be paid an extra day's wages each week, it is felt to be formally unjust if some redheads do not receive the unmerited and discriminatory benefit while yet other redheads do receive the benefit. The idea is that the inconsistent application of benefit- or burden-allocating rules is not a mere technical inefficiency or logical inconsistency, but an actual type of injustice which is quite distinct from the type of benefit or burden in question and from the reasons for having the rules in the first place. What is at stake, it is argued, is simply a matter of the justice of treating like cases alike.

There would indeed appear to be deeply rooted instinctive reactions of resentment which are aroused by 'unequal' treatment in such a purely formal sense. This instinct is manifested at a very early age by siblings who are treated differently by their parents. In the adult world it is evident in arguments about comparability in wage rates, where the demand for greater remuneration is based primarily on what is paid for similar work by other groups. In general it would seem that it is regarded as unjust to confer a benefit or burden on one or more members of a group without doing so on all other members of the group, and that this applies even when the rule in question is regarded as materially unjustified and even unjust.

It may be, however, that, whatever the emotional reactions to imperfect rule implementation might be, there is no real injustice in the incompleteness of the application of unjustified rules in that all such judgements, if they are to be sustained, depend on the assumption that the rule in question is defensible. It is certainly sometimes hard to see the justice of applying an unjust rule merely because it has been applied to others. If we have imprisoned one morally innocent man it can scarcely be regarded as unjust not to imprison all innocent men. The demands for such purely formal justice may be effective in the pursuit of benefits against authorities who have favoured other groups conventionally regarded as similar, but this is because of the *ad hominem* force of such arguments, since the authorities in question are likely to be committed to the justifiability of the rules they have already deployed and this can be used to extract concessions from them.

Whether or not mere formal 'injustice', independently of the content of the rules, constitutes a genuine grievance is a matter of rather fine moral intuition. Certainly it does not seem a substantial enough consideration to explain the significance of law for the pursuit of justice. The missing ingredients in the concept of mere formal justice may be tied up in the associated ideal of the rule of law according to which it is held that political power ought to be channelled through a system of general rules which are impartially applied by an independent authority according to standard procedures which guarantee such matters as a fair hearing for those who are liable to benefit or suffer as a consequence of the application of these rules.

Unfortunately for our purposes the rule of law is a very mixed bag of requirements, not all of which appear to have a direct bearing on questions of justice. The arbitrary uses of political power may of course produce injustice, as when unmerited harms are inflicted on individuals at the behest of the power-holders, but even greater injustices may be perpetrated by the efficient application of unjust rules. Of course, where just treatment does require rule-application, then the rule of law in this sense is a pre-requisite of material justice, but this simply takes us back to formal justice as the instrument of material justice and does not illuminate its alleged independent value as a separate type of justice.

There are, however, some elements of the ideal of the rule of law which are relatively independent of the substance of rules and which do appear to have a connection with justice. These elements are to be found in the so-called 'principles of legality', which are identified by Fuller in relation to his eight ways of failing 'to make law', an activity which he described as 'subjecting human conduct to the governance of rules' (Fuller, 1969, p.46). In accordance with well established principles of the rule of law, Fuller argued that successful law-making requires that rules be general, publicised, prospective, understandable, non-contradic-tory, possible to conform to, relatively constant and consistently applied (see pp.3ff). He further argues that a total failure in any one of these respects does not result merely in a bad system of law but produces something which is not properly called a legal system at all, the reason being that it cannot effectively govern human conduct. If, for instance, the rules in question are totally unknown to the citizens of a polity, then they cannot be used to control their behaviour. On the other hand, the full realisation of all these conditions is an aspiration or ideal to which no actual legal system can completely attain.

What distinguishes Fuller's thesis is that, while allowing that the morality of the content of the law is something that raises issues which are 'external' to the law, he insists that there is an 'internal' morality embedded in the idea of law as he has defined it. He reaches this view by noting that in the case of each type of legal 'inefficiency' there is an associated form of moral outrage. Retrospective laws, for instance, do not merely fail to change behaviour, they are also felt to be grossly unfair. Unclear laws are 'brutally absurd', contradictory laws are 'repugnant', while laws requiring the impossible are brutal as well as pointless. The citizens of Fuller's inefficient law-maker, King Rex, are not only ungoverned, they are also indignant, for they have had to suffer both the disorder of the kingdom and the injustice of being penalised according to unpredictable decisions and rules to which they were powerless to conform.

Fuller has, in general, failed to convince his audience that there is a logically necessary connection between efficiency and morality in law. In the abstract, the morality of the means must be judged by reference to the morality of the ends in question and law would seem to be no exception to this rule. The fact that evil and corrupt regimes utilise clear, consistent and prospective rules in itself seems to add nothing to their morality, any more than efficiency in theft adds to the moral quality of that enterprise.

Nevertheless there would appear to be at least a contingent connection between Fuller's model of law and aspects of moral value which come within the ambit or the rule of law. For instance, where the rules concerned satisfy Fuller's standards it is in principle possible for citizens to change their behaviour so as to avoid the penal consequences of disobedience. This may count for little if such behaviour involves them in what they regard as grossly immoral or undesirable conduct, but the fact that citizens have a choice to make in relation to the rules and their consequences is in some sense a recognition of their status as responsible agents. No doubt Fuller overstates this point, but it has some force:

'To embark on the enterprise of subjecting human conduct to the governance of rules involves of necessity a commitment to the view that man is, or can become, a responsible agent, capable of understanding, following rules and answerable for his defaults.

Every departure from the law's inner morality is an affront to man's dignity as a responsible agent. To judge his actions by unpublished and retrospective laws, or to order him to do the impossible is to convey to him your indifference to his powers of self-determination.' (p.162)

However, since malevolent men can manipulate others through their rational capacities, no reliable inference can be drawn from the fact that someone embarks on rule-governance to the effect that he has a certain subjective attitude towards those affected by the rules he creates. To use the fact that people are capable of conforming to rules does not necessarily imply a subjective attitude of respect for them. Moreover Fuller does not give sufficient weight to the fact that efficiency may often be served by departures from the principles of legality since, for instance, retrospective punishment may serve to deter others and inconsistencies in rule application can be a means of more closely adapting the process to the policy goals being pursued.

However the contingent and imperfect correlation between Fuller's principles of legality and respect for agents does suggest a way in which law and justice may be associated in a manner which does not depend essentially on the content of the primary rules. At its minimum the insight is that it is unjust or 'unfair' to punish someone for doing something that he could not know was punishable, or to induce action on the basis of a proffered reward and then not give the reward for conforming behaviour. Thus there is a sense of 'desert' according to which those that meet the standards publicly required of them 'deserve' either not to be punished, or to be appropriately rewarded, so that it would be unfair not to treat them accordingly. This application of desert is, of course, greatly enhanced when the rules in question are thought to embody material criteria of merit in that they forbid harmful conduct or enjoin useful behaviour, but there is at least a foothold here for the idea of the justice of treating people in accordance with Fuller's principles of legality.

This minimal sense of the rule of law can be filled out by adding other requirements which are clearly much more contingently connected with the very idea of law. These include the standard excusing conditions in criminal law, and the assumption, still normally made, that fault is a necessary element in the attribution of civil liability. These basic and common principles of law fit much more readily Fuller's idea of treating people in line with their dignity as responsible agents, although they can hardly be considered as essential principles of all actual or potential legal systems.

Other normal, but by no means necessary, features of modern legal systems are similarly responsibility-oriented. Some of the standards of so-called 'due process' or 'natural justice' fit neatly into this category. Thus the requirements of due notice to any charges, the opportunity to be heard and cross-question witnesses and have evidence duly considered in open court can be seen as, in part at least, elementary extensions of the treatment of people as responsible beings: 'what makes law an appropriate method of social control is not that it is more efficient than other more manipulative or coercive methods, but that it embodies a proper respect for the citizen as a rational agent' (Duff, 1986, p.97). Not only do such procedures promote accuracy in the application of rules, they also embody a commitment to vindicating the propriety of the procedures to the vulnerable individual: 'rules of procedure do not guarantee that decisions will be just. Rather they constitute necessary, or near necessary, conditions of the decision-making process being a process with which a man could be expected to identify' (Lucas, 1980, p.97). Moreover a fair hearing along these lines is clearly a matter which is fundamentally involved in the sort of justice that is expected in our courts of law.

These considerations connect in turn with the idea that impartiality is an aspect of the justice which applies in relative independence of the content of rules. This ideal may be unpacked in a multitude of ways, many of which we have already analysed as part of formal justice. For instance, the notion that only those factors explicitly contained in publicly expressed rules should be taken into account in the application of rules is part of what it is to judge impartially, as are the other ingredients of 'natural justice' which have just been mentioned. But there are additional aspects in the idea of judicial impartiality which go beyond the notion of accurate and publicly justified rule application and relate more to the use of significant judicial discretion in areas where rules run out or require interpretation. Here the judge who has no personal connection with the parties in court, and who is not regarded as partisan in relation to matters of civil dispute but will nevertheless take a detailed interest in the matters at hand, is preferred. Just as having general rules can be seen as an attempt to transcend individual prejudice or bias, so there is a notion that judges should sustain impartiality in their even-handed dealing with those matters which are not precisely determined by the applicable rules.

Although the ideal of the impartial judge is by no means an analytical requirement of a legal system, this, along with the associated rules of natural justice, is so closely associated with the modern idea of the proper conduct of law as to embody the sort of justice that is expected of the law. Once this is appreciated then it becomes possible to articulate the common element between this enhanced idea of formal justice, on the one hand, and material or substantive justice, on the other hand, since both have to do with different aspects of the treating of people as responsible agents.

Moving, for the moment, to the second level of analysis, material justice may be said to relate to the formulation of rules which embody reference to the deserts which are to be punished or rewarded, or reflected in other distributions of benefits and burdens, while formal justice is a mix of the analytically necessary efficient application of these rules, the existence of second order rules which allow for excuses and exculpations where the standard assumptions of responsibility do not apply, the treatment of individuals as publicly answerable through fair procedure in court, and the underlying assumption of a commitment to judicial impartiality. On this account, the justice with which law is concerned is continuous in kind with the justice of distributions which are not primarily the concern of courts of law, for both 'legal' and 'social' justice have to do with the treatment of persons as responsible agents.

More abstract accounts of formal justice, according to which justice is no more than a matter of logical consistency, especially when conjoined with a theory of material justice which discounts considerations of desert, are more likely to end up with a strong inexplicable disjunction between our ideas of legal and social justice.

Justice and equality

Interestingly, the ideal of judicial impartiality, which we have noted as an aspect of the rule of law, is also deployed as a technique for determining what is to count as materially just. The opinion of the impartial and well-informed judge, in one form or another, is a standard base for what are said to be materially just decisions, including decisions about the proper content of distributive rules. As we shall see, variations on this theme of impartiality abound in epistemological investigations, into the acceptable bases of judgements of material justice, which suggests that there may be further fundamental affinities between the bases of formal and material justice.

This possibly significant deep connection between formal and material justice can be seen in analyses of the idea of judicial impartiality which goes beyond formal interpretations of the principle that like cases should be treated alike, to the more substantive claim that there this principle itself rests on the belief that, in some sense of 'equality', all human beings are 'equal'. This can be seen in some interpretations which are given to the idea of 'treating like cases alike', a formula which, although it can often serve as an example of the pure formalism of routinely applying the relevant rules, can, at the other extreme, be equated with the assumption that all human beings are essentially alike. Hence the association of ideas of justice and some form of human equality.

However it would seem that justice *per se* cannot be identified with a simple idea of equality in which after everything has been taken into account all human beings are placed in the *same* situation as regards the desirables and undesirables of life. Such egalitarianism is routinely contrasted with justice, presumably because justice is in part concerned with distinguishing between persons and groups and justifying their differential treatment. Egalitarianism is at most one possible substantive view of justice and cannot therefore be regarded as essential to the concept of justice itself. Indeed it is arguable that justice, given its connection with merit or desert, in practice presupposes the prima facie correctness of inegalitarian treatment. On the other hand, many proposals for social reform put forward in the name of justice do call for a move towards more equal material conditions for human beings on the grounds that the differences in the material conditions of human life are far too great. This may be because differences in merit and demerit are seldom as substantial as the differences in situation which characterise people's lots in actual societies.

A compromise position on the relationship between justice and equality is to say that there is an assumption that all be treated equally until relevant reasons are given for distinguishing between them, and that this is built into the very idea of justice. This approximates to Honore's position (see p.21). In this case justice may be said to express the specific moral viewpoint, championed by Ackerman (see Chapter 4), that unequal life situations must be justified, so that every theory of justice must seek to explain or justify the basic presumption of the equality of persons as well as demonstrate legitimate grounds for differential treatment.

There are at least two importantly different conceptions of what this interpretation of formal justice entails (see Katzner, 1971). The first interpretation, which may be called 'presumptive formal justice', is the principle that in the distribution of benefits and burdens it should be assumed that all are to be treated equally (that is, given the same amounts of the thing in question) until it is demonstrated that they differ in some relevant respect. The presumptive version of the principle underlying formal justice is really a procedural recommendation according to which all are presumed to be the same until proved to be different, a practice which has certain parallels with the presumption of innocence in criminal trials.

Such a principle may have important practical implications, particularly in situations where there is a general absence of information about the people in question, but it involves no constraint on the possible inequalities of the eventual outcome of distributive situations, for it may turn out that there is no relevant respect in which persons are the same or even similar. Indeed it would be possible for presumptive formal justice to coexist with material judgements according to which some persons were discounted altogether in the eventual distributive outcome.

A more forceful form of treating equals equally is that, in any distributive situation, all persons should be given equal consideration. This is usually taken to mean that each person's interests are given equal weight, so that, whatever the relevant distributive criteria, the effect of their application on each individual is taken into account in proportion to its degree. This is the dogma, attributed by J. S. Mill to Bentham that: 'everybody to count for one, nobody to count for more than one' (Mill, 1863, p.58). Your pleasure is as important as mine and my desires are of equal moral significance to those of any other person. This may be called the principle of equal worth.

The idea that equal consideration, in the sense of the acknowledgement of equal worth, is built into the concept of justice is an ancient and attractive one. If something like this lies behind the notion of formal justice then it would certainly explain the moral significance of that concept. Moreover as a principle it appears to carry with it major substantive implications, since it rules out the total neglect of one person or group of persons: all must be taken into consideration, for all are of equal worth. In reality these implications are not considerable unless certain assumptions are made about what sort of factor ought to be taken into account and given equal weight to whomsoever they apply. The tendency is to assume that, as in the examples given, equal consideration means that it is everyone's welfare or merit that is taken into account, but this is not logically entailed by the principle alone, since the substantive criteria of justice actually adopted may make no reference to such considerations and embody instead such less appealing standards as height, colour or luck. These amoral considerations cannot be ruled out of order by the idea of equal worth unless we introduce a substantive view of the features of humanity which render individual persons of equal worth.

It is, therefore, common to write into the idea of equal consideration a substantive notion of what factors are to be taken into account when determining the import of the idea of equal worth. These factors are those which are thought to be fundamental to the human person or to some aspect of what it is to be a human being, such as the capacity for experiencing pleasure and pain, or the ability to think, choose and be held responsible for one's actions. The principle of equal worth thus becomes the principle that people should have equal consideration as persons, so defined.

Some such idea of the equal worth of all humans is probably presupposed by the concept of justice, but as a principle it does not in itself encapsulate what justice is distinctively concerned with. The principle of equal worth may well be fundamental to the moral point of view in its entirety. Certainly it is a presupposition of classical utilitarianism as well as Kantian autonomy theory. It is possible, therefore, that what distinguishes justice as a moral consideration is that it proposes reasons which justify treatment which results in inequality. Again, however, this is not something which is unique to justice, for any moral consideration may justify unequal treatment. A theory of justice must, therefore, be able to identify and connect the reasons for differential treatment which have distinctively to do with justice. It seems doubtful that this can be done without adopting something like the meritorian thesis that justice has to do with the unequal worthiness of human beings and how this should be reflected in our treatment of them. It may also be that the determination of what counts as equal worth for the purposes of justice involves some reference to those properties of human beings that makes it reasonable for us to praise and blame them. In other words, justice presupposes that persons have equal worth as responsible agents. This makes for a close connection between the ideas of equal worth and unequal worthiness.

The meritorian view that justice is to do with the equal worth and unequal worthiness of human beings is hardly a morally neutral analysis of the concept of justice, but then perhaps justice is not a morally neutral concept. The meritorian position does leave open a vast range of issues within its moral parameters, for it still has to be decided which features of human beings are fundamental to their status as responsible agents, what is to count as merit and demerit, and what implications individual differences in the dimension of desert have for our treatment of each other. It leaves open, also, whether justice, so construed, is always of overriding, or even major, significance in determining what is morally right. Human beings are not only responsible moral agents, they are also, for instance, sentient beings with important experiences of pleasure and pain, something which lies at the base of egalitarian demands which may not be well formulated in the language of justice. Any account of what justice is about must take note that common humanity, or even generous beneficence, may sometimes be in conflict with, and more important than, the claims of justice.

2 Justice as Rights: Dworkin and Minorities

The violation of rights is often cited as a standard example of injustice. It is unsurprising, therefore, that attempts are made to analyse justice purely in terms of rights. Justice is then a matter of respecting rights and providing remedies for their infringement or violation. In accordance with the logic of the concept of justice articulated in Chapter 1, 'to each his or her due' is interpreted as meaning 'to each his or her rights', with differing conceptions of justice giving varying content to the rights in question.

This is a powerful thesis which appears to capture some of the most important aspects of justice discourse identified in the previous chapter. It fits the major significance which is normally attributed to justice, in that to assert something as a right is to assert that it may properly be insisted upon and is no mere optional extra or merely desirable goal. Rights, like justice, are matters of entitlement. They do not depend on the grace and favour of others. Rights generate obligations on the part of others, obligations which are in some sense owed to the rights-holder.

Viewing justice as a matter of rights also points up the emphasis on the interests of the individual which is a feature of justice discourse. For although collectives may be ascribed rights, the rights which justice theorists have in mind are primarily those which protect individuals against the singly lesser but cumulatively greater interests of large numbers of other people. In the words of Ronald Dworkin, whose work features centrally in this chapter, rights are 'trumps', in that they cannot be set aside at the behest of majorities or policies aimed at the overall good of society. The rights he has in mind are those individual rights, such as freedom of speech and equality before the law, which are given special constitutional protection in many jurisdictions, but the same logic, although perhaps in a weaker form, may be applied to rights in general. Consequently, 'justice as rights' fits well the anti-utilitarian flavour of justice.

The idea that individuals have rights captures also the belief that the possession of rights enhances the dignity of the right-holder (see Feinberg, 1970b, pp.243–57), and so exemplifies the idea of respect for persons which is often said to lie at the core of what it is to treat people justly. This contention is often thought to rest on a restrictive analysis of rights which confines the term to one type of right, namely rights which give the rights-holder the opportunity to control the action of others, if he or she opts to do so. However, the wider analysis of rights as rule-protected interests, which makes such optional powers a contingent feature of rights (that is, a feature which characterises some rights but not others) also enables us to see in the language of rights a commitment to the equal worth of every individual and the consequent priority of certain individual interests over consider-ations of the general good.

The idea of justice as rights also accords with the legal associ-ations of justice, and offers a ready explanation as to why courts of law are regarded as courts of justice. Rights have to do with the implementation of societal rules or other authoritative stan-dards, such as are embodied in laws. Similarly, the rights theory of justice can explain the connection between justice, remedies and punishments, and makes it clear why the demands of justice so often involve calls for the establishment of laws whose enforce-ment can be overseen by courts of law rather than left to the discretion of bureaucratic organisations.

On the other hand, it can be argued that rights have a narrower scope than justice. Rights seem most at home in limited areas where individual interests are protected by definitive rules capable of being adjudicated in courts of law. This may be important for the rectification of injustices done to individuals, but it does not seem to have the same foothold where matters of wider collective or 'social' justice are concerned. Unjustified economic inequalities, the absence of educational opportunity and discrimination in employment are all grave social injustices but they are not objectives whose attainment can always readily be effectively pursued by means of legally enforceable entitlements. To take in these wider issues we have to have recourse to some idea of background 'moral' rights whose nature and content are highly controversial and often obscure.

Moral rights are, in general, regarded as standards or values which determine the proper content of rules which affect the welfare and interests of individuals. If this means no more than that they are the rights we ought to have, then the concept is clear enough but the values it encompasses are obviously far wider than justice alone, for the full range of social and political values are relevant to the determination of 'positive' rights (that is, the rights which are embodied in actual laws and social conventions). If, however, it is argued that there are pre-legal and pre-social 'natural' rights which all men and women have independent of the authoritative rules of their society, then it may be that the distinctive properties of these rights will help us to identify what is just and unjust. Unfortunately the nature and reality of such mysterious entities as moral rights are hard to establish.

Moreover, the stress which the tradition of rights places on the freedom of the individual may be seen as a real hindrance to the achievement of the sort of egalitarian and welfare-oriented society which some see as a prime goal of justice. It may be that many rights give individuals unreasonable powers of veto over important social objectives whose justification is their contribution to justice. With its emphasis on individual choice and the liberty of the individual the theory of justice as rights often turns out to be an ideologically partisan theory in which liberty is favoured disproportionately over equality.

Rights and formal justice

Given the difficulties confronting the justice as moral rights thesis, it is common to retreat to a more limited objective and argue that rights are particularly germane to the analysis of formal justice, which may be defined as treating people in accordance with their existing socially recognised positive rights. Questions of material justice are then treated separately by means other than an appeal to rights. This has the advantage that the distinctiveness of the language of rights can be clearly demonstrated. The appeal to rights is seen as an appeal to established rules or conventions which settle the matter in hand without the need to consider all other, possible morally relevant, factors. If rights are conventional entitlements which block further debate in relation to the issues at stake, this enables us, for instance, to make a clear distinction between 'right' and 'rights', and we can then go on to identify justice with the latter.

This response substantially diminishes the claimed connection between rights and justice since it now excludes material questions about the content of rights-conferring rules. It becomes a particularly weak thesis if the arguments outlined in Chapter 1 concerning the moral unimportance of so-called pure formal justice are taken into account, since, as we have seen, formal justice, so conceived, places no real limitations on the possible content of rules and, in abstraction from such content, is of questionable moral significance.

However, since in ordinary and technical legal terminology, not all rules or norms embody rights, it may be that those rules which do confer rights are constrained with respect to their content, and that this constraint is a pointer to what justice is about. In other words, there may be a distinctive rationale for rights-conferring rules which is the real nub of the justice as rights thesis. For instance, if, following the developed analysis of formal justice and the rule of the law outlined in the previous chapter, the rights approach is extended to take in the idea of the equal worth of persons as a basis of the justification for having society governed by a system of rules, then the justice as rights thesis acquires rather more substance, although it still does not give a great deal of guidance as to the content of the rules in question. We could say, however, that rights, and therefore justice, involve a commitment to recognising the equal worth of persons.

The idea of equal worth can itself be developed in the light of theories of rights which seek to state what it is about persons that make them potential bearers or subjects of rights. Thus, if rights are defined, in accordance with the 'will' theory of rights, as normative powers of control over the behaviour of others, powers which the right-holder may exercise or not at his or her discretion (see Hart, 1973, pp.171–201), then the rights thesis could be interpreted as saying that individuals should have such powers, and that justice is done when these are established and upheld by law or social convention. Such discretionary powers may be justified as expressions of individual autonomy or as devices for protecting individual interests, and formal justice is then seen as giving effect to these morally desirable powers.

If, furthermore, we take the will theory of rights to include the proposition that human beings have, or ought to have, rights in virtue of their capacities as rational agents, then we have the beginnings of a pre-legal conception of moral rights of some substance. Such a position, which goes back at least as far as Kant, is exhibited by Gewirth's thesis that persons have rights to the necessary conditions for human action (see Gewirth, 1978, chapter 2). This view, when combined with certain truisms about the nature of action and its empirical prerequisites, carries significant import for the content of rights and hence, on the general approach under consideration, for the nature of material as well as formal justice. Moreover it has the advantage of bringing together the two types of justice — formal and material — in an explanatory way since both involve respecting individuals as autonomous choosers.

The will theory, and the associated idea of rights as the preconditions of human agency, are, however, overly restrictive analyses of rights, for rights are routinely predicated of subjects, such as young children and mentally handicapped people, who lack the capacity for rational choice and autonomous action (see MacCormick, 1977, pp.189–207). Moreover, when subsumed into the justice as rights thesis, the will theory does not account for the formal justice of rules which do not instantiate or protect powers or options. It is normally assumed that formal justice arises in relation to the application of any rules which have a bearing on the welfare or interests of persons, whether or not the rules confer powers or 'options'. The protection of interests can only be seen as a matter of rights if rights are defined so as to include all interests protected by rules from which persons (the right-holders) stand to benefit, as is the case of the 'interest' theory of rights, according to which a right is a rule-protected interest (see Campbell, 1983, pp.92–102).

Because the interest theory of rights is more open-ended, it is better suited than the will theory to provide an analysis of rights which makes it plausible to claim that formal justice normally arises in the application of all, or at least most, societal rules, for such rules normally have some bearing on human interests. Its weakness is that it is rather too broad to distinguish rules which confer rights from those which do not, although it does place some sort of limitation on the content of the rights-creating rules, for it requires that the rules in a system to which formal justice applies be at least conceived of as being in the interests of the persons concerned. This more open-ended requirement not only explains why issues of formal justice appear to arise over the application of a whole range of normal social and legal rules, but also has the advantage of greater ideological neutrality, in that it does not assume that the protection of individual choice has a greater claim to the status of a right than, for instance, the relief of suffering.

It would seem, therefore, that, although theories of rights may help us to some extent in filling out the bare notion of the equal worth of individuals, the more plausible of the rights theories on offer is too broad to provide an analysis which takes us beyond the mere outline of a rationale for having a system of formal justice, namely that it helps to protect and further human interests. If we wish to progress to a theory which can have a more substantial account of material justice it is necessary to have more specific guidance as to the nature and content of the so-called 'moral' rights which, it is claimed, provide standards for the assessment of the justice of the content of rules.

Justice as human rights

In order to extend the justice as rights hypothesis from formal to material justice, we may resort to the distinction between the general idea of moral rights and that sub-category of those moral rights which are deemed to be 'natural' or 'human' rights. The identification of the distinctive nature of such rights is a difficult and controversial task and lack of agreement about what constitutes a human right breeds doubt about the very concept of human rights. Most attempts at analysing human rights start out from the general position that human rights are a sub-category of moral rights which are universal (in that they apply to all persons everywhere and at all times), inalienable (in that they can be neither taken nor given away) and of overriding importance (so that they take precedence over all other considerations).

The problem of identifying more than a very few 'negative' rights — that is, rights *not* to be treated in certain ways — which meet these criteria is also great. Perhaps only the right not to be tortured is completely universal and inalienable, and even that may be doubted. For this reason the criteria are often watered down in various respects, particularly if it is thought desirable to include the 'social' and 'economic' rights, such as the right to education or health care, within the list of human rights. These rights are 'positive' in the sense that they are rights to be treated in certain ways, call for positive action on the part of others and usually depend on the deployment of scarce resources whose availability cannot be guaranteed everywhere and at all times. Unless formulated in an intolerably vague way, such rights cannot plausibly be claimed to be completely universal and entirely independent of particular economic circumstances.

However, if it is possible to arrive at an acceptable definition of human rights, material justice can then be defined in terms of securing such basic or human rights, and/or providing remedies for their infringement or violation. This has the advantage of making justice only one among the many considerations which may lead us to enact positive entitlements and, given the significance attached to human rights, it does much to explain the importance which many attach to the pursuit of justice.

In general the justice as human rights thesis generates, in more acute forms, both the attractions and difficulties of regarding justice as having to do with rights of any sort. Particularly promising is its account of the conflict between justice and utility since human rights cannot, because they are defined as overriding rights, be sacrificed to the general happiness. A weakness of the human rights approach lies in its retreat from a positivist interpretation of rights according to which rights are defined in terms of existing societal or legal rules. Justice as human rights is, therefore, unable adequately to account for the legal flavour of justice. Of course, there is a long history of attempts to translate human rights into legal form, but in general they lend themselves more to political rhetoric than to legal formulation and adjudication. The language of human rights expresses ideals and aspirations which need to be honed down into specific entitlements before the rights they are said to embody have any connection with formal justice and the rule of law, which require the accurate implementation of pre-existing rules.

The criticism that human rights, conceived along the lines of the traditional analyses, are non-justiciable may be thought to run counter to the experience of those jurisdictions which have operative conventions or bills of rights to which appeal can be made through courts against any action or inaction which is seriously detrimental to individuals, even if these are in accordance with the ordinary legislated law of the land. Does not the experience of the European Court of Human Rights, or of the Supreme Court of the United States of America, illustrate the viability of giving the force of positive law to the idea of human rights?

Certainly the notion of rights which have a special constitutional status in that they cannot be overturned, even by the otherwise lawful actions of governments, has become a reality which many political observers welcome as a way of providing some check on the failures and excesses even of democratic governments in matters which can readily be thought of in terms of injustice. If human rights are then defined as fundamental rights, that is, rights with special constitutional protection, then the idea of human rights does seem to have legal application. This is only achieved however by a patently positivistic analysis of human rights according to which they are equated with rules laid down by human decision, in this case through the enactment of the appropriate constitutional provisions. Human rights then become constitutionally entrenched rules which are normally administered by specialist courts, rather than simply a type of moral right of a sort to which appeal can be made to justify the setting up of such human rights conventions and special courts in the first place. It requires to be demonstrated, therefore, that in making their decisions human rights adjudicators are applying pre-existing and specific notions of pre-legal human rights. It may be that all that is going on is the creation of a new system of rules and precedents of a rather indeterminate nature which permit the extensive exercise of discretionary powers by an elite group of lawyers who are constrained only by political considerations and a highly unspecific tradition of human rights discourse as this is embodied in brief and ambiguous lists of human rights. The existence and application of bills of rights, and their constitutional equivalents, does not in itself prove the reality of the human rights in the moral form on which they are alleged to be based (see Campbell *et al.*, 1986, chapters 1 and 2).

Those who would present a view of justice in terms of human rights have to provide a coherent account of these rights and the way we determine what they are. Furthermore they have to indicate that violation of these rights is properly regarded as a matter of injustice, for there may be some things, such as torture, which we ought never to inflict on each other, but which are wrong not because of their injustice but for some other moral reason, such as their inhumanity. It may be that general theories of rights can help here, although, on close inspection, they throw up the very types of moral disagreement for help in resolving which we look to theories of rights. In particular the standard conflicts between liberty (as exemplified in the will theory of rights) and egalitarianism (which has more affinity with the interest theory) may have to be resolved before it is possible to identify either the form or the content of the rights to which special constitutional protection is to be given. At this level of debate the rights approach often appears to have little to offer beyond an appeal to dogmatic self-evidence or unchallengeable moral intuitions. Yet, there are no reasonably specific rights-conferring rules capable of obtaining the agreement of dispassionate and informed persons, even within the same culture, then it is doubtful whether the idea that there are moral rights (let alone that special sub-category of moral rights called *human* rights) is at all helpful in fixing our criteria of material justice. To settle controversial matters by an appeal to moral rights, human or otherwise, may be to do no more than pit one set of prejudices against others.

Given the epistemological blind alley into which rights' discourse often leads us, it may be that we should give up the idea of moral rights except in the 'manifesto' sense which refers to the rights which we believe ought to exist in a morally adequate society. This would be to abandon as unhelpful the notion of human rights, except in so far as it refers to the idea of giving special constitutional protection to some rights as a device for the protection of important human interests. Whether such rights are thought to have a particularly close connection with the concept of justice would then become a matter for subsequent analysis.

These are the sort of challenges to which a rights theory of justice has to respond. Unfortunately such responses are not always forthcoming. For instance, one noted rights theorist, Robert Nozick, simply assumes that men have certain natural rights and then proceeds to base his theory of justice on this essentially unproven assumption (Nozick, 1974, chapter 2). Others, such as Gewirth (1978) and Finnis (1980), do, however, give these issues closer attention. Gewirth, as we have seen, develops a Kantian basis for rights in terms of autonomy, while Finnis follows the natural law tradition of Aristotle and Aquinas. A particularly significant contribution to theories of rights as a basis for justice has been made by Ronald Dworkin who, in *Taking Rights Seriously*, presents a sustained effort to bridge the gap between the notions of moral rights and positive rights in a manner which, if successful, would provide a basis for presenting an attractive form of the justice as rights thesis. It is to this theory that the remainder of this chapter is largely directed.

Dworkin's rights

That Dworkin has not generally been regarded as primarily a theorist of justice is an indication of the extent to which considerations of so-called social justice have become detached from legal contexts but, as his recent writings make clear, he is as much concerned with wide issues of social justice as with the specific nature of legal justice. While it is primarily of rights that Dworkin writes, his analysis of rights is carried out firmly within the assumption that justice is a matter of determining what rights persons have and ensuring that they are treated in accordance with these rights. Not only does he contend that 'it is a matter of injustice when judges make mistakes about legal rights' (Dworkin, 1978, p.130), he also insists that 'the institution of rights rests on the conviction that the invasion of a relatively important right . . . is a grave injustice' (ibid., p.199). This is because, in his view, rights bear on the dignity and equality of persons, factors which are, for Dworkin, the very foundations of justice. Thus, in the Dworkinian scheme of things, justice and rights go together so that, for instance, the question of whether or not a practice such as positive discrimination is unjust is treated as a question about whether or not the practice violates the rights of those affected by

it (see ibid., pp.22, 198 and 231). He is therefore firmly committed
to a rights theory of justice.

Dworkin divides political theories, including theories of justice,
into three groups. The first consists of teleological theories which
are ultimately based on goals (states of affairs that may be
advanced or preserved by political acts). Utilitarianism is one
such theory. The other two theories are deontological ones in
that they rest on convictions about the rightness or wrongness of
acts in themselves, independently of their further consequences.
Of these deontological theories, the first is rights-based and the
second duty-based. In this context he says that a person has 'a
right to a particular political act, within a political theory, if the
failure to provide that act, when he calls for it, would be
unjustified within that theory even if the goals of the theory
would, on the balance, be disserviced by that act' (ibid., p.169),
while a person has 'a *duty* to act in a particular way, within a
political theory, if a political decision constraining such an act is
justified within that theory notwithstanding that no goal of the
system would be served by that decision' (ibid., p.170).

While Dworkin contends that all theories involve goals, rights
and duties, he argues that they differ as to which type of norm is
fundamental from the point of view of ultimate justifications.
Thus goals may be justified because they promote rights or
duties, while rights or duties may be justified, in a rule-utilitarian
manner, on the grounds that, in the long run, they promote
certain goals. Similarly rights may be justified on the basis of
their correlative duties, or duties may be justified in terms of
their correlative rights. Alternatively, goals, rights or duties may
be justified by reference to other more basic goals, rights or
duties or, on the other hand, they may stand on their own as
being in no need of further justification.

Ultimately, however, justifications must be grounded in one or
other type of consideration. Each political theory will not only
have its own particular set of goals, rights and duties but 'will
give ultimate pride of place to just one of these concepts; it will
take some overriding goal, or some set of fundamental rights, or
some set of transcendent duties, as fundamental, and show other
goals, rights, and duties as subordinate and derivative' (ibid.,
p.171). Thus, all theories, except for 'intuitionist' theories, which
present a pluralism of ultimate bases, are either goal-based (like

utilitarianism), duty-based (like Kant's categorical imperative theory) or rights-based (like Tom Paine's theory of revolution). Dworkin permits all three types of theory to have a concept of justice in that all three approaches generate positive rights, but he regards the rights-based theories as preferable for the formulation of a conception of justice.

The focus of Dworkin's theory of rights is not directed towards ordinary positive rights. He interprets ordinary positive rights along the lines of the will theory as having to do with actions that the right-holder may or may not 'call for' as he chooses, and he assumes that in normal circumstances justice requires implementation of these rights. However, his concern is rather with the 'background' rights which act as the ultimate justifications for ordinary positive rights and also set strict limits on the propriety of any goals that may be endorsed. He allows that not all goals are justified in terms of rights but insists that no pursuit of a goal may be of a form which violates a basic right. Basic rights are thus moral or political rights which generate entitlements: 'if someone has a right to something, then it is wrong for the government to deny it to him even though it would be in the general interest to do so' (ibid., p.269).

As is the case with all rights, basic rights act as restraints on behaviour, including goal-seeking behaviour. That is why they are conceived as 'trumps', for they have automatic precedence over or exclude other considerations. This veto power is however a matter of degree in that, while all rights must have some 'exclusionary' force, since they cannot be set aside by every morally relevant consideration (see Raz, 1975, pp.35–48), some rights have greater exclusionary force or trumping power than others. At one extreme on the scale of overridings there are 'absolute rights', which never yield to competing rights or vital goals, while at the other extreme are rights with so little 'weight' that they override scarcely any other rights or goals. Nevertheless every right must have some 'threshold' force which enables it to outweigh other considerations, otherwise it could not function as a right.

With this scheme Dworkin can distinguish between 'background rights, which are rights that provide a justification for political decisions by society in the abstract', and what he calls 'institutional rights, that provide a justification for a decision by some particular and specified political institution' (ibid., p.93). Background rights are abstract rights which constitute 'the grand rights of political rhetoric' while institutional rights are 'concrete' in that they 'are more precisely defined so as to express more definitely what weight they have against other political aims on particular occasions' (ibid.). Abstract rights provide justifications for concrete rights but they carry no immediate remedies, while concrete rights are definitive of what is institutionally due to a person in particular circumstances.

It is a distinguishing feature of Dworkin's analysis of rights that they are not always expressed in rules. Concrete institutional rights are normally formulated in rules which, for Dworkin, means that they can be applied in an 'all-or-nothing' manner. These constitute the paradigmatic legal or positive rights which are the core of normal legal adjudication and which, according to the rule of law, judges should apply in routine courtroom findings. However, Dworkin does not take the standard line of contrasting such positive rights with moral rights and then restricting judges to the adjudication of positive rights, leaving it to legislatures to draw on moral rights for the formulation of legal rules. Rather he argues that the law itself contains 'principles' as well as rules. These principles are distinguished, not by their greater generality or vagueness, but by the fact that, in judicial reasoning, they have a certain 'weight' rather than an 'all-or-nothing' effect, that is, they provide reasons for a particular decision of varying force, but do not definitively dispose of the case in hand. The role of principles in legal reasoning is primarily to decide 'hard' — that is, unclear — cases where there are no unambiguous relevant rules, or where the rules produce results which are unacceptable in terms of certain basic legal principles such as the principle that 'no man should profit from his own wrong' (ibid., p.24). These principles embody or imply rights with a more fundamental status in Dworkin's hierarchy of legal norms than ordinary positive rights.

Dworkin's most influential and controversial work is his attempt to demonstrate that the existence of principles within the law undermines the view of legal positivists, such as Hart (1961), that law is a system of rules supplemented by judicial discretion where this is necessary in order to interpret ambiguities in the rules or to fill in gaps where there is no uncontroversially relevant rule by which to decide a particular case. His thesis is that, if we accept legal principles, then judges have a sufficient basis for arriving at a correct legal decision in every case, however 'hard' it may be. Moreover, since these principles are identified with the background moral principles used to justify concrete rights, it follows that legal validity is not a matter of positive enactment alone but involves a moral dimension. This moral dimension, which represents the basic requirements of justice, is expressed in the legal principles which enable judges to decide hard cases without resort to discretionary power.

Dworkin holds to the line that judges determine what the law is, rather than supplement it with their own personal judgements. In determining what principles there are in law and what weight to give them in particular cases judges do, or should, draw on the morality of their society. However, this societal morality is not the moral fashion of the moment, as it might be expressed in an opinion poll, but is to be found in the abstract rights embedded or presupposed in the legislation and political culture of that society in its historical development. The judge is fitted to determine what these principles are because they are discovered by constructing 'a scheme of abstract and concrete principles that provide a coherent justification for all common law precedents and, so far as these are to be justified on principle, constitutional and statutory provisions as well' (ibid., pp.116f). This is a style of reasoning familiar to lawyers, who seek to determine the law by considering previous legal decisions in the light of relevant enacted laws which they endeavour to interpret as a coherent whole. Such legal method is, according to Dworkin, extended, where necessary, by a broader appeal to that background political theory which can provide the most coherent justification for the settled law. In this the judge may take account of the general role of law in that society and the current standards of community morality as well as the specifics of past political and legal decisions, for 'political rights are the creatures of both history and morality: what an individual is entitled to have, in civil society, depends upon both the practice and the justice of its political institutions' (ibid., p.87).

It cannot be said that Dworkin's strategy for bridging the gap between law and morals, which is insisted upon by the legal positivist, is entirely clear. His objective is to provide a satisfactory delineation of the boundary between legislative and adjudicative decision-making and so preserve the classical doctrine of the separation of powers. He does this by seeking to demonstrate that there is an autonomous mode of judicial decision-making that is compatible with the non-elected status of the judiciary. This thesis rests on the claim that judges are bound by and are able to follow the law rather than create it in every case that comes before them.

To maintain the distinction between legislation and adjudication Dworkin insists on a sharp contrast between decisions based on the rules and principles on the one hand, and decisions which involve some reference to goals, on the other hand. Legislatures may properly make law in order to further collective goals, such as economic prosperity, as well as to concretise background rights or duties, always provided they do not infringe rights in the pursuit of such goals. Judges, however, may decide cases by reference only to rules and principles. In effect this means that they must make their decisions by reference to rights (for principles as well as rules are expressive of rights), not goals. The right answer in a legal case is, therefore, the decision which treats persons according to their pre-existing rights. While some of these rights will have been enacted by legislatures intent on furthering certain policies, judges may not reason in the light of these policy objectives but must restrict their attention to the concrete rights, and where necessary, the background political or moral rights which have weight in that particular sphere.

Thus standards of justice feature in both adjudication and legislation, but in adjudication justice is the sole consideration, the just decision being the one which gives effect to the rights of the accused or the plaintiffs. In legislation, on the other hand, decisions are made according to a combination of goals and background abstract rights. Only where the latter are involved does justice feature. Thus justice may provide a veto on goal-based legislation which infringes upon background rights. In addition, justice is the sole basis for legislation designed to protect or further abstract rights. In the latter cases, Dworkin argues, rights must be distributed equally, a requirement which does not apply if legislation is a matter of policy, when legislatures may distribute benefits and burdens unevenly if they so choose, provided basic rights are not affected.

It is this connection between rights and equality which provides Dworkin with the underlying moral basis for his theory of rights and thus his analysis of justice. Indeed his ultimate basic right is the right to 'equal consideration and respect' which he distinguishes from actual 'equality of treatment', the term he uses to refer to those situations where each person either receives, or ends up with, the same equality of the valued commodity that is being distributed. Justice involves the right to treatment as an equal, not the right to equal treatment.

At one level of analysis it appears that the principle of treatment as an equal is part of the very concept of justice, for it is presented as an abstract right which can be satisfied by many different concrete political ideals, including egalitarianism, meritocracy and average utility or Rawlsian fairness. Treatment as an equal requires only that, whatever the details of the system of distribution, government must treat people with equal concern and respect. In particular, government 'must not distribute goods or opportunities unequally on the grounds that some citizens are entitled to more because they are worthy of more concern. It must not constrain liberty on the ground that one citizen's conception of the good life is nobler or superior to another's' (ibid., p.273).

This version of the principle of equal worth does not imply that the interests of some citizens may not have to give way to those of others, but it does entail that each citizen's interests will be given the same sympathetic consideration when, for instance, liberty is curtailed in the interests of some collective goal. It also means that the ideals of one person or group should not be imposed on those who do not share them.

To give substance to this 'highly abstract' right Dworkin argues that in the determination of collective goals majority preferences should count, but only where these preferences are based on the individual's aspirations for himself (his 'personal' preferences) as opposed to his wishes about what should happen to others (his 'external' preferences):

'a utilitarian argument that assigns critical weight to the external preferences of members of the community will not be egalitarian in the sense under consideration. It will not respect the right of everyone to be treated with equal concern and respect.' (ibid., p.275)

It is because the ordinary democratic process cannot in practice sort out personal from external preferences that the idea of individual political rights is so important, for such rights provide a way of protecting individuals against the external preferences of others, and this:

> 'allows us to enjoy the institutions of political democracy, which enforce overall or unrefined utilitarianism, and yet protect the fundamental right of citizens to equal concern and respect by prohibiting decisions that seem, antecedently, likely to have been reached by virtue of the external components of the preferences democracy reveals'. (Ibid., p.277)

Hence it is the liberal commitment to equality that is the basis for the protection of individual liberties.

The powerful attraction of Dworkin's approach to rights as the basis for an account of justice lies in the way he relates the formalism of treating persons in accordance with their positive legal rights to the background moral rights which can provide reasons why the accurate implementation of concrete rights is desirable, thus bridging the gap between formal and material justice. He seeks to transcend what he calls a 'rule-book' conception of the rule of law which covers only the idea of strict adherence to legal rules and argues for a 'rights' conception of the rule of law which requires the adjudicator to give due weight to the principles which would justify existing legislative enactments. Moreover the way in which Dworkin connects rights with the concept of the individual as worthy of equal respect ties in with the idea of the moral significance of individual responsibility, the exercise of personal choice and the pursuit of self-determination, all of which give substance to the idea of justice as a distinct and major moral ideal.

Nevertheless the principal weakness of Dworkin's theory is its failure to give a convincing account of the relationship between concrete and background rights. This is partly a matter of the difficulty he has in giving grounds for accepting his thesis that there is a right answer to hard cases of law and that this answer is properly described as discovering and applying the rights of the parties involved. Even if it is conceded that there is a correct answer to every legal dispute, the elaborate form of reasoning required to reach this answer makes it difficult to believe that legal decisions are made only on the basis of something we can recognise as pre-existing 'rights'.

In the first place, this contention ignores the substantial role played by appeals to public policy — such as the consequences for governmental objectives like economic efficiency — as the basis for apellate decisions in court. Dworkin has met this difficulty by saying that apparent appeals to policy can always be 'substituted' with arguments of principle. Public policy arguments can readily be rephrased so that they are stated in terms of protecting or furthering the rights of those affected by the policy. This manoeuvre hardly fits in with his contention that goals and hence policies are non-individuated political aims and thus presumably far removed from the idea of individual rights. Indeed, if taken literally, this concession as to the interchangeability of policy and principle undermines all that he has sought to establish about the significance of rights in legal decision-making.

In the second place, it seems a matter of faith for Dworkin to assert that there is an objective way of deciding which decision in hard cases best coheres with the precedents, rules, principles and background political philosophy of a jurisdiction. If the notion of a right answer is merely regulative, in that it does no more than provide an abstract but unattainable goal towards which it is our legal duty to strive, then appeals to rights cannot fulfil their normal function of providing a way of settling disputes by reference to institutional rules or principles, for, ultimately, it simply involves accepting the determinations of persons appointed to make such decisions. Indeed it can be argued that the overt purpose in the formulation of some rules (particularly those which contain references to standards such as 'reasonableness') and many legal principles is to enable the judiciary to deploy general ideas of fairness or desert so that justice may be done in particular cases. These difficulties are not eased by Dworkin's recent deployment of the ideas of 'integrity' as an objective of legal reasoning or his proffered analogy between legal and literary textual interpretation (see Dworkin, 1986).

It follows from these criticisms that the 'moral' judgements involved in determining rights by reference to principles cannot in practice be subsumed under the methods of formal legal reasoning, so that the gap between formal and material justice, which Dworkin seeks to bridge, inevitably re-emerges. Background abstract 'rights' dissolve into generalised moral values which cannot function as rights by giving us a relatively objective and politically uncontroversial way of determining entitlements by reference to an authoritative system of norms.

Moreover Dworkin does not give us any reason to accept that law as such contains rights of the sort that he approves of. Writing within the tradition of American jurisprudence and taking it for granted that the political and legal culture of that jurisdiction are of an acceptable democratic and liberal form, he can readily equate his background 'rights' with moral principles of a specific content. It is relatively easy for us to accept the significance of formal justice, or the rule of law, in a system which seeks to render coherent such evidently acceptable meritorian beliefs as the principle that no man may profit by his own wrong. But this does not render more acceptable the coherence of rules and principles which embody the traditions of offensive political cultures. At this point there is a fundamental ambivalence in Dworkin's conception of the moral rights which are 'there' in the law. Sometimes he argues that these rights are the principles which would give a coherent and consistent justification of legal precedents and legislative enactments already posited. At other times he permits an appeal beyond positive rights and evaluations to the basic principle behind all rights, that is to some explication of the idea that we should treat persons with equal concern and respect.

To meet such criticisms Dworkin would have to argue that the very idea of rights limits the content of principles. In effect he attempts little more than the articulation of the idea of rights as part of a liberal tradition of law and politics. This means that, according to one interpretation, the development of Dworkin's theory requires the Herculean task of seeking the explicit statement of the rights inherent in the American or some other acceptable liberal democratic tradition; that is, the method to discover what rights persons have becomes a task for high-level legal reasoning of the sort he commends.

However on another interpretation of the Dworkin enterprise we must use the background right of equal concern and respect to work out a basis for deciding which positive rights persons ought to have (and therefore in Dworkin's natural law terminology, actually do have). This is to make the central thrust of Dworkin's theory to license appellate courts to decide hard cases by reasoning from fundamental principles to concrete rights. This involves working out the meaning and application of these principles rather than seeking to demonstrate or discover a hidden coherence behind the jumble of statutory provisions, decided cases and historically sanctified political outlooks. At the same time, it would transform Dworkin's approach from a mainly legal to a mainly political philosophy of direct relevance to defining the content of rights independently of past legislative and judicial decisions.

Dworkin's politics

The political dimension of Dworkin's enterprise cannot be carried out by remaining at a level of analysis of 'equal concern and respect' which makes it compatible with a wide range of views on material justice, for we have to be confident that the principle can act as a way of justifying specific decisions where difficult moral choices have to be made. Interestingly Dworkin has embarked on the arduous task of putting flesh on the bones of his fundamental principle of justice so that it can fulfil this problematic role. In a long and complex two-part article (Dworkin, 1981) he develops these ideas in relation to what he calls distributional as distinct from political equality, that is, in relation to resources other than political power. In the first part he dismisses various types of 'equality of welfare' on the general grounds that there is no way of measuring welfare which is at once practicable and acceptable. For instance, 'equality of satisfaction' is intrinsically relative to morally arbitrary or controversial individual tastes and goals while 'equality of success' in achieving preferred objectives is relative to subjective factors, such as individual preferences and ambitions. In other words there are impossible baseline problems in measuring and comparing welfare, whether interpreted as enjoyment, preference or satisfaction, particularly as it is unfair to take into account expensive tastes and unusual ambitions.

An approximation to 'equality of resources', on the other hand, where the individual shares of resources available for private holding are equally distributed, is measurable and manageable through the utilisation of the mechanisms of the market-place in ways which get round the problems of differing tastes and ambitions. In the second part of the article, his basic thesis is that a fair distribution, based on equal concern and respect, will not take into account pure luck, including the distribution of natural endowments, but will allow for the effects of the uses individuals make of their talents and the choices they make in the pursuit of their chosen interests in a liberal economy. In Dworkin's terminology a fair distributive scheme is 'endowment insensitive' but not 'ambition sensitive'. This situation is reached through a combination of an imaginary original auction in which all individuals are given equal amounts of currency and can bid for whatever type of scarce resource they wish to the extent that they can afford, and a progressive taxation system which provides compensations and safeguards to an extent that the average informed individuals would have insured themselves against had they been given the opportunity to do so at the outset of their entry into society. This insurance cover is taken out in a hypothetical situation of equal risk of such disasters as being born handicapped or suffering later misfortunes.

Such an insurance system does not generate literal equality of resources, for those with scarce and demanded skills who choose to work will find rewards way beyond those guaranteed by any rational insurance system, but it will reflect an acceptable balance which embodies the objective of each individual being treated with the same concern and respect. We will not be compensated because of our expensive tastes or below-average skills but we will be safeguarded against seriously debilitating circumstances and gross lack of ability. All this worked out in terms of what is considered to be a fair arrangement for a 'number of shipwrecked survivors . . . washed up on a desert island which has abundant resources and no native population' (ibid., p.285). It is assumed that in these circumstances 'no division of resources is an equal division if, once the division is complete, any immigrant would prefer someone else's bundle of resources to his own bundle' (the 'envy test'). This is taken as constituting one way of arriving at a fair outcome, given that each immigrant can argue that 'no one is antecedently entitled to any of the resources, but that they shall instead be dispersed equally among them' (ibid.).

Some of the complexities of this imaginative and convoluted

scheme will be considered in the next section, but the important point to note here is the distance which we have come from the starting-point of the justice as rights thesis in which we seemed to be promised a way of determining what is just which has some structural similarity to the way in which our actual positive rights are determined in a court of law. Instead we have become enveloped in a controversial exploration of how we determine the basic principles of justice and their practical implications. In other words we are back in the sphere of standard moral and political argument in which the appeal to the rights of individuals settles nothing more specific than, perhaps, a general strategic approach to the issues in question. Such 'rights' are so far removed from the positive rights which feature in determining our day to day entitlements that they have no more distinctive role in moral argumentation about what positive rights we ought to have than any other socially relevant moral ideal. In other words the rights thesis, when deployed in relation to material justice, is in danger of losing its distinctive flavour and promised usefulness.

Justice and minorities

The protection of minorities against the moral claims of majorities has long been regarded as a prime test for a theory of justice, for it is to considerations of justice that we look for the grounds on which to limit the political rights of majorities. The issues here relate to the proper limits to the fundamental democratic idea that, in cases of conflict, issues, including legislative matters, be settled by resort to democratic decision procedures which terminate in a vote in which all members of the community may participate, directly or indirectly, and in which that choice which obtains the greatest numerical support should be binding on all. The question arises whether this majoritarian principle implies that there are no limits to what a majority of persons in a polity may decide to impose on unwilling minorities.

Some such limitations are, of course, inherent in the very concept of democracy, since it must be assumed that the majority decision takes place in a constitutional setting in which all have the right to vote and stand for election. This means that demo-

cratic majorities cannot remove such political rights from minorities without ceasing to be democratic majorities. By filling out the
idea of democracy to include the role of information and communication in making electoral choices 'real', minorities can be
guaranteed freedom of speech, freedom of communication in
general (hence freedom of the press) and perhaps freedom to
demonstrate and protest in order to bring their views to the
attention of others. All this can be presented as presupposed by
the majoritarian principle. By extension of the same mode of
argument, the furtherance of the qualities which are required to
make rational choices in a democracy may be included in the
ideal of a democracy so that it is possible to argue that some form
of educational provision is a democratic right which cannot be
taken away by majority fiat.

These democratic restrictions on the rights of majorities can be
regarded as a matter of justice if democracy itself is justified on
that basis. This may operate at two levels: either the democratic
system is based on self-determination rather than, for instance,
on utility, and self-determination is seen as a facet of justice, or
democratic procedures are in general justified on non-justice
grounds but it is contended that it is just that all have an equal
opportunity to participate in such procedures.

However, quite apart from these constitutional-based arguments, the question arises as to whether there are other considerations which bear on the limits which may be placed on the
substance of the decisions imposed by majorities. That there are,
or should be, such limitations is a principal motivation for the
enactment of bills of rights and other constitutional curbs on
majority powers. Such arrangements can be seen as the dominant
background context for Dworkin's discussions of abstract absolute
rights. The question therefore arises whether the principle of
equal concern and respect gives us any substantial leverage
against majoritarianism by providing a basis for constitutionally
protected minority rights beyond those which are logically entailed
by the majoritarian principle itself.

Dworkin himself has discussed these matters, mainly in the
context of the politics of discrimination, holding that 'the argument in favour of anti-discrimination statutes, that a minority has
a right to equal respect and concern, is an argument of principle'
(1978, p.82). Thus, when confronted with the contrast between

two racial discrimination cases, one in which 'a black man named Sweatt applied to the University of Texas Law School, but was refused admission because state law provided that only whites could attend' and another in which 'a Jew named DeFunis applied to the University of Washington Law School; he was rejected although his test scores and college grades were such that he would have been admitted if he had been a black or Filipino or . . .' (ibid., p.223), Dworkin is able to support the Supreme Court decision in favour of Sweatt on the grounds that his exclusion violated Sweatt's constitutional rights, while, at the same time, maintaining that no fundamental right of DeFunis had been infringed.

His argument is that in such cases there is no right to equal treatment because educational places of this type are not something to which every individual has a prior right, so that what matters is whether the persons concerned are being 'treated as equals', that is 'with the same respect and concern as anyone else'. However, while it may be self-evident that Sweatt is not being treated in such a way, the same would appear to be true for DeFunis, whose scholastic achievements are not being given the same weight as those of other persons.

Dworkin's response to such a contention is to point out that, since neither DeFunis, nor anyone else, has the right to a place in a Law School, it is proper for those deciding on entrance policies to have regard to social policy or community goals, such as the desirable racial balance of lawyers who have to serve the different communities within society. This is a matter of policy, not of rights, so DeFunis may be excluded as a consequence of goal-based decision-making.

But is the same not true in the case of Sweatt who also did not have an antecedent right to enter Law School? In this case the answer is different, however, not because there was no policy behind the University of Texas Law School entry criteria (racial harmony might indeed be served by it) but because a fundamental right is violated by the application of its criteria. It is not enough, in Dworkin's view, merely to point out that minority groups feel insulted by discriminatory practices, so that 'If we wish to distinguish *De Funis* from *Sweatt* or some argument that uses one concept of an insult, we must show that the treatment of the one, but not the other, is in fact unjust' (p.231).

To demonstrate this Dworkin brings in his distinction between personal and external preferences, that is, between preferences which relate solely to the individual's aspirations and desires for himself or herself, as opposed to his or her wishes about what they would like to happen to others. Racial segregation policies are based on external preferences to the extent that they involve the majority enacting their wishes for the lives of the members of other racial groups, whereas such considerations do not decisively affect the policy decisions for affirmative action in the absence of which DeFunis would have been admitted.

The distinction between personal and external preferences is a powerful one, if only because it echoes the assumptions of classical utilitarianism and modern welfare economics that rational preferences are preferences based on individual self-interest. However it is doubtful whether it is a powerful enough distinction to achieve such an ambitious objective as the identification of the fundamental rights which prohibit the exploitation of minorities. Rather it serves more as an *ad hoc* device of particular relevance to what is nowadays referred to as 'discrimination', namely the disfavouring of a group on irrelevant grounds where there is an element of dislike or denigration involved. There does seem to be something particularly offensive in a group being disadvantaged as a result of being despised and undervalued, and this is clearly a factor in racial, and also in religious and sexual discrimination, which accounts for the element of insult experienced by those who are discriminated against for these reasons. There is thus a basis for saying that, in the distribution of social benefits, we should exclude external preferences, such as whites not wishing blacks, or men not wishing women, to have certain opportunities.

However, while such a device may, in certain political circumstances, open up the prospect of greater equality to such groups and while there may be something to be said morally for discounting this sort of external preference as distasteful or worse, it is hardly exhaustive of the grounds for condemning discrimination and is of dubious relevance to other types of unjustified minority disadvantage.

Thus in discrimination it is the injustice and inhumanity of systematic deprivation in line with racial, religious or sexual differences, as well as the element of insult in the reasons why such inequality is brought about, that is to be condemned. If, for whatever reason, the merits or sufferings of such 'minorities' are not given the same weight as are accorded to the merits and sufferings of the privileged groups, then wrongs have been identified and call for rectification. Thus, if as a result of decision processes which involve nothing more than the self-interested inputs of the 'majorities' certain groups are in fact systematically worse off, as is the case with much 'indirect' discrimination where there is no explicit or even covert use of the basis of the group classification (sex, race or religion) but these groups nevertheless suffer disproportionately, then injustice and perhaps inhumanity are in evidence whether or not external preferences are involved. Dworkin's approach appears to bypass these basic moral insights and highlights another aspect of immorality which is, in most cases, of lesser significance to discriminated groups, to whom the injury is worse than the insult which is so often added to it.

The same points may be made, *a fortiori*, where any individual or group in society suffers as a result of the preferences of the majority, for the fact that majorities take only their own interests into account is, in many respects, grounds for doubting the moral authority of their decisions, the point being that they ought to take into account the welfare of all members of society and to do so in proportion to the needs and merits of each individual. John Stuart Mill's fears concerning the pressure of unenlightened public opinion and the untrammelled political decisions of the enfranchised working classes were not based only on the worry that the progressive elite would be coerced through the application of an inferior morality but also on the grounds that social and political arrangements would be made to suit the uninformed and misguided personal preferences of the majority. Anxieties on this score are not alleviated by excluding external preferences, even if this were a practical alternative.

Indeed it is far from clear that external preferences are always irrelevant to social decision-making, particularly where we are in the realm of public goods that cannot be parcelled up into little bits and distributed to individuals as separately valuable items. National defence, adequate policing, architectural preservation, and public goods in general, are more securely sustained and more readily justified by approaches which embody a concern for the welfare of the community as a whole rather than as an aggregation of self-centred preferences. Certainly there is nothing that is insulting and little that is dangerous in permitting external preferences a role in the determination of policy in such matters.

If the distinction between personal and external preferences is not a prime or exhaustive guide to the distinction between policies which infringe rights and those which do not, then it may be that more mileage can be got from Dworkin's model for just distribution of private goods. Would indirect discrimination, for instance, not be excluded by the combination of an equal auction and a hypothetical insurance market?

Due to the complexities and abstractness of Dworkin's more recently formulated decision-making model it is not easy to determine what its actual outcomes would be. This in itself is a major drawback to a theory of justice which is meant to be based on rights, for the advantage of a rights approach should be to set up an authoritative source of guidance as to the entitlements of persons. As far as it is possible to surmise on these matters it would appear that the equal distribution of resource-commanding tokens (whether it be clamshells suggested by Dworkin in his desert island example, or other forms of currency) in combination with the 'perfect' auctioning of all individualisable resources would not produce a distribution skewed against all the minority groups which are at present worse off in existing societies. But since differences in taste and need are not allowed for, and different abilities will inevitably lead to legitimate inequalities through the ensuing processes of economic choices in a market economy, it is clear that other 'inequalities' will emerge which will seem unjustified from other standpoints, such as the merits or needs of those involved.

Dworkin certainly seeks to avoid some merit-based inequalities by using the taxation system to compensate for some (it would appear, extreme) differences of endowment, so that handicapped persons would not be left to starve. And there is no doubt that a properly organised market economy will give higher rewards to some persons who are meritorious because they choose wisely and work hard in proportion to their genetic endowment. However there is little ground for the optimistic view that a society based on Dworkin's ideal of initial equality of resources will approximate to one in which there is a systematic proportionality of resources possessed to the merits and demerits of its citizens, and his approach is undoubtedly ill-adapted to providing for equality of satisfaction of needs. Indeed the correctives of Dworkinian taxation, however progressive, specifically exclude the objective of attaining 'equality of welfare', that is, an equality of satisfactions or 'success' in one's chosen life-objectives.

Dworkin has, or course, a host of pertinent arguments against such ideals as 'equality of welfare', most of which are aimed at the impracticality of seeking to ensure equal satisfactions and success, due to the absence of objective and workable measures of 'satisfaction' or 'success'. There is, however, an obvious sense in which equality of resources is a second best choice for an ideal of justice since it is hard to avoid the feeling that its intuitive plausibility depends on the assumption that equality of resources gives an equal chance of equal satisfactions. Resources are, after all, not ends in themselves but means to achieve human purposes. Further, the fact that this equality of resources does not adjust for major differences in tastes and needs would appear to entail 'discrimination' against those with tastes or needs for goods which are scarce and in high demand (which is a matter of fortune) or which simply require more than the average amounts of a given resource to satisfy. Which new oppressed minorities would emerge from this desert island fantasy it is hard to determine, but it is clear that there would be some such. The Dworkinian scheme could only take account of these inequalities if they are of such magnitude and likelihood that the average immigrant to a new social arrangement would think it wise to insure against them. Dworkin however admits that there will be systematic underinsurance in that it will not be rational to pay high enough premiums to ensure full compensation for misfortunes particularly where misfortunes include the absence of advantages that, given better luck, persons might have had.

It is not intended to argue comprehensively in this section against Dworkinian equality, or to prove that rights cannot be powerful instruments for the protection of minority interests. In fact a constitutionally entrenched system of rights embodied in rules rendered specific in the course of a history of judicial decision-making and political debate may well serve as an important means of protecting minorities against unjust treatment at the hands of majorities. It is often of immense value when faced with a decision which favours most but not all of the members of a society to be able to point to considerations which veto that decision on grounds which cannot be overturned by utilitarian considerations alone. Rules which give entitlements that are inviolate against majority decisions both symbolise and protect the objective of justice for all.

What is in question, however, is whether, in the effort to formulate the content or scope of such rights, it is of much use to appeal to some pre-existing 'moral' rights for guidance. Our discussion of Dworkin's account of justice confirms that, once we go beyond the identification of rights with rule-protected interests and move into the realm of general moral principle (and here I use the term 'principle' in its ordinary sense in which it implies vagueness as well as variable moral weight), we rapidly enter the arena of general moral and political argument in which the issues are to do with what rights we should have and what weight these rights should be given, rather than what 'trump' rights we, in some obscure sense, already have and can therefore call to our aid in a peremptory manner. The sort of basic or fundamental rights which Dworkin seeks to provide us with through the efforts of Hercules, the infinitely able and knowledgeable judge, or through the imaginative model of clamshell auctions and hypothetical insurance markets, cannot serve as the basis for an appeal to entitlements which preclude the necessity for further moral debate, as should be the case if we are dealing in rights as they feature in their characteristic contexts and distinctive uses.

What we have, instead, is a series of significant moral considerations which are on all fours with competing moral arguments based on such factors as merit, need or choice. In other words, at this level of justificatory argument, talk of rights has nothing distinctive to contribute beyond a sense that judicial procedure is an appropriate forum for the allocation of values. Indeed it may be dangerous terminology in that it leads people to expect that we may discover certain self-evident deontological truths to which we can give absolute practical priority. There may be serious epistemological and, in the end, moral objections, to the pretensions set up by the proposition that there are fundamental moral rights which are there to be discovered once we have acquired the necessary insight or refined the most illuminating set of distinctions and techniques of legal and political argument. The history of the thesis that justice is a matter of treating persons in accordance with their rights is a warning that there are no shortcuts to the determination of what is just. In the end Dworkinian rights leave us in a muddy pool of moral argument from which we are unlikely to be rescued on the chimerical life-raft of so-called moral rights, however fundamental they are alleged to be.

3 Justice as Contract: Rawls and Welfare

It is a measure of the immense influence of John Rawls that it seems appropriate, when going beyond the formalism of the 'justice as rights' approach, to give first consideration to contractual theories of justice. In many respects Rawls's major work, *A Theory of Justice* (1971) has set the current agenda of issues to be discussed, and provides the terminology in which much of this discussion proceeds. It is important therefore that both the force and the limitations of Rawlsian contractarianism are appreciated before alternative approaches are examined.

There are at least two ways into the analysis of the conceptual ties between justice and contract. The first is to note that the obligation to keep promises and the justification for enforcing certain voluntary agreements (or providing other forms of redress) have traditionally been regarded as part of what justice is about. It has normally been seen as unjust to break binding agreements and just to provide a remedy for breach of contract. A theory of justice has to account for this part of material justice but this is secondary to the thesis that justice is best understood in relation to the idea of contract.

This second and more profound tie is alleged to hold between the idea of a social contract and the very foundation of all principles of justice. A social contract is an agreement between potential citizens (or between such persons and a potential ruler or rulers) about the terms on which they are to enter into either social or political relationships (or both). Social contract theory posits a situation in which persons who have no existing political (and perhaps social) rights or obligations reach (usually unanimous) agreement about the basis on which to establish a social and/or political system in which they have such rights and obligations, including the obligation to conform to the agreement reached. The social contract may be used both to explain the general obligation of citizens to obey the law (and the possible limits of this obligation), and to provide a way of determining the proper content of the rights and obligations which bind members of a civil society. It may serve, therefore, both to establish the grounds of social, political and legal obligation, and to justify a particular set of positive norms. The two objectives may of course be closely connected in that the general obligation to conform to societal norms usually involves reference to the content of the rules agreed in the 'state of nature' – as the pre-social or pre-political situation in which the agreement is reached has traditionally been called.

The idea of a social contract came to the fore in political philosophy during the period when a non-theological ethical foundation was being sought for the emerging modern state as an independent political entity. The state came to be seen as an omnicompetent institution within which the sovereign has the right to make binding laws in accordance with a constitutional structure that sets out the scope and content of the powers of the ruler and the duties and rights of the citizens. The social contract model took many different forms which varied in their descriptions of the state of nature, in their analyses of human nature and in the terms of the contract reached. In Hobbes's *Leviathan* (1651), the horrors of the state of nature and the egoistic rationality of Hobbesian man go with a contract between citizens that established almost unlimited allegiance to an almost unlimited sovereign power. The less serious drawbacks of the state of nature, together with a more balanced view of man as a creature with moral capacities, depicted in Locke's *Second Treatise of Government* (1690), produce a social contract between potential citizens that established governmental power as something which is entrusted to the sovereign who had to rule within the law of nature and maintain a degree of continuing consent from his subjects in order to retain his legitimacy. Rousseau's yet more attractive state of nature, outlined in *The Social Contract* (1762), in which uncivilised peopled enjoyed certain physical freedoms and securities, although little economic and moral development, leads to the affirmation of a democratic system in which each citizen would continue to bind himself by his own legislative enactments alone.

Clearly the notion of a social contract is a form into which many different political views can be fitted, but all these views involve some recognition of the significance of acquiring the consent of individuals to the norms which limit their presupposed initial freedoms. As such social contract models assume an individualistic view of society according to which persons are the sources of their own political rights and duties, and embody the liberal view that encroachment on the freedom of such individuals requires justification. In all its variations social contract theory encourages us to see actual political societies as a form of association whose object is to secure the interests of their members in a way which is consistent with the intrinsic equal autonomy of all.

Within this framework two rather distinct interpretations of the state of nature and social contract emerged early on in its development. In the first, considerable weight is placed on the historicity of the phenomenon, so that it is assumed that there were persons in a state of nature who did enter into actual agreements. This claim is clearly important if political obligation is said to derive directly from the social contract since only actual agreements are binding.

Developing awareness of the historical implausibility of the contract led to its modification, first into a view of what *might* have taken place (conjectural history), and then into the idea that the actual agreements involved are being made all the time in that persons in actual political societies continuously make tacit or implicit agreements (for instance by not choosing to leave the polity), a modern variation of which is the idea that voting in an election is a tacit agreement to abide by the outcome of that election and adhere to the political system as a whole.

The second, more radical, approach is to abandon entirely the idea of an historical or actual contract and reinterpret the concept in hypothetical terms so that the contract becomes the agreement that persons of a certain sort in a certain type of situation *would* have reached. The rationale for this second, hypothetical, interpretation of the social contract is less easy to determine and depends considerably on the ingredients that go to make up the initial recipe for the state of nature. Most often the hypothetical contract is said to be a basis for determining the proper content of social and political rules, constitutional and otherwise. For instance, it may be argued that just rules are those which would be agreed to in a hypothetical state of nature as the basic norms of social life.

The intelligibility of this thesis depends crucially on the characterisation of the imagined state of nature, including the qualities of the persons who participate in it. In the historical version of the contract these matters could be settled by considering what, given a certain view of human nature, life must have been like without the benefits of social and/or political organisation and the reasons which would motivate people to reach agreements on the basis of social order.

Hypothetical contractual theorists, on the other hand, do not speculate on what pre-social life must actually have been like, although they do tend to follow the same basic lines in that the imaginary contractors are described as free and equal, and are said to be living without the benefits of political arrangements, so that they are motivated to secure an agreement which is mutually beneficial. However, the characterisation of the state of nature changes, from the simple absence of social and political constraints on the one hand and the approximate physical and mental equality of persons on the other, into a more idealised and artificial model in which freedom is a matter of uncoerced and informed choice (autonomy) and equality has to do with equal capacity to bargain on the basis of equal procedural rights and equal claims on the outcome.

The effect of these developments is to render more plausible the claim that the outcome of such an agreement is just, since it seems intelligible and perhaps attractive to say that what persons who are free and equal in these ideal senses would agree to has a claim to be regarded as just. This is because the situation in which the agreement is made seems to be fair, in that it is uncoerced and based on no unreasonable advantages of initial precedence. If the circumstances are fair then it seems natural to regard the outcome as reasonable and the rules which would be agreed to as just.

Extending this line of thought it is also possible to base political obligation on such a hypothetical contract by adding the premise that citizens have an obligation to obey just laws. Since just laws are identified as those which would be agreed to in the ideal hypothetical contract we can then say that the contract is the basis of political obligation. Indeed, it is possible to go further than this and infer a general obligation to conform to arrangements which fall within the hypothetical contractual agreements, not only because the hypothetical contract is a standard for determining justice, but also because we are in principle bound by what we would have agreed to in certain specified circumstances.

Thus the justification for paternalistic action, in relation to children or adults who are temporarily unconscious, the mentally ill or even persons who are seriously misinformed about matters which vitally affect their interests, may be that we can say that they *would* have agreed to what is in fact a coerced or non-consenting intervention in their lives *if* they had been grown up, or conscious, or mentally well, or informed. Although such persons did not actually agree, the fact that in more normal circumstances they would have agreed is taken as an independent reason for justifying the paternalistic acts in question. Such an argument is hypothetical in form, in that it makes appeal to counter-factual situations – for the persons were not grown up, or conscious, or mentally well, or informed – but it involves a claim to factual accuracy, in that it is maintained that it is true that the person would have agreed if, contrary to fact, they had been in a different situation or had different characteristics. Such hypotheses are not entirely fanciful and may indeed be subject in some cases to empirical testing, and they remain in this sense historical, at least in the sense of conjectural history. It may be claimed that this mode of reasoning applies equally to the situation of 'primitive' people who lacked the developed intelligence and experience to choose for themselves.

In both versions of the contract theory there is an unresolved tension between fact and speculation which until recently had been thought to be fatal to that theory. This tension emerges in various guises. In the case of Hobbes it is to be seen in the fact that his empirical claims include the thesis that, in the state of nature, men have no moral obligations while, in his theory as a whole, he has to contend that men have a pre-political obligation to keep their promises, otherwise there could be no moral basis for our obligation to conform to the original contract. How can a contract which is entered into in an amoral context set up the moral presuppositions required to make that contract itself binding?

This problem may be got round by the Lockean method of assuming that there are certain natural moral rights which predate the contract. Men have a natural right to life, liberty and property and institute government between them to protect these moral rights. While this may seem logically more satisfactory, it has the disadvantage that the contract cannot now be used to justify these basic rights which exist prior to the contract and these must therefore be given a justificatory basis elsewhere. Moreover the Lockean modifications may undermine the basis for an agreement in the historical contract because of the differing moral views of the contractors. In the historical contract this reduces the prospects of agreement and in the hypothetical contract it reduces the moral relevance of the contractual model, since we will not be inclined to accept its outcome unless we share the particular moral outlook of the contractors.

A more subtle problem of the same basic form is that the relevance of contracts, historical or hypothetical, depends on the continuity of social reality between the contracting situation and our own. On the other hand, too much accuracy in this respect inevitably renders the contract which is entered into morally suspect because it does not then meet the characteristics of a fair agreement. Actual societies are not fair and contracts in them reflect unequal power and wealth. Contract theorists are therefore in great difficulties when they seek to characterise a state of nature which has sufficient similarity to empirical reality for us to see its connection with our own nature and social experience, and yet is still a situation in which any agreement reached, whether actual or hypothetical, is fair, in that it is not the outcome of the sort of coercion, inequality or material ignorance which is commonplace in actual societies.

These are formidable difficulties which had long been considered to count decisively against the idea of a social contract in political theory. The choice between empirical accuracy and moral relevance seemed unavoidable. However the stakes involved are high and the advantages of a successful contract theory considerable. If it is possible to found social and political obligation in the idea of voluntary agreement, this not only gives strong support to the value of individual autonomy (and so of individual rights) but provides the best possible justification for having binding laws, namely that those bound have in some sense agreed to be bound by them, so that the obligations involved are self-imposed. Moreover, the idea of the social contract appears to offer the prospect of reconciling differing individual interests and values by a familiar device of compromise and discussion in which apparently incompatible objectives and incommensurable values can be brought under a single decision procedure. It is perhaps not so surprising therefore that the most striking contribution to the theory of justice in recent times has been a restatement of the hypothetical social contract as a counterposition to the utilitarianism which had for so long dominated political philosophy. Nor is it surprising that many of the criticisms which have been made of this neo-contractarianism echo the traditional attacks on the classical contract theories.

Justice as fairness

Justice as fairness is the theme elaborated by John Rawls in *A Theory of Justice* (1971) and developed in his subsequent writings. Rawls's model is based on the idea that the procedural fairness of an 'original position' (Rawls's version of the hypothetical state of nature) transfers itself to the principles of justice which would be agreed in the original position as applying to the basic institutions of actual societies. In other words, a fair bargaining is assumed to produce fair results. As far as the original position is concerned there is no antecedent standard by which to assess the results, as there would be in what he calls 'perfect procedural justice' where the idea is to have the most efficient procedure to get a result which is independently known to be correct. The acceptability of the result of the agreement reached in the original position depends solely on the acceptance of the procedure. Rawls calls this a matter of 'pure procedural justice' (1971, p.85).

Rawls insists on the procedural purity of the original position, not because he thinks that we cannot more directly assess the principles chosen in the original position, but because he wishes to present the contract as an independent justificatory source. Indeed the basic strategy of his method is to demonstrate that the principles adopted in the original position coincide with those which his readers would in any case accept once they had reflected systematically upon them. His hope is that 'the principles which would be chosen [in the original position] match our considered convictions of justice or extend them in an acceptable way' (ibid., p.19). There are thus two sets of moral standards at work in Rawls's synthesis. One represents the limitations on argument we do in fact accept when we argue about justice. These are embodied in the description of the original position. The other represents our moral intuitions or judgements about what is just once these judgements have reached a condition which he calls 'reflective equilibrium'. It is only when – perhaps after further processes of compromise and adjustment – the two independent moral bases produce a common outcome, that we have reason to think that we have the appropriate principles of justice.

The method of reflective equilibrium involves selecting our strongest and surest moral convictions as the provisional fixed points and then working backwards to the principles which would justify such intuitions. Thus we are certain that slavery is wrong and justify this conviction by reference, perhaps, to the idea of the fundamental equality of all persons. In this way we move towards the elaboration of a set of consistent principles which, together with knowledge of social circumstances, lead us to make the judgements we do for the reasons we make them. In pursuing reflective equilibrium we then seek to apply such principles to other everyday situations with respect to which our intuitions are more obscure and less certain and then determine whether the principles we have arrived at produce acceptable results in these more difficult cases, always being prepared to revise our original intuitions on the grounds that they may be 'distorted' or 'irregu-lar'. And so, by a to-and-fro process of reflection in which judgements are developed and revised and principles tested and refined, we finish with an 'equilibrium' of consistent judgements and principles with which we can proceed to tackle more contro-versial moral issues. It is these 'considered convictions of justice' whose coincidence with the principles chosen in the original position constitute the liberal ideal of justice.

The idea that in a hypothetical situation of equal liberty, rational and disinterested persons would choose the principles which accord with our sense of justice is said both to explain and to justify a particular conception of justice. The explanatory force comes from the demonstration that the principles of justice would be adopted by rational persons as the basis for social co-operation, it being assumed that there is some rationality in human affairs. The justificatory force comes from the coherence of considered moral judgements.

The elaborate coherence theory of moral appropriateness developed by Rawls is vulnerable to the charge that the fundamental intuitions on which it appears to rest are not themselves reliable raw data on which to proceed. What, it might be asked, is the point of establishing a reflective equilibrium based on moral intuitions if we cannot show that these intuitions provide at least an approximate insight into moral truth? Such questions are particularly pressing if we have to take account of the variety of 'senses of justice' which have existed and do still exist and the difficulties which arise in trying to mould them into a consistent position.

Rawls's initial response to such questions is first to limit the application of his theory to the sense of justice which is pervasive in modern liberal democratic societies. These are not specified, but he clearly has in mind principally the United States of America and other western democracies. Further 'justice as fairness' is restricted not only to a particular type of society, but, within that, it is confined to questions of justice in relation only to the basic institutions of society; in particular his concern is with the distribution of the benefits and burdens of social co-operation.

In his later writings (Rawls, 1980, p.518) Rawls is more explicit in his rejection of any deep philosophical underpinnings for his theory of justice. Not only does he reject the idea of rational intuitions as a justificatory test of universal moral truths, but he also abjures any search for epistemological or metaphysical bases for justice as fairness. Instead he argues for the autonomy of political philosophy as an activity aimed at furthering a consensus of fundamental political ideals in a particular polity as an essential prerequisite for the attainment of what he calls a 'well-ordered' society. His claim is that, despite the variations of political belief even within his own country, there is a degree of underlying agreement as to the terms of co-operation between citizens, and further there is a prospect of obtaining further consensus, a goal to which he hopes his own theory will contribute. The coherence of moral intuitions is not based on a philosophical ideal of moral truth but on this pragmatic political objective. His social contract approach is, then, simply a method which facilitates a desirable consensus in one type of society. However, despite these disclaimers, Rawls's followers are often less restrained in their ambition for his method of political argument and take it to be a basis for more universal standards of justice.

Rawlsian justice

If we accept Rawls's limitations on the scope and relevance of his contract approach to justice, the theory is best presented by a fairly detailed account of the hypothetical original position, including the procedures and reasonings which lead to the adoption of his favoured principles of justice, including the now famous 'difference' principle.

In order to achieve fairness, persons in the original position must be free and equal. By 'free' Rawls means not only that the parties in the original position are uncoerced and not under any prior obligations or constraints but also that they are independent and autonomous sources of claims on the benefits of social co-operation. They are not limited by prior moral conceptions in the pursuit of their own interest. Rawls denies that the parties are egoists since they do not seek to harm anyone else, but says they are mutually disinterested in that they care only about their own welfare, taken in isolation. They feel no envy, nor interest in the benefiting or harming of others for its own sake. In pursuit of their disinterested claims the parties are free to propose and argue for the principles of justice that they believe would be of greatest benefit to themselves and it is assumed that they, as rational persons, will agree only to the best bargain they can obtain in return for the benefits of social co-operation. People in the original position possess what Rawls calls 'rational autonomy', a property he equates with the notion of rationality found in Kant's hypothetical imperative or in neoclassical economics, in other words the rationality of the intelligent and prudent person.

'Equality' in the original position applies first to equal freedom as defined above, including equality in procedural rights and equality as sources of valid claims on societal resources in relation to basic social institutions. All parties have 'equal worth', so all are described in the same way and situated equally in the original position, which means that they are 'symmetrical with respect to one another' (1980, p.521).

The nature of this equality is not, however, completely abstract, for it is grounded in the equality of persons as moral agents, a notion to which Rawls traces the entire rationale of the contract model. For this reason he calls his method 'Kantian constructivism'. It is Kantian because it embodies the idea of persons as moral agents. This, for Rawls, means that each person has, first, a conception of the good (that is, a set of convictions about what personal goals are worth pursuing) and, second, a sense of justice (that is, a set of beliefs about the terms of fair social co-operation). It is also assumed that persons are capable of acting on a long-term basis in relation both to their conception of the good and their sense of justice. The method is 'constructivist' because the content of the principles of justice is generated from the ideal of the moral person through the model of the original position. From the point of view of the original position this means that the constructing parties are equal in that they all have the minimum properties necessary to be moral persons and also that their claims are of equal force and validity.

In order to ensure that this theoretical equality is given effect in the original position Rawls introduces his novel conception of a 'veil of ignorance' which is designed to remove all possibility of unfairness in the decision to be made by rendering each of the parties entirely ignorant of any particular fact about themselves which might lead them, as rational choosers, to favour themselves at the expense of those with different qualities. This means, for instance, that while they know that they have a conception of the good, they do not know its specific content, and cannot, therefore, slant the principles of justice to suit their particular goals. Similarly they know other general facts about human nature and society, but not their own particular nature, their sex, their social class, their size or intelligence, or talents. In this way we 'nullify the effects of specific contingencies which put men at odds and tempt them to exploit social and natural circumstances to their own advantage' (1971, p.136).

Furthermore the parties are, *ex hypothesi*, ignorant of the content of their sense of justice for even though this might not divide them in the same way as their knowledge of their own conception of their interests or their good, it is essential for the logical independence of the contract method that the motivation of the parties is the furtherance of their own interests, albeit they know that they are creatures who will have a sense of justice in actual society.

As important as the characterisation of the free and equal parties is the specification of what it is they are called upon to decide. Fundamentally their choice relates to the principles which will be used to construct the basic institutions of their society which will in turn determine the distribution of the benefits and burdens of social co-operation. They know, however, that in making this choice, they must have in mind life in a 'well-ordered' society. This involves a number of crucial features which relate to the type of social existence appropriate for morally autonomous agents with a sense of justice. The parties know that, in actual society, they will move beyond the rational autonomy of the original position to *full* autonomy, which is 'that of citizens in everday life who think of themselves in a certain way and affirm and act from the first principles of justice that would be agreed to' (1980, p.521). The implications of this condition are considerable. It means that, in the society to which the principles of justice are to apply, there will be an effectively regulated public conception of justice, so that the rules will be known, accepted as 'reasonable', and largely followed. Further the members of society will have mutual regard for each other as free and equal moral persons and thus as independently legitimate sources of varying and developing demands on the common pool of resources and people whose co-operation can be expected only when arrangements are fair, and therefore not simply 'rational' but 'reasonable'.

Under the rubric of a public conception of justice Rawls takes in what he calls 'the formal constraints of the concept of right', which require that the rules of justice be general, universal, public and capable of ordering social claims with finality and comprehensiveness. In this way he brings in some of the basic idea of the rule of law as it relates to equal treatment and impartial adjudication. Also the formal constraints of right rule out 'first-person dictatorship' in which the will of one person is paramount and also ensure that there are no 'free-rider' arrangements whereby named individuals are granted special privileges. More specifically, since the principles of justice apply to the basic structure of society, the parties are to choose 'a public system of rules which defines offices and positions with their rights, duties and immunities and the like' (1971, p.55) in the main spheres of social life, rules whose proper administration is a matter of formal justice in that 'similar cases are treated similarly, the relevant similarities and differences being those identified by the existing norms' (ibid., p.58).

All this is assumed, rather than chosen, by the rational choosers who are parties to the social contract. The parties in the original position are taken to 'represent' the full autonomy of moral persons in a well-ordered society, but they are allowed only such knowledge as is necessary for them to choose the principles of justice. Knowledge that it will be a well-ordered society does not in itself enable them to determine a particular set of principles so they must proceed on non-individuated knowledge about the nature of man and the empirical realities of social life, including economic and sociological information, and the general conditions on which social co-operation is necessary and possible.

If all divisive information is removed from the parties it appears that there is then nothing for them to bargain about, for each individual will have the same set of considerations to take into account, the same motivation and the same ability to reason. It has therefore been argued that the Rawlsian contract needs only one party since equality entails identity of relevant features amongst the contracting parties. Nevertheless Rawls assumes that there will be residual differences of opinion not related to arbitrary differences between the parties which will give rise to actual debate, although it is not clear to what these disagreements might amount. At any rate we are asked to accept that the contracting parties will know, or will be able to work out, that there are certain 'primary goods', that is, things which any person will require in order to pursue any conception of the good in a well-ordered society which respects the individual's moral powers to follow out in his life a conception of the good and an ideal of justice.

Primary goods, that is, the social background conditions and general all-purpose means normally necessary for developing and exercising the two moral powers and for effectively pursuing a conception of the good, include the basic liberties, such as freedom of thought and liberty of conscience, necessary for developing moral agency, freedom of movement and free choice of occupation, income and wealth, and 'the social bases of self-respect', by which he means the conditions necessary for individuals to maintain a feeling of their worth as moral agents. Primary goods are those things which are necessary for the pursuit, not of any human objective, but of any objective which is compatible with the exercise of moral agency.

Given that the parties in the original position have sufficient information and motivation to agree as to what constitutes primary goods the question then arises as to how these goods are to be distributed. Here Rawls assumes that it will be rational for the contractors to proceed with caution. After all, they are dealing with the vital matters affecting the ground rules of their society. The contractors are unlikely, therefore, to take risks. He also assumes that they will not adopt a number of disparate principles but will seek an ordered set of guidelines which will give precedence to some considerations over others. In particular they will use the idea of 'lexical' ordering, according to which it is required that one consideration, which is said to be lexically prior, must be satisfied before going on to deploy the other considerations, which may also be lexically ordered *vis-à-vis* each other.

Rawls conjectures that two principles will be agreed in the original position. The first is that 'each person is to have an equal right to the most extensive total system of equal basic liberties compatible with a similar system of liberty for all' (1971, p.250). This principle, he contends, is lexically prior, so that it must be met before we can turn to the second, which is that 'social and economic inequalities are to be arranged so that they are both (a) to the greatest benefit of the least advantaged and (b) attached to offices and positions open to all under conditions of fair equality of opportunity' (ibid., p.83), with the proviso that (b), fair equality of opportunity, is lexically prior to (a), the 'difference' principle). In other words, once basic liberties have been maximised to the highest point compatible with their equal distribution, unequal distributions of other goods may be introduced if they have the effect of maximising the lot of the worst off group (the 'maximin' strategy), provided that there is genuine equality of opportunity with respect to the inequalities licensed by (a). In all these respects the 'right' is prior to the 'good'.

The basic liberties which are to be equally distributed and given priority over all other considerations are in part those which are included in the set of primary goods already identified, particularly freedom of expression and liberty of conscience, but he extends basic liberty to cover those democratic rights which are necessary for the protection of other individual interests, and also to freedom of the person, the right to hold some private property and other liberties involved in the idea of the rule of law, such as freedom from arbitrary arrest. To some extent, therefore, both the content of the primary goods and their priority is predetermined by the choice presented in the original position. But beyond this there is a sense in which political liberties are seen as an indispensable safeguard against unacceptable treatment. Priority is given to these liberties because, it is alleged, no rational chooser would risk putting himself in the position where his interests (which might turn out to be those of a small minority) are endangered by a non-democratic regime. It is only safe to put such liberties first. The rather controversial thesis that fundamental liberty should be sacrificed only for the sake of other fundamental liberties and never traded to any degree for greater economic prosperity is, however, not applied where these liberties cannot be secured, or where the economic development of the society is at some unspecified low level.

The first part of the second principle of justice takes in what Rawls terms 'efficiency', in that it proposes maximising other primary goods provided these are equally distributed and permits inequalities where these benefit the worst off class of persons (the difference principle). The assumption is made that a measure of the self-centredness of the original choosers will carry over into actual society so that people will sometimes require incentives to make a contribution to socially productive enterprises. Here again envy is ruled out as reason for reducing inequalities and, in contrast to Nozick, no question of any prior right to the benefits of exercising personal abilities is allowed.

It is the rational decision to avoid risk by the parties to the contract which leads them to choose this difference principle as grounds for limiting social and economic inequality. The parties to the contract are concerned to guard against the worst possible outcome for themselves as participants in actual societies and will not hazard their future security by adopting, for instance, the utilitarian principle of maximising the total quantity of such primary goods without reference to the way they are distributed.

They do not know how likely it is that they may find themselves much worse off than under a maximin strategy and are unwilling to take the risk of coming out badly despite the fact that, on the basis of probability, they are likely to do better under a utilitarian arrangement. In these circumstances it is as well to insure against catastrophic bad luck.

Nor, as rational persons, will the parties permit inequalities in positions for which they might not be able to compete on equal terms. This requires not only equality of legal rights but also of the educational and material resources necessary for the development of the individual's inherited talent. This does not mean that positions will not be given to those best qualified – that is an acceptable requirement of efficiency – but it does mean that irrelevant factors related to family, wealth or education of the citizens will be inoperative as causes or ground of the selection to office. If this is ensured then we will have 'fair equality of opportunity'.

There are many ramifications in the working out of what Rawls calls his 'special conception of justice'. For instance, he outlines four stages in the emergence of an actual system of social institutions: in the first the two principles of justice are chosen; in the second there is a constitutional convention to set up a system of government; in the third ordinary laws are legislated and in the fourth these laws are applied by judges. During this process the veil of ignorance is progressively lifted somewhat so that at the second stage the constituent assembly knows the nature of the society in question, at the third stage the legislators know the basic economic facts about their society and at the fourth stage the veil of ignorance is totally removed so that for the first time citizens know their own circumstances and characteristics.

In order to place some limits on what can count as a person's good for the purposes of the theory, Rawls makes a number of empirical assumptions about human desires, needs and abilities, the most controversial of which is the 'Aristotelian principle' according to which, 'other things being equal, human beings enjoy the exercise of their realized capacities (their innate or trained abilities), and this enjoyment increases the more the capacity is realized, or the greater its complexity' (1971, p.426). This follows the precedent of John Stuart Mill's modification of classical utilitarianism to distinguish between the 'higher' pleasures of Socrates and the 'lower' pleasures of pigs.

However Rawls does not seek to justify in detail the way in which basic liberties and other primary goods are derived, nor does he say what sort of democratic constitution and specific legislation will be adopted. His aim is rather to set out a method for understanding the role of justice in society and to gain general acceptance for it as a method of political reflection in a liberal society.

The primary normative objective is to provide an alternative basis for social choice to the prevailing utilitarian outlook, which, he contends, does not take seriously enough the 'distinction between persons' (1971, p.185). By submerging of the interests of the individual in the welfare of all utilitarianism encourages the erroneous idea that society is akin to one individual who may rightly sacrifice some of his desires in order to further others. It is for this reason that he favours his own path to impartiality over the alternatives represented by the 'ideal observer' theory derived from Adam Smith, or the 'universalisability' theory derived from Kant, both of which, in his view, also tend to submerge the individual in society as a whole.

It is also in order to counter the attractions of utilitarianism that he insists on a closely integrated set of principles of social choice which determine priorities in cases of conflict. One attraction of utilitarianism over the pluralism of competing incommensurable moral outlooks has long been that it is able, in principle at least, to provide a solution to all distributive problems because of its unitary standard of rightness. Rawls believes that his own theory provides a viable alternative to utilitarianism in this respect as a social decision procedure.

Problems for Rawls

Some of the most damaging criticisms of Rawls's theory are to the effect that persons in the original position would in fact adopt average utility as the rational choice in such conditions of uncertainty since this offers them the best chance of the best life. To many it seems desperately *ad hoc* for Rawls to rule this out by insisting on the unrealistic proviso that rational individuals would not be prepared to take the risks involved in such a strategy and do not know the probabilities involved. Yet, if he does not introduce these arbitrary provisos, there seems little to choose between contractarianism and direct appeal to the principle of universal beneficence as the basis for social choice.

Similarly it seems far from obvious that basic liberties must be given priority by purely self-regarding individuals with a sound knowledge of human nature, for actual men are prepared to forgo political rights for economic gains well beyond the point of economic subsistence. Rawls's carefully constructed method of settling these points of competing priorities is therefore always in danger of lapsing into pluralism. Controversy has also attached to the exclusive emphasis which the difference principle puts on the situation of the worst off group. Surely, it is argued, more weight would attach, for instance, to those whose position is only marginally better than this one class of persons?

That these issues are hard to settle one way or the other is a further problem for the hypothetical contract approach in that it seems impossible to know what such unusual individuals in such special circumstances would decide. The danger is that in attempting to use the model we will simply hold onto our own moral assumptions about natural justice. Certainly it seems wildly optimistic to regard this process as a form of 'moral geometry' through which we can discover 'the only choice consistent with the full description of the original position' (ibid., p.121).

More specifically, the degree of ignorance which is required to ensure fairness takes away much of the information that is required for rational choice-making, in that the individual's particular conceptions of the good can have considerable relevance to the basic structure of society. For instance, it is evident that differing tasks and differing ideals will make differing demands on economic resources and political organisation. The pursuit of pleasure is in general more expensive than the pursuit of learning and the interests of the physical activist are less dependent on political structures than those of the political enthusiast. The fact that knowledge of different interests affects partiality does not mean that these factors are inherently irrelevant to the choices proffered in the original position. In particular the comparison of persons in terms of their needs cannot be carried out on the basis of primary goods alone. As we shall see this problem is especially acute if the 'least advantaged' group is identified only in terms of the primary goods they possess. The fairness of the contract appears to be promoted at the expense of the realities of moral choice in determining actual priorities.

Rawls's response to such difficulties is in part to reassert that he is not taking a morally neutral approach to the problem of distribution but is in fact seeking to explicate a particular moral point of view, namely that in which the autonomous moral agent is supremely valued. This is in fact the main grounds on which he identifies and protects basic liberties and insists on equality of opportunity. It is also the reason why he insists that in a well-ordered society there will be a public system of justice with general rules that allow individuals to co-operate on the basis of mutual respect. Again his Kantian starting-point is what determines the fact that self-respect depends, not on wealth, but on the dignity of autonomous living and enables him to erect tolerance as a prime value protected by the veil of ignorance. It also enables him to accept so readily the empirically questionable Aristotelian principle.

All these liberal assumptions are presupposed by the theory not proved or even justified by it. As a source of inviolable rights which might be used to control the extent and method of economic progress for the majority any theory of justice from contract remains, therefore, subject to the suspicion of idealogical partiality.

Surprisingly, however, there is one element in the traditional liberal doctrines which Rawls does not endorse, and that is the significance of natural desert in the allocation of resources. Taking the view that the capacity to develop natural endowments is as much inherited as the natural endowments themselves, he takes all abilities as in principle part of a social pool of common assets on which no one has a prior claim. He argues that desert requires that there be a public set of rules laying down the rewards for certain performances which generate legitimate expectations, something which can come into existence only after society has been set up and after the principles of justice have been chosen. Thus, once the requirements of fair equality of opportunity have been satisfied, the inegalitarian outcomes of the chance distribution of natural resources remain unchecked by considerations of desert.

This is one way in which the logic of the original position does seem to have overborne our collective considered judgements in reflective equilibrium. Moral intuitions in themselves would surely have found some place for the idea that those who have earned our praise and thanks by socially beneficial and effortful activity would be allocated extra goods on that basis, and for that reason. Rawls might argue that this is never fair in the case of primary goods or in relation to the basic institutions of a society, but this is hardly beyond contention.

The issue of desert is complicated by Rawls's idiosyncratic initial analysis of justice which takes in any morally relevant consideration which bears on the distribution of the benefits and burdens of social co-operation. This means that the intuitions on which he bases his reflective equilibrium are not really connected with 'justice' as a specific type of distributive consideration but must include any rationale which is 'overriding' in this context, including the subsidiary parts of his complex lexical system of principles which promote efficiency. He does not therefore ask us to confine ourselves to things which are specifically identified by the language of justice and fairness, rendering it doubly difficult to specify the intuitional bases of our sense of justice. This is particularly evident when he intrudes into justice the forward-looking criterion of the appropriate level of incentives to produce maximally efficient returns.

Justice and welfare

Justice has inescapable and firm ties to the treatment accorded to those who fare worst in whatever social arrangements exist in a society. Not only is 'social' justice closely associated with the relief of poverty and the care of the less fortunate members of society, but justice in general is inextricably linked to the idea of the interests of the oppressed, the weak and the exploited. Any theory of justice must, therefore, have regard to its implications for the most needy persons within a community. This does not mean that 'need' as such must be the prime criterion within an acceptable conception of justice, but no approach which does not address itself adequately to the problem of what constitutes 'fair' treatment of the most deprived citizens can be seriously considered as an acceptable normative theory of justice.

The connection between justice and welfare is obscured by the use of the term 'welfare' in Welfare Economics to cover the satisfaction of any human preferences which can feature in economic choices, so that the maximising of welfare is adopted as the modern equivalent to the maximisation of utility. Interpreted in this way a concern for welfare may be regarded as distinct from justice in so far as the former is a matter of aggregation and the latter a matter – at least primarily – of distribution. In contrast, the relevant connection may be between justice and welfare in the sense of the satisfaction of the basic needs of those who are unable to provide adequately for themselves, an objective which is often given priority over the demands of others upon the same scarce resources. This relates welfare, in the sense in which it is tied in with justice, to some conception of fundamental human needs.

The basic need analysis of welfare is, however, as it stands, rather restrictive if we are seeking to take in the characteristic activities of the 'welfare state' whose operations cover more than helping those who cannot provide the essentials of material living for themselves. The Welfare State extends to the provision of general health and educational services for everyone, including those who would be able to see to these matters for themselves and their family, if they had to do so. The crucial features of the Welfare State are that its services promote the well-being of citizens and are provided more or less free of charge, or in other words through a system of insurance or taxation rather than payment for services received. Normally the fiscal arrangements for such services are such that the poorest persons in society do not in fact pay for what they receive in that insurance is paid by those in employment or, more substantially, through a system of progressive taxation. Services are then provided on the basis of need rather than ability to pay, hence the affinity between caring for the poor and the Welfare State. The conceptual boundaries here are fuzzy in that there is no clear distinction between giving direct material aid to those in need and providing an environment in which those previously unable to care for themselves have the effective opportunity to do so, but the general drift of welfarism is clear enough – it is directed to the satisfaction of fundamental needs and thus has to do particularly with those in greatest need, although this may be within a system of universal benefits funded via the fiscal mechanisms of the State.

Theories of justice must relate the conception of justice involved to the justification, or otherwise, of welfare provisions. Merit-based theories can either justify the relief of poverty on the grounds that gross suffering is in general undeserved and therefore unjust and requiring remedy, or else they may classify poverty relief as a matter of beneficence or prudence rather than justice, a strategy which need not carry the implication that it is not a proper activity for states.

Need-based theories have no immediate difficulty in accommodating welfarism but require, along with other theories, to identify what counts as a fundamental need, and to assess the relative fairness of the mechanisms they propose to use for the promotion of need-satisfaction. Rights-based theories, which characteristically interpret rights in terms of respect for individual choices, have more difficulty in determining what should be done about persons who fare badly under such a choice-based system, either through making bad choices, or through not having the wherewithal to make effective choices in relation to their own well-being, perhaps through lack of capacity, ability or wisdom. The first move of rights' theorists is often to equate welfarism with providing individuals with the opportunities to develop and deploy their abilities as rational or moral agents, but this leaves untouched the problem of those who are unsuccessful in making use of these opportunities, to say nothing of the wider problem of the possible injustice of the unequal outcome of even a strongly interventionist form of 'fair' equality of opportunity, which must still depend in part on morally contingent matters such as inherited natural endowments and favourable family circumstances.

One of the attractions of Rawls's theory is that it appears to marry the entitlements of human choice with a lively concern for the less fortunate members of society. Once the equalities of basic liberty and fair opportunity are taken care of as inviolable rights, the difference principle sees to it that such inequalities as emerge are only permitted in so far as they benefit the least advantaged in society. This seems not only strongly egalitarian in its tendencies, but tailor-made to a system which gives the sort of priority to the well-being of the poor which is to be looked for in a conception of justice. The worst-off group in society not only enjoy the self-respect which comes from the possession of full and equal political rights and the material assistance which is necessary for them to develop their abilities to the same level as those of similar ability and motivation, but the whole subsequent economic system appears to be directed to ensuring that they are not excluded from its benefits of increased wealth which comes from social co-operation. No inequalities are allowed which do not improve their position.

Deeper investigation of Rawls's difference principle and related features of his theory which bear on the lot of the worst-off segment of society does not entirely bear out these expectations. This is hardly surprising in view of the recurrent problems which arise in bringing together in one system the prime value freedom of choice and the virtues of fair contracts on the one hand, and effective commitment to the provision of welfare on the basis of need on the other. Not only does it turn out that Rawls's scheme permits far greater economic inequalities than might be imagined, but it also becomes clear that the difference principle is not directed primarily at those most characteristically identified by the concept of fundamental need. Consequently it becomes diffi-cult to see how the Rawlsian approach can adequately opera-tionalise the provision of welfare at an acceptable level to essen-tially needy groups.

One of the features of the original position which is taken to be 'realistic' in that it is also a feature of actual societies – at least modern democratic ones – is that a free-market economy is efficient as a means for co-ordinating the efforts of economic agents, who are assumed to be basically self-interested. People are taken to require incentives to work and to develop their socially useful talents. Rawls holds that there is no effective way of ascribing relative values to resources except by recourse to the laws of supply and demand as the crucial determinants of who gets what is an economically efficient system. However he con-tends that 'there is no essential tie between the use of free markets and private ownership of the instruments of production' (1971, p.271) and takes up a neutral position as between the private and public ownership of the means of production and exchange, simply assuming that both property systems are compat-ible with a market economy.

From Rawls's point of view the economic efficiency of the free market is a fortunate empirical fact since the liberties which are essential to the operation of a free market – including the absence of slavery, and the right to a measure of private property – also feature amongst his list of basic liberties. However, beyond the requirements of efficiency and basic liberty, there is an independent insistence that the competition be 'fair'. This is spelt out in Rawls's full conception of equality of opportunity which requires large transfers of resources to ensure that all those with similar abilities and motivations have similar educational opportunities, not just formally, but in effect, through the provision of adequate facilities and material support. This is extended to cover equal economic rights in a free market which is then seen as a case of 'pure procedural justice'. If markets are reasonably competitive and open then the fairness of the competition transfers to the fairness of an outcome which is not independently known to be just.

Despite the happy coincidence of economic efficiency and pure procedural justice, which gives Rawls's economic theory the flavour of Adam Smith's 'invisible hand', Rawls does not believe, any more than Smith, that the fair competition of the open market can be sustained without proper governmental background institutions. Accepting that there is a tendency for wealth and power to accumulate, thus distorting competition and undermining equality of opportunity, he requires the state to police economic activities to prevent monopolies and trade restrictions, which threaten both efficiency and fairness. He goes further than Smith, however, not only in the substance of his ideal of fair equality of opportunity, but also in his use of the difference principle to justify taxing the better-off members of society to provide a 'social minimum' of resources for the least well-off group through what he calls the 'transfer' branch of government. In Smith's system of natural liberty this tendency to more equal distribution happens naturally through the expenditure of the wealthy, and not artificially as a result of state-organised re-distribution of resources.

Before looking into the significance of the difference principle in this context we must note that, once all these corrective actions and background fairnesses have been taken into account, it is still the case that some will use their talents better than others and that some have more talents than others, so that, given freedom of contract and freedom of choice in employment, significant inequalities are bound to emerge if different employments are rewarded differently as, *ex hypothesi*, they must be in an incentive system. However 'fair' the starting point, therefore, inequalities will rapidly emerge and accumulate, for the individual is free to spend his income to pursue further wealth and opportunity. The general idea that differences in natural and developed abilities should lead to differences in income is not of major concern to Rawls. He does not hold that individuals have an antecedent natural right to use their capacities as they think fit to gain whatever they may, as Nozick contends, but he does not regard it as problematic that natural differences lead to material inequalities, given a free-market incentive system. If differential rewards need to be offered to increase the general wealth of a society, then those who, in a 'fair' competition, are chosen to fill such offices and positions on the basis of ability, 'deserve' or are entitled to these higher rewards. Anything less would be an infringement of legitimate expectations and a denial of basic freedoms of choice.

The question then arises whether the difference principle turns this apparent meritocracy into something more like a welfare system. The argument that it does so is to the effect that the inequalities in question all have to be justified by their beneficial effects on the worst-off group. However, while it might appear that this will produce a roughly egalitarian society there is in reality no reason to think that it will do so. Self-interested individuals will be able to benefit from the possession of scarce skills, differentials which bring small increases in resources to the worst off may bring much larger benefits to other groups, and in general the outcome of the difference principle is compatible with very significant inequalities. Moreover any tendency it has to equality is contingent on particular circumstances, in the same way as the alleged egalitarian outcomes of the principle of utility depend on the empirical variables which affect supply and demand. It is possible, therefore, that in a Rawlsian society the worst-off group may be very badly off indeed both in absolute and relative terms.

Anxieties of this sort are heightened by investigation of the membership of the worst-off group in society. It might be thought that this will include those unable to work through sickness, mental or physical incapacity, or lack of opportunity; but this is apparently not so. In the first place, such persons are in general not represented in the original position, where the parties are confined to those with the capacity to take part in society and who must, therefore, have the minimum requirements of moral agency; that is, they must, *inter alia*, have the capacity to have and, effectively pursue, a conception of their own good. This makes no allowance for the special needs of those without these capacities. Moreover, within the class of moral persons, the worst-off group are identified in relation to their possession of primary goods, particularly economic and material resources, and not according to their available satisfactions which are, of course, affected by their state of health and other sources of suffering and felt misery, and do not depend simply on the resources available to them irrespective of their physical and mental condition. Further, it turns out that Rawls, in thinking about this group, identifies them with the group which is in employment, but is paid least, rather than with those who are in what might be considered a worse position of being unable to work. The 'social minimum' is 'wages plus transfers' (1971, p.277).

It is not clear how basic to Rawls's theory is this characterisation of the least favoured group. He gets to this position initially through considering normal social and economic life, putting to one side the problem of those who do not come up to participant level in a society of free and equal moral agents: 'everyone is capable of honouring the principles of justice and of being full participants in social cooperation throughout their lives' (1980, p.545). However, this assumption may be considered to be a relatively superficial part of the model. Certainly the problem of the unemployed appears to be mitigated by the fact that the principle of fair equality of opportunity requires that governments ensure that there is a choice of suitable employments available, but this is a highly problematic practical suggestion in a free-market economy which cannot simply create jobs to provide employment without distorting the market and, if the problem is a large one, creating massive 'distortions' in the economic system, thus reducing the wealth available to help the worst-off group. Further, in an incentive system, jobs that are created to provide employment in this way must presumably be paid less than the lowest paid socially useful job, which may be very low indeed. And, of course, this solution, even if practicable and possible in a free market system, does nothing for those unable to work, whose special needs may be much greater than can be met by the resources of the least-favoured class.

Another tactic for reducing Rawlsian embarrassment on this point is to take the temporary conditions of childhood, unemployment, transient illness and old age into the normal life-cycle of the worker and see benefits in relation to such needy categories of person as part of the total rewards of employment. This would not, however, deal with those whose course-of-life needs of this sort are exceptional due to the abnormality of their health or accidental misfortunes. Also, such arrangements would not be confined to the worst-off group so that we are not here dealing with an application of the difference principle.

Moreover to take special needs into consideration would be to make a major change in Rawls's assumptions. In the first place, it takes us away from an uncontroversial list of primary goods to an idea of equality of life-satisfactions which is less manageable in general. It also inevitably brings in different conceptions of the good. Thus a physical disability may make a person particularly badly off if the individual has objectives calling for normal or developed physical skills. There is, secondly, the problem of what to do about disadvantages which cannot be specifically rectified, but only compensated for, such as liability to serious and painfully incurable illness. Clearly, even an equal share of resources will be insufficient to redress such imbalance of satisfactions and medical care in itself will not greatly alter the situation. Does this mean that the difference principle would involve putting more and more resources towards marginal improvements in the lot of persons with such a low quality of life? Society would then become one large hospital or welfare institution, to which end all social co-operation would be ultimately geared. This would certainly seem to be the outcome if the difference principle takes in not only the sickly worker but those persons unable to work at all.

The reason why Rawls does not take this to be the result of his difference principle may be that he does not take persons disadvantaged in these ways to be 'normal' members of society, in that his model is designed to deal with the distribution of the benefits of social co-operation to which all members contribute. He sees society as an organisation for mutual benefit in which everyone participates to some degree and from which all should benefit, hence the justice of viewing natural abilities as a form of collective asset whose fruits can legitimately be used to improve the lot of the least well-off set of contributors.

To allow non-contributors to be represented in the original position would be to remove the basis for a bargained agreement, but to exclude them seems inhuman, especially as Rawls is prepared to allow representatives of future generations a say in the contracted outcome, in so far as the parties to the contract do not know in which generations they will be born. We seem, therefore, to have a clash between the logic of the original position and the sentiments of justice which the outcome of the social contract is said to match.

Moreover the seemingly minor move to improve the theory by allowing the maximin strategy to be applied by the parties in the knowledge that they might turn out to be non-persons, in the sense of lacking the minimal capacities for moral agency, and hence, almost certainly, non-contributors, in that they have no useful natural assets to place in the common pool, would in fact tend to subvert the whole free-market system, for such persons are not part of the structure of incentives. For instance, a serious application of the difference principle to those unable to contribute anything useful to the co-operative enterprise would lead to them being given more primary goods than many who are in socially productive employment. Similarly, when jobs are in short supply, as surely in real societies they must often be, those unable to work will include those who cannot find work, despite the government's efforts to create jobs. If these are – problematically – included in the least well-off group, then their income cannot be raised above that which they would receive in employment or else, as self-interested persons, they would have no incentive to seek work.

Such problems may not be a major drawback to Rawlsian justice if those unable to work are few and unemployment is virtually eliminated. In this case relatively minor adjustments through the transfer system can meet the special needs of these groups as well as benefiting the least well-off category of workers. However, as Rawls points out in his argument for creating the transfer branch of government, in general 'the market is not suited to answer the claims of need' (1971, p.277). Indeed, allocation on the grounds of need undermines competition, so that if the transfer programme becomes a major element within a distributive system then it may well turn out to be practically as well as theoretically at odds with the moral agency values of 'justice as fairness'. Rawls will therefore have very serious problems with a welfare state which seeks to go beyond seeing to the exceptional needs of the very poorest and least able section of society.

These are standard problems which arise at the interface of distributing resources according to contribution – as a free market system is bound to do – and distributing resources according to need. Despite promising appearances the difference principle, not surprisingly, fails to cope with the transition from providing resources to providing the opportunity to earn resources. In the end Rawls's system, using as its basis the original position, comes down in favour of choice and opportunity for those with the ability to grasp it, rather than of a sort of full-blooded commitment to satisfaction of needs which is bound to undermine a free-market system but nevertheless seems to be an element in our sense of justice. This is evident, for instance, in his identification of self-respect with equal political rights rather than equality of economic resources, and his consequent readiness to accept a degree of economic inequality which marginally increases the lot of the least advantaged group of employed persons. This accords with the priority of liberty, political and economic, but it may do less than justice to those who are really worst off in the community of free and equal moral persons. It seems then that, in the event, there is an unresolved tension between the libertarian ethos of the original position and the reflective equilibrium of our considered moral judgements which incorporate treatment in accordance with basic need.

It is another question again, however, if distributions which are based solely on need are, in any case, a matter of justice, rather than humanity or benevolence. Rawls's broad definition of justice as having to do with 'the way in which the major social institutions distribute fundamental rights and duties and determine the division of advantage from social cooperation' (1971, p.7), and his emphasis on the overriding force of justice, do not enable him to exclude the provision of basic welfare from the sphere of justice without undermining its social and political priority.

Finally, Rawls's rejection of desert as an element within justice debars him from making the alleviation of undeserved need a matter of justice, thus closing off another way of bringing at least some categories of need within the scope of justice in distribution.

4 Justice as Dialogue: Ackerman and the Law of Contract

No analysis of justice is sufficient by itself to enable us to make determinate judgements about the justice or injustice of particular states of affairs. This is not simply because of the independent requirement for accurate factual information relating to the actual situations under review. Actual justice assessments also require a specification of the normative criteria involved which is much more detailed than can be provided by any manageable explication of abstract concepts like merit, need or choice. Judgements on specific states of affairs presuppose specific norms which lay down not only what is to count, for instance, as merit, but also the weight to be given to such factors in the distribution of specific types and quantities of benefits and burdens. As far as these details are concerned philosophical presentations of conceptions of justice do little more than point us in a particular direction. Within the parameters of relevance established by any theory of justice much remains to be done before individual determinations of justice are possible.

We have already seen how, if a rights approach is adopted, the pursuit of justice requires us to move beyond the generalised rhetoric of 'moral rights' and calls for the enactment of a set of detailed rules laying down entitlements and obligations for specific types of situation. Apart from this concretisation of abstract rights, every system of rules requires interpretation and refinement in the process of application. No theorising about the existence of right answers actually provides a right answer to a particular case. Nor can a method of reasoning, such as Rawls's reflective equilibrium, dispense with the need for the exercise of judgement. Other approaches place even more stress on the need for a complex process of assessment if we are to approximate to the attainment of justice in historical situations.

In effect this means that any practical theory of justice must allow a place for wise and well-informed judgement as well as explicit criteria and rule-defined priorities. Indeed there is a tradition, going back to the ancient Greeks, according to which justice is attained through the qualities of the judge rather than the properties of the judged, so that justice resides not in the situations assessed but in the individuals making the assessments. The characteristics of the just man, not the features of the just state of affairs, then become the focus of theoretical interest.

In such cases the role of the just judge, or just assessor, is not confined to the mechanical application of rules, but requires also the exercise of practical wisdom, which is said to be a matter of knowing how to judge justly rather than knowing that justice consists in this or that state of affairs. Impartiality, intelligence, experience, sympathy and the indefinable quality wisdom are some of the characteristics demanded of the good judge, whose decisions are the measure of justice.

Few theorists today would consider such an approach adequate to the task of formulating a theory of justice, but something of this approach surfaces when it comes to developing a methodology for determining how we are to arrive at and apply appropriate criteria of justice. In fact the method recommended for determining as well as deploying the substantive norms of justice is often akin to an appeal to the judgement of the wise and impartial adjudicator.

While all theories of justice must pay some attention to what are essentially problems of normative epistemology – that is, how we come to have knowledge of right and wrong – those theories which make the mode of arriving at and using adequate criteria of justice the main thrust of their endeavours are the theories which have the closest affinity to the tradition of the just judge approach. In such theories justice is largely identified with whatever emerges from properly conducted decision procedures carried out by decision-makers with certain approved characteristics. Justice thereby becomes principally a style or mode of judgement rather than a particular set of criteria or principles.

A large part of Rawls's approach to justice is essentially an epistemology of impartiality, although he explicitly rejects the ideal observer theory of the benevolent and well-informed spectator, which he regards as no more than a covert version of utilitarianism. The model of the original position, the features of the choices to be made, first about basic principles and then about detailed social arrangements, together with the facilities and limitations placed on the choosers, are designed not only to provide principles of justice with which we independently agree, but also to give moral weight to those principles through the nature of the decision process that gives rise to them. Justice as fairness is, in this respect, the thesis that those principles which are the outcome of a fair procedure are just – Rawls's 'pure procedural justice'. Rawls himself goes further than this in that he invites our endorsement of his principles of justice irrespective of their origins. He also retreats from the procedural aspect of his theory by allowing our views on the outcome of the decision process to alter the specification of the original position. But the general idea that justice is approachable as a matter of method and style of decision making is evident in Rawls's method.

As Rawls indicates, when utilitarian theorists adopt the just judge approach they tend to invoke the model of the ideal observer or impartial spectator who is said to take an informed and non-involved but sympathetic overall assessment of different distributive possibilities. Justice is thus associated with impartial benevolence, or in the case of Adam Smith, for instance, with impartial resentment, in that he identifies justice with the proper response to injuries sustained at the hands of other people. The measure of this response is the approval of non-participant bystanders. By generalising from the observer's responses rules of thumb are arrived at by a process of induction from particular judgements of the observer and then used to set up standards of social conduct.

The main criticism of the ideal observer theory is that, like utilitarianism in general, it is said not to take sufficient account of the distinction between persons. By treating individuals as if they were no more than different experiences of the same person which can be traded off one against the other, utilitarianism is alleged to submerge the interests of the individual in a communal pool of experiences. Another important criticism is that all actual observers are inevitably influenced by their existing moral beliefs to that the 'impartiality' derived from their status as observers is insufficient to give them the necessary moral neutrality to act as genuinely impartial judges. The sympathies of the spectator are said to follow, not lead, the formulation of moral standards.

An alternative contribution to decision making or just judge approaches to justice, which seeks to transcend the arbitrariness and abstraction of hypothetical contractarianism and the circularities of ideal observer or impartial observer theories, centres on the method of interpersonal 'dialogue'. This approach is adopted by Bruce Ackerman, whose *Social Justice in the Liberal State* (1980) is the main subject of this chapter. By imposing what he calls the conversational constraint of 'neutrality' on dialogue concerning the distribution of desired but scarce resources, Ackerman believes that he has identified a method which is capable of generating general principles of justice and, more importantly, providing a way forward in the effort to achieve a solution to specific distributive disagreements in a liberal state. Neutral dialogue is said to achieve this, not primarily by proving a particular set of principles of justice but rather through devising a method by which all justice-related disputes can be legitimately settled, so that 'a particular procedure of dispute resolution – here, the process of constrained conversation – can be transformed into a commitment to particular substantive outcomes' (Ackerman, 1980, p.14). In other words, adopting the appropriate procedures produces the appropriate results. The norms of justice are the outcome of properly conducted conversation.

The central concern of this chapter is to explore whether Ackerman's bold epistemology of justice generates more specific and defensible conclusions than the rights and contract approaches.

Neutral dialogue

Ackerman's *Social Justice in the Liberal State* is lightweight in tone but underneath its folksy style and entertaining dramatic presentations, the book contains an ambitious thesis about liberalism and justice. Ackerman offers no analytical definition of justice but simply takes off from a wider version of Rawls's description of the conditions of justice. In this case we are told that justice has to do with the legitimation of power in situations of scarce resources. In other words, justice has to do with the justification of inequality in relation to desired and limited goods.

Ackerman sets about the task of establishing which power distributions are legitimate by expressing what he takes to be the essence of Liberalism, namely a style of verbal interaction in which individuals are prepared to defend their holdings of scarce resources by reasoned argument of a type which he described as being subject to 'neutral conversational restraints'. This approach is exemplified in a simplified model which he refers to as 'the spaceship myth'. This fantasy postulates a constitutional assembly of fellow space travellers who come upon an uninhabited planet containing one valued resource designated 'manna'. Manna has the fortunate features of being divisible and malleable but is, less fortunately, particularly when measured against the extensive desires of the space colonists, scarce. The Assembly must decide how this resource is to be distributed among the prospective colonists. It must do so by a process of debate or dialogue in which all may participate, provided that they abide by certain ground rules as laid down by the all-powerful spaceship Commander. The nub of the theory lies in the determination of these ground rules, for once the rules of debate are known, agreed and enforced, the substantive principles of justice will eventually be worked out and, *ex hypothesi*, fully implemented, since it is another feature of the myth that a perfect 'technology of justice' is available to the community of space-colonists in that 'there never is any practical difficulty in implementing the substantive conclusions of a Neutral dialogue' (ibid., p.21).

To engage in such a thought-experiment is clearly to follow in the general wake of Rawls's revival of social contract and state of nature models. However, Ackerman believes himself to have improved on the state of nature device, in its traditional form, by avoiding the dubious postulate of pre-social natural rights on the basis of which moves can be made for the setting up of a society in order to guarantee and develop these rights. In other words, Ackerman accepts the strictures on 'moral' rights presented in Chapter 2 of this book. He does this in his typically engaging and elliptical way. In what is presumably a gentle dig at Nozick and his alleged ideological forebear, Adam Smith, Ackerman quips that 'rights are not the kinds of things that grow on trees – to be plucked, when ripe, by an invisible hand' (ibid., p.5). Rather, rights are human structures to serve human purposes.

On the other hand, historical social contracts are also found wanting because they do not represent a genuinely rational decision process. Actual social contract procedures involve bargaining, manoeuvring and coercion and make too much depend on the idea of keeping to a once and for all historical agreement. The Rawlsian hypothetical version of the contract is dismissed for other reasons, principally that the veil of ignorance requirement robs the contractors of the informational basis on which real social choices can be made.

Dialogue is said to be superior to contract as a method for determining social values because it involves in a simplified but realistic position (relative scarcity) real (although culturally diverse) people who are engaged in genuine debate which can, Ackerman claims, generate effective and applicable criteria of justice without presupposing any pre-existing rights or controversial values. This makes it a method which can be deployed in actual societies to solve real disputes. In another work he argues that neutral dialogue is in fact a mode of discourse akin to that used in certain forms of legal argument (Ackerman, 1984, pp.96ff).

The spaceship myth is not, of course, entirely value-free. Indeed not only is the commitment to dialogue rather than force and suppression a matter of positive evaluation, but not just any type of dialogue qualifies as 'neutral'. As we shall see some of these additional requirements are not really additional since they simply spell out what it is to engage in dialogue as opposed to diatribe or incoherent ramblings, but other ground rules of the dialogue of justice represent an elucidation of an ideology, namely liberalism, which carries here its North American connotations of a mildly progressive commitment to social welfare and strong associations with the ideals of liberty, autonomy and diversity.

Given these assumptions, it is hardly surprising that the end product of the model is a vindication of 'the liberal–democratic welfare state' (Ackerman, 1980, p.30). But, while Ackerman does not seek to disguise the value commitments involved in his endorsement of a modern liberal welfare state, he claims that the core of liberalism is to be found purely in the rigorous application of its anti-paternalism to the process of political debate. The 'key to the liberal enterprise' is the idea of 'constrained conversation' and the crucial constraint in question is 'the liberal's opposition to paternalism' (ibid., p.10). Once this is appreciated then not only can the coherence of liberal ideals and the liberal state be demonstrated but we also have in our possession a method of settling political disagreements on which liberals can agree. The liberal state is both the product of this method and its embodiment.

As it turns out, the first principle of neutral dialogue is not in fact exclusive to liberalism, although Ackerman would hold that it is one of its most basic features. The principle, termed 'Rationality', sets out the object of the project, the justification of power:

'Whenever anybody questions the legitimacy of another's power, the power holder must respond not by suppressing the questioner but by giving a reason that explains why he is more entitled to the resource than the questioner is.' (Ibid., p.4)

Ackerman asks us to note that this purely formal principle is general in that it requires all forms of power to be rationally defended. This applies to private property as well as state power, genetically determined and educationally developed capacities as well as contingencies of time and place. He also takes out of the principle of Rationality the view that arguments used to attack or defend power over resources or holdings of manna must imply or propose distributional rules which *could* provide a possible solution to the problem of scarcity. Thus 'all distributional rules must be *harmonious*: the material resources under the rule cannot add up to more than the total available for distribution', and they must be '*complete*' in that any admissible distributional rule 'must specify how *each* colonist will fare if the distributive proposal gains the Assembly's acceptance' (ibid., p.35). He also takes out of the Rationality principle the requirement that 'to count as a reason, a statement cannot contradict the very idea that power can conceivably be exercised illegitimately' (the '*conceivability* test') (ibid., p.38), and the requirement of '*comprehensiveness*' by which he means that any argument for a distributive rule must show that it is actually superior to its rivals (ibid., p.41f).

As Ackerman acknowledges, these initial moves do not take us very far. The requirements that proposed rules be harmonious, complete and comprehensive represent the familiar formal requirements for the selection of rules of social choice, while the conceivability test seems to add nothing that is not explicit in the original statement of the principle itself. Disappointingly, the explication of the first principle does not clarify what it is to give a reason in favour of a distributive rule. However it does enable him to insist that no aspect of power relations – including the institution of private property – is above scrutiny.

Nor is the second principle – 'Consistency' – any more substantive. Although this principle is presented as an expression of the familiar dictum of formal justice – 'treat like cases alike' – he interprets this dictum as no more than a demand that:

> 'The reason advanced by a power wielder on one occasion must not be inconsistent with the reasons he advanced to justify his other claims to power.' (Ibid., p.7)

A similar constraint is placed on all participants in the dialogue. Rather misleadingly, Ackerman debars inconsistency on the grounds that it renders the protagonists unintelligible, whereas in practice inconsistencies only become apparent when the offending utterances are clearly understood. Nevertheless we may allow that consistency of this minimal sort is a requirement of rational thought, whether inside or outside the liberal tradition, so that material contradictions which have a bearing on the conclusions proffered cannot be permitted.

It is clear that neither Rationality nor Consistency place any effective constraints on the positions that can be argued in the constituent assembly. The most outrageous views may be consistently argued and effectively determine social choices. The main thrust of the method emerges, therefore, only with the third principle – 'Neutrality' – which is used to rule out of order some consistent and rational arguments. Here

> 'The germ of the idea is that nobody has the right to vindicate political authority by asserting a privileged insight into the moral universe which is denied to the rest of us.' (Ibid., p.10)

The Neutrality principle is the one which expresses the antipaternalism of Liberalism and sets the basis for all subsequent legitimating dialogue. Interestingly, it is formulated in terms of a right which must, *ex hypothesi*, be regarded as a 'natural' or moral right in that it is presupposed by the Assembly, whose task is to determine what positive rights the colonists are to enjoy. It is from this right that Ackerman generates the full panoply of a radical and in many respects welfare-oriented liberal state.

The full statement of the Neutrality principle is in fact rather more complicated, and indeed rather different, for it refers not to a claim to superior insight but to other, perhaps related, forms of superiority. It reads:

> 'No reason is a good reason if it requires the power holder to assert:
> (a) that his conception of the good is better than that asserted by any of his fellow citizens, or
> (b) that, regardless of his conception of the good, he is intrinsically superior to one or more of his fellow citizens.' (Ibid., p.11)

In view of what has gone before, it might be thought that this dual principle is to be interpreted as disallowing claims to the possession of superior insight into the good, or to have priority over other citizens based on such superior insight, but this turns out not to be the case. In interpreting (a), which he calls the bar against *selectivity*, a conception of the good is defined in terms of persons' aims or objectives in life (even if these are to act spontaneously with no preconceived specific goals), so that what is ruled inadmissible is an argument to the effect that one goal or set of goals is superior to another. This would presumably apply even if the argument does not presuppose a claim to superior moral insight. In other words the requirement is that all *objectives* of action are on a moral par for the purposes of the debate.

Similarly with (b), which Ackerman calls the constraint on '*unconditional superiority*' (ibid., p.44), what is ruled out is any claim that the individual has superior worth which gives him or her priority irrespective of his or her particular aims in life. In other words the requirement is that all *persons* are on a moral par with each other for the purposes of the debate.

This interpretation of the Neutrality principle seems to exclude any argument which presupposes that one moral view or person is to be preferred to any other, so that complete moral relativity must be assumed in the Assembly, at least in so far as morality involves the ordering of acts and affairs. This is a very much more sweeping requirement than the disqualification of claims to privileged moral insight, since not all arguments for priorities presuppose such epistemological elitism. In effect this means that, as far as superiority and inferiority go, no moral judgements at all can be made, for anyone who makes a moral judgement must intend that it should be better than its rivals. The only alternative to a claim to moral correctness is complete moral agnosticism.

As an interpretation of Ackerman's principle of Neutrality, this account could be challenged on the grounds that it gives no place to the role of the word 'intrinsically' as it occurs in (b), and also in a reformulation of (a) on p.41, where it is stated that the citizen cannot affirm one conception of the good to be '*intrinsically* superior to others' (my italics). Does this not imply that Ackerman rules out only judgements of moral priority which assume privileged access? Ackerman might well claim that this is indeed the case but argue that in practice all claims to superiority must be based on privileged access because, *ex hypothesi*, any claim to superiority will be challenged, and no moral judgements can be forced on another person, since moral judgements are not susceptible to proof (p.11). In this case what is ruled out is a claim to knowledge in an area in which knowledge, as distinct from privileged access, is not available. Yet, while claims to privileged access involve an obviously illegitimate epistemological selectivity, this does not apply to all statements of opinion in areas of incorrigible uncertainty. Ackerman does not have arguments to show that persons are always wrong to follow the advice of Aristotle and John Stuart Mill and proceed on the basis of such certainty as they can achieve in political matters.

Another interpretation of 'intrinsically' which accords with some of Ackerman's many glosses on the principle of Neutrality is to the effect that what is prohibited is any argument of the form 'because it is me', or 'because it is mine', that is, the egoistic view that a goal or person is superior for no reason other than that it is his or her goal or that he or she is that person. This is what is ruled out, for instance, by the rule, championed as a utilitarian device by Hare (1952), that all candidates for moral principles must be 'universalisable' in that they should contain no references to particular persons or unique situations. Few moral theorists would have difficulty in following Ackerman in rejecting egoism of this type but he lumps this together with the use of any criterion, even if it is formally universalisable, which leads to an assertion of superiority. This is a much more controversial stance, since some people do accept principles even where these do involve hierarchical orderings of values which when applied are unfavourable to themselves.

It would appear, therefore, that the all-important principle of Neutrality comes down to the assertion that, because there is no such thing as moral knowledge or certainty, we are never justified in commending a distribution of manna on the basis of judgements about the superiority of any persons, actions, goods or ways of life. This means that there can be no judgements of utility, no appeals to desert and no limitations placed by prior moral rights, save those which are embedded in the rules of the dialogue itself.

All this puts tremendous normative weight on the reasons which lie behind the Neutrality principle. These are set out briefly in the opening chapter and returned to, also briefly, in the closing one. What seems to justify the Neutrality principle is Ackerman's liberal premise that, because of the intrinsic value of the individual living an autonomous existence, people should be free to make their own mistakes. This means each person choosing and pursuing his own conception of what is good or worthwhile even if it means 'going to hell in his own way' (ibid., p.377). Clearly, for Ackerman it is self-evidently an attractive idea that everyone should be able to follow their own path without having to answer to others for their thoughts and actions, at least as they relate purely to their own lives and their non-coercive interactions with other people. What Ackerman values is 'a form of community in which each participant is guaranteed the right to live his own life regardless of what his neighbours may think of him' (ibid., p.376).

Without denying that there may be other things whose goodness may be known to us he claims that 'the capacity to develop a rational life plan' is 'the best thing that there is', and asks, 'Are you prepared to deny this? What could be better for a person than his own development of a plan of life that seems to him good?' (ibid., p.368). The only extended argument that Ackerman has for this position is the one we have already noted to the effect that any alternative position involves a controversial claim to moral knowledge. He does gesture towards the argument of Mill that experimentation is the path to progress, and draws on the Kantian insight that moral goodness is not something that can be forced on anyone, since it requires that persons act out of personal moral conviction. He also reminds us of the danger of entrusting political power to any corruptible human being:

'Even if you think you can *know* something about the good life, there are several good reasons for imposing liberal constraints on political conversation. Most obviously, you might think that you can only learn anything true about the good when you are free to experiment in life without some authoritative teacher intervening whenever he thinks you're going wrong. . . . Even if you don't think you need to experiment, you may adopt a conception of the good that gives a central place to autonomous deliberation and deny that it is possible to *force* a person to be good. . . . Assume, finally, that you think you know what the good life is and that it is of a kind that can be forced on others; then the only question is whether the right people will be doing the forcing. A single glance at the world suggests that this is no trivial problem.' (Ibid., pp.11ff)

Ackerman does not develop these arguments for and against paternalism in any detail. Nor does he consider the extensive literature on the subject. Yet it is interesting to note that he does bring in some reference to contingent consequences of the dialogic method which render his arguments open to falsification. Also noteworthy is the fact that he does not appeal to the idea of autonomy as a presupposition of treating persons as responsible, in the sense of being answerable for their actions, although this is the flavour of his initial requirement of Rationality. This may be due to the association between the responsibility view of autonomy and the idea of justice as desert, a connection which he wants to rule out on the basis of the correct assumption that it involves making value judgements on individual conduct.

Nevertheless there is a curiously meritorian connotation to much of the terminology he uses to express his principle of Neutrality. The most frequently repeated of his formulations in his simulated dialogues is the claim that 'I am at least as good as you are' – a highly ambiguous phrase that could refer as much to the moral qualities and insights of the individual as to his worth or value as the author of a rational life plan. It is the denial of 'superior moral worth' (ibid., p.374), 'moral superiority', (p.91) as being 'specially deserving' (p.55) or being a 'better person' (p.57) that is reiterated, as much as the claim that the pursuit of a life plan is as important and valuable in the case of one person as in the case of another.

It might be surmised that Ackerman's prohibition of any argument which requires the acceptance of one valued objective or form of life or type of person as morally superior to another would produce complete stalemate in the Assembly Hall of the spaceship. However, perhaps because the space travellers are anxious to get their feet on *terra firma*, agreement is eventually reached after strong rulings from the Commander, whose task it is to see that all the contributors keep within the rules of the dialogue. This is achieved by using arguments of the form: 'Since I am just as good as you are, I should get at least as much of the stuff we both desire – at least until you give me some Neutral reason for getting more' (ibid., p.58).

The move from the initial rejection of superiority to the affirmation of equal worth is an interesting and crucial one, since it would appear that the thoroughgoing moral sceptic would not be able to be so positive about such a controversial matter as A being at least as good as B. Moreover, as we noted in Chapter 1 (p.33) such an initial presumption of equality can have a profound impact on the eventual outcome of a distributive decision. Ackerman holds that, since all can agreee that their 'own image of self-fulfilment has *some* value' (ibid., p.57), Neutrality will enable them all to make a claim on scarce resources on exactly the same bases, namely (1) that they are morally autonomous and (2) that no one can say that their values are worse than anyone else's. Hence, with respect to initial resources at least, all are to be given equal amounts. This may not satisfy everyone or enable them to get all that they desire, but it is a practicable division which passes the requisite dialogic tests.

It is doubtful whether even this formulation of the argument takes seriously the scepticism on which Neutrality is said to be based. It may not be possible to be sure that everyone's pursuit of their good is as valuable as everyone else's, either in its mode or content. Individuals will manifest more or less of the typical characteristics of autonomy, such as critical reflection, rational pursuit of objectives and constancy of effort, and there may be differences in the value of the lifestyles they adopt. Ackerman insists that we cannot know how these differences are to be evaluated, but this does not mean that we have to make the controversial assumption that they are, for practical purposes, equal. Yet he presents this as the obvious starting-point against which criticism may be directed. Consequently, no critics can unseat the assumption of equality without violating Neutrality and equality is therefore, by default, declared the winner, its critics being eventually reduced to silence and thus to political defeat. With a principle, like Neutrality, which is incompatible with the deployment of any value judgement, clearly everything depends on where the burden of proof lies. If it is equality of resources that has to be unseated, then equality is bound to win.

It may be, however, that a covert underpinning of Ackerman's egalitarian initial distribution of manna is to be found in the meritorian flavour of the phrase 'at least as good'. It is reasonable to assume that, at the outset of adult life, persons are approximately equal in their deserts, since they have not yet acquired merits and demerits, which largely accrue in adulthood. We might note in passing that, given the equal starting-point which is said to be the implication of the dialogue, it is easy to think of subsequent unequal outcomes as more or less deserved, given that they represent the working out of a situation of greater equality of opportunity than has yet been attained in any society. However, these are not the considerations to which Ackerman overtly appeals.

At this stage in Ackerman's mythical spaceship adventure the crucial arguments are directed against those who might wish to move from 'at least as good' to a distribution of manna which produces either 'equal satisfaction' of everyone's desires, or an 'equal chance' for everyone to reach their personal objectives in life. Both these alternatives have the apparent advantage of taking some account of the fact that manna is valuable essentially for what it can be used to achieve, and that this will vary from person to person. Equal satisfaction is rejected because it involves reaching agreement that satisfaction is good (ibid., p.49), thus violating Neutrality. The second, equal opportunity, option is dismissed because we cannot reduce everyone's plan of life to one clear objective or limited series of objectives, so that a number of people would be left out of such a distribution (ibid., p.53). Yet the equal distribution of manna is also open to question because it neglects the evident fact that not all life plans will be equally expensive, and it is hard to know why this difficulty is not as fatal to the egalitarian solution as the other difficulties are deemed to be fatal to its alternatives. Ackerman, acknowledging that tastes differ, and that some objectives are more expensive to pursue than others, holds that we must simply put up with such inequities on the grounds that scarcity is an inescapable fact of life.

Applying the same mode of argument to the situation of an ongoing, but still ideal, society, Ackerman reaches the following sweeping conclusions: A political community of diverse individuals can organise its power struggle consistently with Neutral discourse if it takes steps to assure that:

a. No citizen *genetically dominates* another.
b. Each citizen receives a *liberal education*.
c. Each citizen begins adult life under conditions of *material equality*.
d. Each citizen can *freely exchange* his initial entitlements within a *flexible transactional network*.
e. Each citizen, at the moment of his death, can assert that he has fulfilled his obligations of *liberal trusteeship*, passing on to the next generation a power structure no less liberal than the one he himself enjoyed.

If a social world fulfilled all these conditions, I shall say that its inhabitants enjoy the condition of *undominated equality* that is required by an undeviating insistence on liberal dialogic legitimacy.' (Ibid., p.28)

In the process of justifying these further conclusions Ackerman deals in turn with issues of citizenship, birthrights, education, free exchange and generational trusteeship, wealth having been considered already in the discussion of manna.

The idea of genetic domination arises in the context of the power of one generation to use futuristic techniques of genetic manipulation to alter the characteristics of the next generation, thus threatening the pluralism which liberal society treasures. Like all exercises of power this choice must be subjected to the test of Neutral dialogue. Neutrality rules out control by parents over the genetic make-up of their children because, in order to exercise this control, they would have to use their own conception of the good as a basis for choosing the capacities of others, and this is unacceptable even if those others are their children. However, 'if *every* X in the Assembly Hall says that B's genetic equipment places him at a disadvantage to A in the pursuit of the good, as X understands the good, then the Commander may declare that A *genetically dominates* B' (ibid., p.116). This formula ensures that the absolutely evident genetic handicaps, which everyone agrees are handicaps, will be eliminated, but is nevertheless compatible with 'an enormous range of genetically diverse outcomes' (ibid., p.121). There is thus no danger of dull uniformity descending on society. It also follows that citizens, once born, cannot complain that their genetic make-up could and therefore should be better, since it can be demonstrated to them that such manipulations would have violated Neutrality by assuming the superiority of a particular conception of the good.

Education comes into the picture as a necessary requirement for the individual to attain his life's objectives, but it is also problematic because of the paternalism that it involves. Children have to be brought up according to a particular set of values before they can be in a position to choose their own futures. Ackerman solves this familiar liberal conundrum by licensing such adult control as is required to prepare the child to become a member of a liberal society, the entry test for which is the ability to engage in Neutral dialogue. This educational programme requires a degree of stability or 'cultural coherence' and, in the early stages, a good deal of parental control, at least until such time as the child learns to internalise restraints on his anti-social instincts. Beyond this there must be a good deal of parental guidance about which goals are realistic, guidance which comes increasingly to be shared with a broad range of educators, all committed to using the minimal constraints compatible with preparing the young for autonomous living in a diverse society.

A liberal education will concentrate on preparing children for the choices which they will progressively be able to make as they come to adulthood, thus making them well equipped to take advantage of the various opportunities that life offers in a liberal society. Children are not to be brought up in a social vacuum but parental and adult rights are essentially subordinate to the interests of children whose eventual conception of the good has equal standing with those of earlier adults. Indoctrination, or the unnecessary imposition of adult values, are illegitimate uses of power in a liberal society.

Adding, to their equal share of manna, the fruits of a liberal education, adults enter on their citizenship from a situation of essential equality, despite their individual differences. At this point they become fully free to enter into whatever agreements they wish with their fellow citizens in order to further their own conception of the good, as long as these do not involve the illegitimate exercise of power over others. This is the central liberal outcome of the process of Neutral dialogue for 'the entire point of our earlier liberal conversations was to set the stage for a world in which everybody could use his *legitimate* initial endowments in the way he thinks best' (ibid., p.182).

All this takes place, it must be emphasised, in a situation which is 'ideal', not only with respect to the effective implementation of social values through a 'perfect technology of justice', but also in that there exists ways of ensuring what is called 'transactional flexibility'. This is a matter of using technological devices which include methods of communication that enable everyone to possess full information about the agreements which others may be willing to enter into and efficient and costless means for communicating with and entering into arrangements with any other person or persons. Further, there being no limits on the use of these techniques, there is no censorship or monopolisation. Other devices enable individuals either to share their use of manna with others or to shield their activities from the view, or participation, of others. This means that there need be no free-riders gaining unpaid-for benefits from the choices of others. Individuals can also isolate themselves from the effects of the behaviour of other people, thus cutting out 'externalities', that is, unwanted costs arising from their agreements or activities.

Given this amazing technology, which is made possible by Ackerman's costless 'transmitter-shields', anything that is compatible with undominated equality goes, provided that the interests of future generations are taken into account and not subordinated to the illegitimate use of power by their elders. For, although the members of each generation are free to make what use they wish of their original allocation of manna, they are under a burden of trusteeship to the next generation, a burden which must be given the same adult starting-point of undominated equality and a share of manna at least as great as that with which the previous generation started out on adult life. This follows from the fact that each generation can claim to be at least as good as any other.

The limits of dialogue

The details of Ackerman's scheme are complex and fascinating, but they are of less significance than the method by which he derives substantive principles of justice from such an abstract conception as Neutral dialogue. The attempt to move towards a concrete image of a liberal society, while presupposing no more than the equal worth of each individual or of each individual's plan of life, has the appearance of a spectacular conjuring trick. A great deal depends, as we have seen on the move from the exclusion of claims to superiority to the dubious working premise of each being at least as good as the other. Ackerman seems blind to the fact that the absence of proof that A is better than B does not imply that A is as good as B. Yet almost everything in Ackerman's dialogues depends on this crucial move, the flow of which depends more on the need for the discussants to proceed on some basis or other, rather than continue in deadlock.

Putting this criticism more substantively, it is by no means evident that there is moral agreement that a person's pursuit of a life plan is a good which is quite independent of the substance of that life plan. Indeed it is arguable that we cannot have a conception of the good at all unless we have a working distinction between the good and the bad, and having this distinction, we are bound to use it to assess the quality of other person's choices and actions. In some cases, at least, this is likely to lead to the conclusion that the good of a person being able to choose his own life is overridden by the harm that is caused by the life he chooses. Borrowing Ackerman's terminology, we may say that the intuition that there are limits to the range of choices that are open to the liberal citizen is at least as good as Ackerman's intuition of the value of individual autonomy.

Difficulties about the limits of liberal tolerance are masked by the availability to Ackerman of the retreat to his original assumption about the prior place of legitimating dialogue in any acceptable political system. Any behaviour which is inconsistent with participation in this dialogue can thereby be declared illegitimate. Violence, fraud, lying and anti-social behaviour in general are said to be incompatible with participation in Neutral dialogue and, for this reason, unacceptable.

This is a rather topsy-turvy approach to the exclusion of such importantly immoral forms of conduct. Is violence really to be excluded simply because it interferes with Neutral dialogue? It so happens that Neutral dialogue cannot proceed without a prohibition on violence, but this is hardly the reason why violence is in general unacceptable. Also odd is Ackerman's contention that we can limit membership of the Liberal state to those who are able to participate in Neutral dialogue and his justification of immigration controls on the grounds that aliens are by disposition not part of the dialogic community. It puts the cart before the horse to argue that persons are entitled to a citizen's share of manna only if they are able to assert their claims to it and only if they happen to be already members of the relevant debating society.

Ackerman is also able to protect himself from having to bring in substantive values to the political decision-making process by means of the wonderful technology which pertains in the ideal world he describes. The effect of this technology is to remove many of the problems of social conflict which required political resolution. If we can shut ourselves off from the harmful effects of the actions of others, then the bulk of our problems in living in the same society are removed at a stroke. And while the perfect technology of transactions may be introduced to fill out the idea of free choice, it also enables us to escape from the difficult value-laden choices that are involved in choosing and paying for particular means of communication and methods of transfer in the real world.

The objection we have noted to an equal distribution of manna on the ground that it ignores human diversity becomes even more forceful when the inequalities which emerge as a result of free exchange in conditions of transactional flexibility are noted.

Ackerman is quite sanguine about the fact that, given human diversity, even with undominated equality, at the end of a lifetime 'some will have used the transactional system to gain enormous wealth; others will die with nothing but their name' (ibid., p.201). Given his assumptions, he cannot argue that this is deserved, only that it is legitimate. If he had explored the issue of desert (something which is excluded in the initial stages by the artificiality of the spaceship myth) then he would have had to take account of the fact that the outcome of free exchange (even with undominated equality) is a matter of luck as well as creditable choices and efforts. The fact that he can see no grounds for correcting these inequalities in an ideal society, except in the interests of the next generation or in order to maintain Neutral dialogue itself, suggests that something has gone radically wrong.

These criticisms are directed at Ackerman's principles of justice as they apply in an ideal society with a perfect technology of justice, perfect transactional flexibility and sustained undominated equality. However, he devotes equal attention to showing how things change when we move to the real world in which none of these conditions pertain. Existing inequalities cannot be justified where citizens start adult life with unequal quanta of material resources, have different educational opportunities, and live in societies in which power is held illegitimately, authoritative rules are broken, often with impunity, the market is riddled with imperfections and externalities are the norm.

Where these failures bear hardly and cumulatively on particular persons and groups Ackerman speaks of 'exploitation' and contends that his scheme would require massive redistribution in order to rectify the injustices of the past and deal with the technological inadequacies of the present. It is here, however, that another weakness of Ackerman's theory emerges, for it is powerless to determine how the required rectifications and compensations should proceed. As Ackerman points out, in a world of scarce resources, economic and political life must proceed without waiting for the full correction of exploitation. Even where there is in theory the technology to accomplish such rectification, the priorities which have to be established require that value judgements, of the sort ruled out of order by Neutral dialogue, must be made. For instance, the polity has to determine what its priorities shall be in the rectification of the various aspects of exploitation.

Ackerman acknowledges that actual people will put more weight on the attainment of their goals than on the achievement of the ideal liberal society in which Neutral dialogue flourishes. Full liberal education, for instance, will be subordinated to economic growth, and the latter may call for increased incentives which actually increase rather than correct material inequalities. Similarly the improvement and subsidy of means of communication may have to take second place to the compensation of those who, due to the absence of the requisite genetic technology, have serious genetic handicaps. Decisions about resource allocation in these circumstances require evaluation of the content of people's wants and needs, a matter which goes beyond the maximisation of their autonomy.

In these circumstances, the principle of Neutrality provides us only with the rule that, initially at least, sacrifices of the ideal rights which pertain in the perfect society must be equal:

'The constraint is the idea of equal sacrifice: since everyone is at least as good as everyone else, no one can be called upon to sacrifice more of his ideal rights than anyone else. Within this constraint, the statesman's task is to choose the budget that best fulfils the liberal ideal of undominated equality.' (Ibid., p.261)

However, it is not clear how we are to assess equality of sacrifice without making potentially discriminatory value judgements with respect to which ideal rights are to be curtailed, and, in any case, Ackerman acknowledges that even this constraint is vulnerable to modification in the light of the need to encourage socially beneficial activities through incentive taxation. In practice, Ackerman has to hand these issues over to the decision of the democratic majority, albeit guided by Herculean statesmen and limited by some allowance for constitutional rights and other devices which go some way towards protecting the equalities and liberties which mark life in the ideal society. Such decision-making procedures cannot however utilise only Neutral dialogue which must, at this point, abdicate and leave the field to more substantive principles of utility and justice.

Justice in contract

The substantive thinness of Neutral dialogue becomes more apparent as we enter the realm of the real world. This is apparent in Ackerman's treatment of contract law, an area in which he has taken a particular interest as an academic lawyer.

The system of ideal rights set out in *Social Justice in the Liberal State* clearly amounts to a strong endorsement of the liberal ideal of free exchange and the implied corollary that persons be held responsible for the agreements into which they freely enter. Ackerman, in contrast to 'contract' theorists such as Rawls, emphasises *actual* agreements rather than hypothetical ones, but argues that 'in protecting any relationship that is the product of a free exchange between consenting adults, ideal liberal theory attempts a *rapprochement* with voluntaristic ideas central to the contractarian tradition' (ibid., p.196). Both the contract and the dialogue approaches agree on the centrality of freedom of contract, but Ackerman claims that his is by no means a blanket endorsement, for free exchange is not a postulate of the theory but simply one of the outcomes of Neutral dialogue: 'the dialogic principles regulating free exchange are an inextricable part of a larger liberal theory of social justice' (ibid., p.195).

This means, for instance, that if the requirements of an ideal transactional system are not met in some way then the person who is as a result unfairly treated 'may demand that government intervene to help them approximate the outcomes they would have reached under an ideal transactional network' (ibid., p.189), for 'the liberal state is deeply committed to the ideal of free exchange – *provided* that mutually beneficial trade occurs within a power structure legitimated by liberal dialogue' (ibid., p.263).

If there is censorship, so that the citizen does not know of, or cannot make, certain offers; if there is monopoly, so that the citizen is not free to take up any of the variety of offers made; if there are externalities such that the citizen is adversely affected by the exchanges of others; or if there is free-riding in that the citizen cannot prevent his goods being available to the benefit of others who have not worked for them, then the exchanges may be illegitimate and unenforceable in law. Moreover, when there has been inequality in the original holdings of adults, or defects in their liberal education or unacceptable uncompensated genetic handicaps, then the assumption of enforceable unrestricted mutual bargaining does not hold even where the transactional network is perfect.

Here Ackerman criticises Nozick for his too easy assumption that what holds in an ideal world more or less holds in the real world. The systematic inequalities in material starting-point, education and grossly defective transactional arrangements cast the gravest of doubts on any actual entrepreneur's extensive holdings. Ackerman is at pains to distance himself from actual *laissez-faire* political philosophies which ignore or condone such background injustices. Nor is Ackerman prepared to go along with the idea that citizens be held to their bargains in all situations, even where undominated equality and perfect flexibility of transactions do obtain. There must be a 'continuing insistence that the claims of free contract be appraised against a background of power relationships established by the transactional framework and the distribution of wealth, education and ability' so that the liberal can at least wonder whether a 'promise, once fairly made, must *always* be kept' (ibid., p.199).

Ackerman also gives the broadest of hints that contracts between those with different levels of relevant knowledge may not be sustained, so that it may not be permissible to 'exploit ignorance' (ibid., p.188), even where perfect transactional apparatus and opportunities do exist. There is also the suggestion that enforceable contracts must be 'mutually beneficial' (ibid., p.263).

All these qualifications could add up to a situation in which Ackerman appears to give a central place to the voluntaristic ideal of free exchange unquestioned in its content, but in effect places so many conditions on it as to render it, after endless corrective interferences, no more than a vestigial residue. The systematic and persistent exploitations and imperfections of actual societies would appear to tower over and negate the freedoms of the ideal world of equal starting-points and perfect exchange mechanisms. What then is left of the liberal commitment to voluntary agreements?

A crucial issue here is the extent to which Ackerman permits inequality of wealth and hence 'economic duress' to affect the enforceability of contracts. Typically in a free market society economic duress – that is, being 'forced' into an agreement out of financial necessity – does not absolve a contractor from his obligations. 'Fair' prices are simply those set by the market and the poor man's limited purchasing power is part of that market. The law of contract is, by and large, blind to the 'justice' of the price agreed.

Ackerman cannot think that it is always proper to take economic pressure into account for, given undominated equality, he holds that whatever is agreed is proper, and we have seen that undominated equality does not remove the element of economic competition between persons of different abilities, motivations and interests. But where exploitation exists, this is a factor which must in principle lead to a form of unconscionability or extortion which negates the normal obligation to fulfil the contract. Also, where the market is imperfect and the communications inadequate it would seem that defaulting contractors must have a case for non-enforcement in citing the alternative bargains they might have made under more ideal conditions. This question takes us nearer to Ackerman's transition to the real world, or 'second best' arrangements which deal with the technical and liberal defects of actual societies.

Most of the discussion on this transition to the real world concerns the quantity of the community's resources that is to be spent on rectifying its liberal defects, together with the decision-making procedure for determining social priorities in what must be an incomplete endeavour: is it to be education before improved transactional networks, or compensation for genetic defects before efforts to prevent monopolies? On these questions the principle of Neutrality in dialogue is said to provide clear guidelines for dealing first, and at considerably more expense than would be acceptable in a minimalist state, with the most evident forms of 'exploitation', that is, clear deprivations of ideal rights in one respect or cumulative deprivations relating to a number of rights (ibid., p.297). And then, as we have seen, there is the principle of equal sacrifice to make sure that any shortfalls from perfect liberal conditions are evenly distributed. Beyond these factors, Ackerman believes there is room for the infinite amounts of 'good faith' disagreement, which has to be settled by a method that is at least compatible with Neutral dialogue, which turns out to be a form of democracy which includes certain constitutional safeguards that specify what is beyond normal democratic intervention. In the end, therefore, it is a democratic procedure which determines the budget that best fulfils the ideal of undominated equality in actual societies. Such a budget inevitably involves a series of trade-offs to which there is no one right answer (ibid., p.255). Unfortunate choices have to be made between perfect liberalism and exploitation, or between freedom and starvation.

Such generalities leave us in the dark as to the limitations which will emerge in the area of contract law. What will Neutral dialogue and constitutional democracy come up with in relation to error, duress and unconscionability – the traditional grounds for releasing contractors from their unfair bargains? Will the favoured procedures add to the grounds on which agreements may be set aside the fact that one contractor had a less liberal education than another, or started off with a serious genetic handicap, or an unequal store of worldly goods?

No doubt wisely, Ackerman does not attempt to give us detailed answers to such questions. Indeed to do so would be out of line with his method which is to leave such matters to the outcome of Neutral dialogue between actual members of real jurisdictions. Each group will have to hammer these things out for themselves in the light of their situation and conceptions of the good. His theory provides only a 'framework within which the concerns of traditional theories may both be refined and reformulated' (ibid., p.196).

Nevertheless Ackerman does give us some guidelines with which to direct our use of Neutral dialogue in relation to 'second best' contract law in non-ideal societies. First, he urges us not to forget that we are dealing with people whose prime concern is the pursuit of their conception of the good. The process of free exchange helps them with that, therefore, other things being equal, free exchange is favoured as a device for enabling people to get what they want. To be effective in this regard there must be some stability in its operation and, therefore, contracts must, by and large, be enforced. There can be no question of waiting for total absence of undominated equality before enforcing agreements.

Secondly, however, it is held to be proper to restrict freedom of contract for reasons of background unfairness. Indeed it is evident from his work on slum landlords and housing codes (Ackerman, 1971) that Ackerman is open to the use of contract law for redistributive purposes. There he argues that enforcing housing codes in slum areas could significantly contribute to righting the injustice which arises from the imbalance of incomes in actual housing markets. If, with a housing subsidy, it is more redistributive to require landlords to acquire certificates of habitability than it is to pursue equality through negative income tax then this is the correct way to further justice. Thirdly, there is the basic assumption that there is an intrinsic value in free exchange because it is a manifestation of the individual pursuing his own conception of the good, which is what liberal society is all about. This value is not necessarily always overridden by the presence of non-ideal factors.

We can see, then, that Ackerman's approach to the reform of contemporary contract law would give weight to factors of economic efficiency, background inequalities and respect for individual commitments. This does seem an attractive mixture of affirming the importance of free exchange, and thus keeping people to their contracts, for both instrumental and intrinsic reasons, while making the commitment to freedom of exchange radically defeasible, in that it may be overturned in an open-ended number of ways for reasons which include not only questions about the involuntariness of the exchanges through duress, ignorance or mistake, but the economic, educational and genetic inequalities that can make enforcing such agreement seem essentially unfair.

This general approach opens the way for arguments which set aside bargains which prove to be disadvantageous to particular groups whose general position is the result of illegitimate inequalities. Several important points of criticism can be made of this position and these cast doubt both on the coherence and the power of the dialogue approach to justice as a whole. For instance, the power of the dialogue method may be doubted because crucial questions, such as the vital issue of the extent to which background injustices should feature in the legal overturning of ordinary commercial transactions, cannot be settled by Neutral dialogue alone, even if all the relevant facts are not in dispute. Allowing contracts to be enforced against a background of injustice is bound to favour some groups and individuals over others for reasons which cannot respect the idea that each person's good is as important as everyone else's. The choice between non-ideal worlds is an essentially discriminatory one in precisely the way that Ackerman wishes to avoid.

Further, the coherence of Ackerman's approach to contract, and hence to justice in general, is compromised by the uneasy combination of radical equality at the start of adult life and what is in effect purely formal equality of opportunity thereafter. It is hard to imagine how an appeal to equal worth, which has such force at one stage of the individual's life-cycle, can be so irrelevant at a later stage. The cumulative inequalities of adult life in a diverse free-enterprise adult society seem bound to work to the selective benefit of some, such as the genetically more able, in ways which have no evident basis in Neutral dialogue and for which Ackerman's method can suggest no effective remedy.

One aspect of this problem is that Ackerman declines to make any direct use of the idea of desert beyond his assumption that a person is entitled to keep the fruits of his own endeavours at least in a society of undominated equality. Such 'fairness' as he does incorporate in his model is not at any point the consequence of using a notion of desert that could set reasonable limits on the inequities of adult life. Thus the undoubted relative fairness of the equal starting-point is not arrived at because it constitutes fair equality of opportunity but because it is the only position said to be compatible with Neutral dialogue. But Neutral dialogue has – at least ostensibly – no place for the value-laden idea of desert and incorporates arrangements which connect with desert only through the fortunate fact that, in the moritorium on value judgements imposed by Neutral dialogue, the only consensual position attainable is a form of equality of resources and education. In consequence, since liberal dialogue has no capacity to determine these practical issues, we are left without a ready alternative to help us contain the free-enterprise society that Ackerman seeks in vain to confine within the limits of justice.

5 Justice as Efficiency: Posner and Criminal Justice

Although it is common to draw a sharp distinction between justice and utility, utilitarians themselves vigorously dispute the validity of this antithesis, and claim that utilitarianism can account for the significance of justice as a subordinate ethical and political standard whose importance can be explained by the ultimate ethical principle that the right act is that which maximises overall utility. In contrast, non-utilitarians often ascribe to justice those moral judgements which are routinely used to curb the application of utilitarian reasoning, while some go so far as to define 'justice' as a distributive ideal which totally excludes the aggregative goal of bringing about the greatest quantity of good.

Inevitably, therefore, utilitarians are on the defensive when articulating and defending their conception of justice and they usually feel impelled to demonstrate that adherence to utilitarianism does not radically conflict with commonsense notions of what is just. Often, in the process, they reinterpret classical utilitarianism so as to accommodate the demands of justice. Indeed, one contemporary theorist of justice, Richard Posner, whose work is very much in the utilitarian tradition, presents his theory almost entirely by way of contrasts with his interpretation of utilitarianism. Later in this chapter I shall consider Posner's 'economics of justice' and its applications to criminal justice. But first, by way of introduction, the main elements of the justice versus utility debate are reviewed.

Justice and utility

Utilitarianism – in some shape or form – has been, in recent times, a working hypothesis for most western economists and constitutes a fair reflection of the concentration on economic growth as the central policy goal in modern politics. Present-day utilitarianism is, perhaps, best exemplified by 'welfare economics' which adopts as the basic economic norm the maximisation of human utility or 'welfare', an approach which has also been applied to democratic theory and, more recently, to the common law. Utilitarianism has also been vigorously championed by R. M. Hare (1962) as a logical outcome of the universalisability of moral judgements.

The central tenets of utilitarianism constitute a powerful combination of empirical and normative dogmas, expounded first by the nineteenth-century Philosophical Radicals, particularly Jeremy Bentham and – in a less orthodox vein – John Stuart Mill. The Philosophical Radicals held the apparently contradictory theses that (1) as a matter of fact, all men seek to maximise their own pleasures and minimise their own pains, and (2) as a matter of value, the morally right act is that which maximises the pleasures and minimises the pains of *all* those affected by it. With these premises, the classical utilitarians embarked on a detailed critique of social arrangements and produced a multiplicity of specific proposals detailing ways in which the self-centredness of the individual could be harnessed to generate happiness for all. What, for Adam Smith, had been a wonder of divine design whereby the individual's pursuit of his own economic benefit, in the context of free market competition, results in the 'wealth of nations', became, for Bentham and his followers, a mechanism to be developed and improved in all spheres of social life by the scientific methods of human social engineers. Thus Bentham proposed to reform the criminal law by having effective sanctions to deter harmful conduct and supported the extension of the democratic franchise to provide similar market-type controls over the behaviour of politicians. Smith's 'natural' harmony of interests was thereby transformed into an artificial harmony whereby the manipulation of incentives produces 'the greatest happiness of the greatest number', a slogan which was taken to mean the largest possible quantity of pleasure over pain in a community where every member's pleasure and pains are given equal weight in the calculus of social happiness.

Given that this historical association of psychological egoism and ethical consequentialism – which became the dominant orthodoxy of late nineteenth- and early twentieth-century capitalism – still features in many public policy debates, it is difficult to treat the twin pillars of classical utilitarianism separately, particularly as the psychological doctrine is frequently deployed to demonstrate how ethical utilitarianism may be used to support ordinary standards of justice. This is done by showing the need for rules which allocate benefit and burdens as inducements for self-interested individuals to act as the general happiness requires. Indeed, although utilitarianism is usually considered to be an essentially ethical doctrine, many theorists are counted as utilitarians more because of their adherence to the postulate that people are rational maximisers of their own happiness (or interests) than on account of any unshakeable commitment to the normative consequentialist thesis that general utility-maximising is the sole ethical and political value. However, the two elements of the classical theory are, in principle, separable and both have been developed in different ways from the various forms of modern utilitarianism.

In modern economics the psychological doctrine concerning the self-interestedness of human motivation has been transformed, for theoretical purposes, into a working hypothesis to the effect that, in order to predict the outcome of economics and social arrangements, it should be assumed that people act rationally, in that they consistently choose those options which bring most benefit to them as individuals, the associated assumption being that economic agents base their choices on relatively constant preferences or desires. The theoretical standing of this hypothesis depends on the extent to which it can be used to generate verifiable predictions concerning the social effects of economic or legal change. Its effectiveness as a postulate does not, therefore, depend directly on the extent to which it applies in fact to the reasoning processes of particular individuals. Thus the idea of maximising behaviour has been described as 'a useful fiction for analysing the behaviour of groups' (Burrows and Veljanovski, 1981, p.3) although it is clearly intended by most of its proponents to be a realistic, if selective, fiction, which adequately encapsulates the dominant tendency in human behaviour.

For Bentham utility-maximising means choosing pleasant and avoiding painful sensations – pleasure and pain being the two 'masters' of human conduct – but the implausibility of this view in relation to many forms of behaviour led to the substitution of 'want-satisfaction' as the measure of utility, a more open-ended variant which enables the maximising assumption to achieve the status of a truism at the price of excessive vagueness. To render this interpretation of utility operational the test of want-satisfaction has been taken to be the preferences of individuals as expressed in the choices they actually make. This turns the maximising hypothesis into the tautological truth that people choose what they choose, since the satisfactions which are said to determine choices are evidenced only by the choices which are made.

In economics this vacuity is remedied by concentrating on strictly economic preferences which involve the effort to gain command over scarce resources by increasing purchasing capacity, and hence gaining control over goods and services which the rational maximiser hopes to obtain through his choices. Since, by extension, anything may be given a 'price' according to what individuals are prepared to pay for it in an open market, all want-satisfactions can in principle be given a monetary value by the application of such ideas as 'opportunity costs', whereby the value that a person places on an apparently non-monetary activity may be equated with the amount of money he could have earned in that time (this representing the 'opportunity cost' of his indulging in the activity in question). In this way we pass from happiness to want-satisfaction, and thence to monetary wealth, as the value which individuals or aggregates are said to pursue. In the case of wealth, however, it is not always clear whether – unconvincingly – wealth is taken to be the ultimate objective or – more plausibly – wealth is assumed to be a measure of enjoyment value of the resultant experiences, the capacity to achieve felt want-satisfaction, or some other further objective for which wealth is merely the instrumental or proximate goal.

The normative ethical principle of classical utilitarianism has undergone similar modifications in the face of comparable difficulties. Thus the empirical problems of measuring pleasures and pains or other psychological states, such as feelings of satisfaction, has prompted the abandonment of happiness-maximising as the all-inclusive ethical value, in favour of some form of preference utilitarianism according to which utility-maximising is giving people what they choose rather than what will enable them to increase their pleasures or enjoyments. Again there is often an ambiguity here about whether realising preferences is a means of increasing happiness or obtaining felt satisfaction, or is itself the valued objective. In the latter case what may be called preference utilitarianism approximates to its standard rival – the ethics of autonomy – in that it treats the exercise of the capacity for choice rather than happiness or satisfaction as the ultimate moral value.

Preference utilitarianism, as an ethical doctrine, looks almost as circular as its behavioural counterpart since, if moral principles are intended to guide choices, it appears to suggest that we ought to choose that which we do in fact choose, in which case it cannot offer guidance about how we ought to exercise our capacity for choice beyond requiring us to be consistent in our preference orderings. However, as we have seen, the ethical dimension of the maximising principle relates not to individual choices directly, but to social choices – that is, to choices which affect the welfare of many or all members of a social group. Ethical utilitarianism is the principle that the right act is the one which gives as many people as possible what they choose. In economic matters this becomes equated with maximally increasing purchasing power and, again, by extension, promoting those non-monetary preferences for which people would pay most.

The preference version of ethical utilitarianism has the advantage of helping to circumvent one of the major difficulties of the classical theory, namely, how to make inter-personal comparisons of utility, particularly when utility is equated with such subjective factors as pleasure or pain. Despite Bentham's valiant efforts to provide a 'felicific calculus' for the aggregation of the hedonic experiences of a community by measuring such factors as the intensity, duration and pleasurable or painful nature of their sensations, it has always seemed impossible to ascertain the truth of claims such as that one person's pleasure is four or five times as great as that of another, or that one person's intense but brief pleasure can be counterbalanced by another person's weaker but longer-lasting pain.

Inter-personal comparisons of this sort are avoided by attending to the choices that individuals make rather than the pleasures and pains they experience. The principle of utility can then be met by giving everyone what they say they want. However, since this can rarely if ever be achieved, particularly when social choices about institutional arrangements are under consideration, in practice it is necessary to resort to a democratic interpretation of preference utilitarianism by making social and political choices in accordance with the wishes of the majority, despite the fact that this may have the disadvantage of effectively excluding the interests of minorities. The move to democratic utilitarianism can be resisted if utility-maximising is given a more restricted democratic interpretation by requiring unanimity in the making of social choices.

This approach is exemplified by the use of the idea of 'Pareto optimality', according to which one situation is superior to another if at least one person is better off (or prefers that situation) and all other persons are equally well off (or think that the situations are equally acceptable). The Pareto optimal situation is that which it is impossible to change in a way which improves the lot or meets the wishes of at least one person without at the same time conflicting with the welfare or wishes of other people who are affected by the change. This uncontroversial concept is not only of very limited application in practice but has the disadvantage of giving to every member of a community a veto over any proposed changes, thus giving unjustified weight to the *status quo* and in effect making an infinite number of different social situations Pareto optimal, since there will always be those who stand to lose by alterations in existing arrangements.

An apparently more classically utilitarian variant of Pareto optimality is the Kaldor–Hicks principle according to which one social situation is to be preferred to another if the gains to some members of the community would be sufficient to compensate those who are the potential losers in the change from one to the other. The changes so justified do not depend on obtaining agreement of all those involved or actually paying the compensation to those who stand to lose from them, so that, while the Kaldor–Hicks approach has the flavour of a maximising happiness principle, it removes the element of consent involved in the Pareto principle, which potential losers could use to block proposed changes. One problem with the Kaldor–Hicks principle is that, when we seek to establish appropriate levels of compensation, it takes us back into the problem area of inter-personal comparisons, for the measurement of gains and losses involves comparing the satisfactions of the different persons involved.

The empirical realism conferred on the normative principle of utility by the Pareto optimal formula has to be offset against its diminished political applicability. Nearly all political choices benefit some at the expense of others. Of more direct bearing on the topic of this book is the objection that Pareto optimality rules out criticism of existing social arrangements as unjust, at least as long as they are more beneficial to at least one person than the suggested alternatives. The Kaldor–Hicks formula has more political uses and in its talk of compensation seems to be moving in the direction of justice, despite the fact that the compensation is notional rather than actual. But this too assumes that justice must take a *status quo* as a reference point for determining compensation. These normative limitations of tests of general social welfare illustrate one of the most serious criticisms of utilitarianism in general, namely its failure to take seriously the distribution of the valuable goods it seeks to maximise. This criticism can be made most forcibly from a meritorian standpoint, according to which it is essential to justice that benefits and burdens are allocated on the basis of the praiseworthy and blameworthy conduct or character of those affected by the distribution, but similar criticisms are put forward by everyone who considers some degree of egalitarianism to be an essential ingredient of justice.

An initial utilitarian response to such charges is to reiterate the Benthamite dictum that, in the calculus of pleasures and pains, 'each counts for one and no more than one'. However, this form of equality means only that no one's pleasure and pain are to be excluded from the calculus, or given less weight than a similar pleasure or pain experienced by any other person. While this requirement is entirely consistent with utilitarianism, and does rule out certain decision procedures on grounds which have at least a semblance of justice, it is still compatible with the many gross inequalities which are routinely denounced as unjust. It permits the 'victimisation' of minorities whose sufferings can be outweighed by the increased pleasures these sufferings bring to others (perhaps in the form of slave labour), and lacks the ability to make relevant moral discrimination between different types of enjoyable and painful activity.

Utilitarians have a number of further arguments with which

they hope to accommodate their theory to commonsense notions of justice:

1. Drawing on the concept of diminishing marginal utility, according to which the enjoyment to be derived from a given quantity of any commodity diminishes as the individual obtains more of it (so that the wealthy person derives less pleasure from receiving an additional sum of money than the same sum of money brings to a poor person), it is to be argued that an approximately equal distribution of money or other desired commodity will maximise the sum total of happiness in a society. To this extent utilitarianism has distributive implications which may be described as 'egalitarian', since it tends to produce an outcome of approximate equality of holdings.

2. According to ethical utilitarianism, an act is right if it maximises the happiness of all those affected by it and wrong insofar as it causes suffering to others; this means that the best utilitarian social arrangements will reward those who act altruistically and punish or burden those who cause suffering to others. It is not, therefore, the case that utilitarianism is indifferent to the moral quality of the behaviour of individuals for, through a system of incentives and penalties, those who act rightly will tend to be allocated a greater share of society's resources than those who act wrongly. This may not mean rewarding moral goodness, if this is seen as doing good for its own sake, but it does give credit for socially beneficial behaviour, thus avoiding the charge of moral insensitivity.

3. The distinctive importance placed on justice as a political value is compatible with utilitarianism because the happiness of human beings is particularly vulnerable to certain types of injury or harm, so that utility is maximised by prohibiting actions which tend to inflict such serious damage. These prohibitions may be regarded as the particular sphere of justice which has to do with the prevention of the major forms of human suffering in contradistinction to the wider utilitarian objective of encouraging the performance of socially beneficial actions. In a variant of utilitarianism – called 'negative' utilitarianism – it is held that pains or pleasures are not commensurate, in that a pleasure cannot outweigh a pain

and, in addition, the relief of suffering is said to take moral precedence over the increase of pleasure. This position is associated with the thesis that law should be concerned solely with the prohibition of pain-causing behaviour, leaving the pursuit of happiness to the private sphere.

4. Finally, stressing again the function of justice as a political ideal rather than an ethic for private life, the utilitarian, drawing on the premise of psychological egoism, can demonstrate that a society organised on utilitarian lines will be a society of rules and therefore of formal justice. Not only will social decisions be taken according to certain generalisations about the normal consequences of types of behaviour, but these types of behaviour will be encouraged or discouraged by the enactment of rules laying down appropriate sanctions (both negative and positive). While these rules, or laws, will be evaluated on utilitarian grounds, so that the net sum of harms prevented and pleasures elicited will maximally exceed the totality of pains inflicted by the imposition of negative sanctions (such as punishments or taxes), individual actions will be judged in accordance with the rules and not by a direct appeal to utility. This 'rule-utilitarian' approach is to be distinguished from the classical 'act-utilitarian' theory, according to which it is the individual act, rather than the rule, which is assessed by the utilitarian standard. Under rule-utilitarianism, it is argued, individuals will be treated with the formal equality required by ordinary standards of justice and the problem of victimisation will thus be reduced, if not eliminated. In this way the rule-utilitarian thesis explains why justice is essentially a matter of social organisation rather than personal morality.

In combination these points constitute a formidable defence of utilitarian justice, but each is open to objection. One general difficulty is that most of them appear unfortunately *ad hoc*, in that they rely on contingent facts, rather than moral principle, to produce acceptable results. Thus, if diminishing marginal utility does not hold in a particular context, can its standard egalitarian consequences be ignored? Or, if punishments do not deter certain types of harmful behaviour, does this mean that they should not be penalised? If disobeying a generally useful rule increases happiness can it not be ignored in that instance? Even when utilitarianism does get the morally right answer, it does not appear to do so for the right reasons.

It is also doubtful whether the combination of arguments (2) and (3) above really meets the full charge of moral inadequacy. Critics are concerned not simply with the fear that the unmerited sufferings of some will be inflicted or permitted just because they maximise overall utility. They also have the feeling that some pleasures, such as those of the sadist or the racist, ought not to be counted at all in the calculus of social values, because they have, if anything, negative moral quality. In a milder version of the same point it is argued, along the lines of Rawls's Aristotelian principle (see p.81) that some types of pleasure are inherently superior to others in a way that does not relate to their felt intensity.

The admission that it may be necessary to pick and choose amongst pleasures and pains undermines hedonistic utilitarianism, according to which these are the only values of consequence, and thereby takes away one of the main advantages of utilitarianism, namely its unitary measure of value. However, there are various types of 'ideal' utilitarianism according to which the rightness and wrongness of acts (or rules) depends on a number of different types of valued consequences. These versions of utilitarianism, which can accommodate the significance of beauty and truth as well as pleasure and pain, are, in general, morally more acceptable, although they do not directly confront the distributional issues characteristically posed by justice.

Rule-utilitarianism does appear to meet some of the distributional objections to making utility the sole measure of political rightness but, if taken strictly, it appears to be a radical departure from classical utilitarianism. The genuine utilitarian cannot surely be committed to following a rule even when this does not – and sometimes this must surely be the case – maximise utility? Moreover, not only is rule-utilitarianism a departure from the classical purity of the theory, it does not in practice avoid all forms of victimisation, some of which are group rather than individual victimisations, and may therefore be perfectly compatible with rule-based institutions, such as slavery or other routinised forms of discrimination.

For reasons such as these, the consideration of utilitarianism tends to generate a search for a more substantial basis for the minimal equalities and particular protections against victimisation which are felt to be prerequisites of any tolerably just society. Typical in this context is John Rawls's critique of utilitarianism's failure to take seriously the distinction between persons and his attempt, through the idea of the social contract, to provide a basis for rights which limits but does not eliminate the application of utilitarian considerations. However, if absolute rights – whether or not they are based on contract or mere moral conviction – are deployed in this way, it is open to the utilitarian to counter with the charge that these rights tend to place unjustifiable restraints on the pursuit of the general welfare and in practice serve in large part to protect the interests of a privileged minority over against the prospective advantages of the majority. Rawls's defence of the priority of liberty and, more evidently, Nozick's stand on the unlimited transactional rights of the property-owning individual can be taken by the tough-minded utilitarian as exemplifying the moral inadequacies of non-utilitarian theories of justice.

More generally, the utilitarian can cast doubt on the common assumption that justice is always an overriding moral consideration and adopt the view that the rights protected by utilitarian rules are indeed no more than positive rights which may be overridden, when appropriate, by wider considerations of utility. This hard-line utilitarian approach may involve overturning some accepted ideas about what is just and requires us to revise our views on the significance of justice within the overall moral framework, but utilitarianism has traditionally been a reforming and radical philosophy and it may be that, in the last resort, the utilitarians' best line of defence is the characteristically iconoclastic one of attacking the questionable outcomes of non-utilitarian principles. A contemporary example of such tough-mindedness is the work of Richard Posner, to whose economic theory of justice I now turn.

Posner's 'economics' of justice

The title of Posner's book *The Economics of Justice* (1981), suggests that his concern with justice is principally to do with the cost-effectiveness of the administration of law. This is certainly one of his interests, but it is a theme which is more central to his recent work, *The Federal Courts, Crisis and Reform* (1985), in which he deals with the case-load crisis facing the federal judiciary in the United States of America. *The Economics of Justice*, on the other hand, focusses more on presenting an economic conception of justice which equates justice with economic efficiency. particularly within the sphere of common law. While this book by no means sets out a systematic and rigorous defence of the idea that justice comes down to the benefits of wealth maximisation, it is noteworthy as a rare attempt to argue for a modern utilitarian analysis of justice (although it must be stressed that Posner himself sharply distinguishes his theory from Benthamite utilitarianism). Since Posner is a leading advocate of what is called the 'economic analysis of law' (EAL), his account of justice provides us with important insights into the contemporary implications of a type of theory which has close associations with the normative economics of free market economists such as Milton Friedman. Posner's achievement has been to apply the type of individualistic economic theory – which has been given new life by recent Chicago-based economists – to the substance of common law doctrines in areas such as negligence, contract and criminal law. Posner's work therefore represents the sort of economic reductionism against which Ackerman is reacting and with which other liberal theorists, such as Rawls, seek some sort of accommodation.

In terms of general ideological standpoint, Posner's theory of justice closely resembles that of Nozick, for both offer vigorous defences of capitalist libertarianism, giving general endorsement to private ownership of productive resources and free exchange untramelled by government interference. However, while Nozick's position is based on the assumption of socially pre-existing rights to life, liberty, the product of one's labour and the outcome of voluntary agreements, Posner adopts a typically utilitarian scepticism regarding moral rights and argues instead, on basically consequentialist grounds, for positive rights which, in the event, turn out to be extensionally identical to Nozick's fundamental moral rights. This is in line with his general thesis that social and political arrangements are subject to the test of 'wealth maximization' – the essential tenet of EAL, which seeks to articulate an economic perspective on law that will help us both to understand and assess legal process in the light of economic 'efficiency'. Like most overarching theoretical approaches EAL is partly descriptive in that it claims that, at least in common law, decisions, whether intentionally or otherwise, are determined by considerations of economic efficiency, and partly normative, in that laws are criticised if they are not consistent with the basic economic logic of the law.

Posner's version of EAL is well set out in a series of essays contained in *Economic Analysis of Law* (1977), where he defines 'efficiency' as 'exploiting economic resources in such a way that human satisfaction as measured by aggregate willingness to pay for goods and services is maximized' (p.4) or, alternatively, 'the aggregate satisfaction of those preferences . . . that are backed up by money' (p.61). An efficient society is one in which goods are in the hands of those who are able and willing to pay the highest price for them, since these are the persons who value them most highly. In other words, in the traditional language of utilitarianism, 'utility' is increased through voluntary exchanges in which one person purchases something from another. Those exchanges would not happen unless the purchasers valued the objects concerned more highly than the sellers, so that such exchanges, by placing goods in the hands of those willing to pay most for them, maximise overall social wealth.

Generalising from this assumption, maximising utility (or wealth) is achieved in the main through the operations of a free market in which participants are allowed to produce what they wish and offer their products in the market place for potential consumers to purchase according to their wishes, means and the other available alternatives. This form of preference satisfaction uses the rational maximising assumption of classical utilitarianism that is part of the standard utilitarian defence of the capitalist system of private production of goods for exchange in a free market: self-interested producers will compete to provide the goods and services demanded by self-interested consumers at the lowest feasible prices, thus unintentionally contributing maximally to the overall wealth of the economic community. Given a reasonable number of non-impoverished consumers, a pool of potential producers ready to enter into competition, and inexpensive ways of entering into bargains on the basis of adequate information (that is, low 'transaction costs'), the economic system will gravitate to a specific form of Pareto optimality in which neither producers nor consumers can improve their wealth in one respect without reducing it more in another.

EAL is an extension of this economic mode of analysis to law, which is interpreted as a way of regulating, in the interests of overall social utility, the behaviour of wealth-maximisers through a system of rules and sanctions administered by lawyers and judges who are themselves motivated by the same considerations as the agents whose interactions are regulated by law. Citizens break the law if the economic benefits to themselves outweigh the advantage of law-abidingness and litigate their disputes if the likelihood of equivalent economic benefits is greater than the likelihood of equivalent economic burdens. Further, judges determine the cases that came before them in the most economically efficient way, attaching the strongest sanctions to the most economically destructive behaviour, allocating rights to those litigants who would be prepared to pay most for them in a free market, and determining liability and damages so as to ensure that resources are in the hands of those most able to capitalise on them.

The law of tort, for instance, concerns itself with the efficient distribution of the costs of accidents in terms of the losses caused by accidents, the costs involved in guarding against them and the processes for allocating these costs, the general principle being that liability for accidents should rest on the party who could have avoided or minimised the risk of such accidents at the lowest cost to himself so that, according to Judge Learned Hand's now famous judgement in *US* v *Carroll Towing* (1947) negligence is a failure to take care when the cost of care is less than the probability of the accident, multiplied by the loss if the accident occurs. The application of this principle gives an incentive to reduce accidents, and hence the resultant losses, to those who can do this with least impact on the community's total wealth. Similarly, efficiency is best served by having a system of property giving individuals exclusive use of 'possessions' which can be alienated only by voluntary transfer, so that rights in property will be acquired by those able to make the most productive use of them.

Posner holds back from the contention that judges always decide cases on such overtly economic grounds. Nor does he believe that all citizens routinely alter their behaviour as the result of conscious economic calculations. But he does maintain that the economic model is theoretically sound in that, in general, it enables accurate predictions to be made about the common law legal process.

It should be noted that EAL, as it is presented by Posner and others, is restricted in scope, in that its descriptive application is primarily to judge-made common law, although there is a suggestion that the common law is ethically superior to the legislative decisions of political authorities which tend to depart from efficiency norms. It is also important to realise that 'wealth maximization' is a specific form of economic analysis which goes far beyond the more limited assumptions of simple Pareto optimality and sets out to act as a standard for choosing between various possible Pareto optimal situations. A society bent on placing all goods and services in the hands of those able and willing to pay for them is 'efficient' in a highly specific way which has no claim to be *the* economic standard of efficiency and is, in general, more resonant of the pretentions of classical utilitarianism than the more cautious normative claims of modern welfare economics.

The practical implications of EAL might appear to be that legal process be replaced by purely economic transactions, at least in civil as opposed to criminal matters, leaving courts to do no more than enforce bargains which are concluded in the market place. For instance, those who are liable to suffer from accidents will agree to pay those who are able to be the cheapest accident 'cost-avoiders' to take the necessary precautions, and the law will then enforce such agreements. This, however, ignores the crucial place of transaction costs in actual markets. It may be prohibitively expensive for individuals acting alone or in concert to gain the information and make the agreements necessary to achieve economic efficiency. In such situations, therefore, law has the more positive role of helping to reduce the market inefficiencies which result from high transaction costs. The contention is that the courts do, or should, allocate rights to those who would pay most for them if there were a relevant free market with no transaction costs.

Similarly, other problems arise in real markets because of 'externalities', that is, the uncompensated losses which fall on third parties as a result of such factors as pollution, environmental damage or accidents which do not feature in the 'cost' of the activities as paid by the voluntary participants. The function of law is to mitigate these market 'failures' also:

'Not that judges can or do duplicate the results of competitive markets, but that within the limits set by the costs of administering the legal system . . . common law adjudication brings the economic system closer to the results that would be produced by effective competition – a free market operating without significant externality, monopoly or information problems.' (Ibid., p.6)

Posner's thesis about the function of the common law is derived from the work of R. H. Coase who, in an influential article ('The Problem of Social Cost', 1960, p.1), argues that in situations where there is assumed to be low transaction costs the actual allocation of legal rights is immaterial with respect to the efficient outcome since the party who values a right more highly will always purchase that right, or its benefits, from the party to whom it is allocated by the courts. One way or another, therefore, the right in such hypothetical circumstances will end up in the hands of the party willing to pay most for it, which is the wealth-maximising solution to economic conflict between litigants. In the real world of high transaction costs the law best promotes efficiency by adopting the solution which *would* have emerged in a costless free market.

Posner's thesis, then, is that 'the common law method is to allocate responsibilities between people engaged in interacting activities in such a way as to maximize the joint value, or what amounts to the same thing, minimize the joint cost of the activities' (Posner, 1977, p.178). Furthermore he contends that, in so doing, the common law is 'just', a surprising conclusion in view of the fact that the maximisation of wealth, as he defines it, gives weight to preferences of individuals in proportion to their capacity to pay for what they want, which appears to be an embodiment of the sort of stark economic inequalities which are routinely denounced as unjust.

In the first part of *The Economics of Justice* which deals with 'Justice as Efficiency', Posner defends this equation of justice with wealth-maximisation by pointing to its alleged advantages as an ethical theory over classical utilitarianism. He argues for the view that 'the criterion for judging whether acts or institutions are just or good is whether they maximize the wealth of society' (p.115) by seeking to demonstrate that it is a satisfying blend of Benthamite utilitarianism and Kantian autonomy.

The defects of Benthamite 'happiness' utilitarianism are said to be, first, the indefiniteness or 'sponginess of the utility principle as a guide to policy' (p.42) due to the absence of an empirical method of identifying, measuring and comparing happinesses (see p.54) and, secondly, the notorious 'moral monstrousness' of utilitarianism with respect 'both (a) to its inability to make distinctions amongst types of pleasure and (b) its readiness to sacrifice the innocent individual on the altar of social need' (p.57).

The problem of indefiniteness is overcome by substituting wealth for happiness since wealth, it is argued, can be objectively measured by market mechanisms: utility thus becomes 'the sum of all goods and services in society weighted by their values', which is 'based on what people are willing to pay for something rather than on the happiness they would derive from having it' (p.60).

Whatever advantages wealth-maximisation may have in terms of precision, at least where actual markets exist, it has no evident intrinsic moral relevance. The value of wealth would appear to depend entirely on its contribution to other goals, such as the utilitarian satisfactions from which it is designed to extricate us. In fact Posner allows that this is indeed its moral grounding, for 'Value and happiness are of course related: a person would not buy something unless having it would give him more happiness, in the broad utilitarian sense, than the alternative goods and services (including leisure) that he must give up to have it' (pp.60f), but he goes on to argue for the difference between wealth and happiness as a criterion of justice by saying that the measure of wealth does not generate satisfactions for *all* since it excludes, for instance, the preferences of the destitute. While he is on relatively strong ground in arguing that there are limits to the moral force of happiness-maximising, he gives no good reason for the particular limitations imposed by wealth-maximisation, as there is no clear reason why an increase in wealth, as he defines it, has any moral significance in itself. Indeed, the fact that wealth as a measure of justice gives systematic preference to the producers over consumers and to the wealthy over the needy, is directly counter to the use of the language of justice to denounce unjustified inequalities of wealth.

As Posner's defence of justice as efficiency develops it becomes clear that, in the end, he does not found it on efficiency as the ultimate moral standard but regards it as merely the subordinate instrument whose significance depends wholly on the further values served by efficiency. This is only to be expected, given that efficiency is an instrumental term which always invites the question: efficient for what purpose? Any answer to this question in terms of wealth creation, if this is interpreted in monetary terms, simply raises the same question about the purposes for which money may be used. It is part of Posner's utilitarian flavour that he brings us back to the value of wealth for satisfying human desires and eschews any moral evaluation of these desires. However, he also justifies wealth-maximising as a way of increasing liberty, for in the wealth-creating markets he describes individuals are free and able to make choices according to their own preferences and personal desires. Echoing Nozick, his claim is that the maximisation of wealth also involves 'greater respect for individual choice than in utilitarianism (p.66), a claim he bolsters by arguing that participants give implied consent to the outcome of all market transactions, provided these are not the result of fraud or duress (see p.94).

Posner's commitment to freedom of choice is not, however, open-ended, for he equates it with the protection of those freedoms which are a necessary part of a free market private property system. In other words, overriding importance is given only to the positive rights which are intrinsic to capitalism. It is only because these rights are not vulnerable to 'the appeal to general utility' that he is able to claim that wealth-maximisation provides more adequate protection for individual rights than does utilitarianism, a theory which, in his view, justifies constant infringements of personal liberty. It turns out that wealth-maximisation limits as well as protects liberty, for it requires that effective restrictions be placed on some activities, such as the formation of monopolies, which restrict the creation of wealth.

We are, therefore, left with the ambiguous position that wealth-maximisation is an intermediate objective ultimately justified by its effectiveness in increasing happiness and liberty and yet also serves as a limiting consideration which enables us to discount certain forms of happiness and favour some liberties over others.

In *The Economics of Justice*, Posner retains the utilitarian's willingness to subordinate rights to utility by allowing that, where transaction costs are high, certain matters cannot be left to voluntary agreements for 'rights are not transcendental or ends in themselves' (p.71). Logically this vulnerability to the claims of utility must apply to the most basic rights of all, including the right to sell one's labour, but Posner argues that, because transaction costs are high, 'the wealth-maximizing principle requires the initial vesting of rights in those who are likely to value them most, so as to minimize transaction costs' (p.71). In this way he can ascribe to everyone the basic rights of liberty and freedom of contract, although he cannot maintain that these rights are in principle absolute.

As many critics have pointed out, this represents a rather unstable basis for the defence of rights, for it might turn out, for instance, that slavery in some form or other is in some circumstances the most efficient wealth-creating system. Moreover, as with all such *ad hoc* utilitarian justifications of rights, this approach seems to reach the right answer for the wrong reasons, in that our objections to slavery are based on considerations other than its disutility. Few would agree with Posner that apartheid is wrong simply because it is 'unlikely that ostracism, expulsion, or segregation of a productive group would actually increase a society's wealth' (p.85). Nor might we feel that the utility monster has been slain if the sadist's pleasure is admitted into the system provided that he pays for his pleasures even though, as Posner points out, the high cost of indulging his tastes will place some limits on his activities. Similarly, while it is welcome that the satisfaction of envious desires is given no moral weight, it is a disappointment that the reason given for this gesture to ordinary moral sentiments is that envy is felt primarily by those without market power, whose desires are therefore irrelevant to efficiency.

The strategy of Posner's defence of justice as efficiency is the familiar utilitarian combination of showing, on the one hand, that wealth-maximisation is a satisfactory rationale for standard moral views about such matters as honesty, truth telling and promise keeping – the 'conventional pieties' (p.67), which are vindicated by the fact that they are vital for a flourishing commercial system (see p.84) – and, on the other hand, in effect modifying the purities of crude utilitarianism by introducing counterbalancing considerations to formulate a more 'enlightened utilitarianism'

(p.107). Posner leaves obscure what happens when the pronounce-
ments of enlightened utilitarianisms conflict with ordinary moral
intuitions. It is also unclear how we are to establish the correct
balance between utilitarian and non-utilitarian elements which
Posner is happy to interpolate into his system. The attractiveness
of Posner's thesis, at this point, is that it does offer us what is in
effect a device for determining that balance, and hence avoids
intolerable vagueness, but in the end he gives us no good reason
to suppose that wealth-maximising is a reliable guide to the
correct mix of utility, liberty, merit and equality which he seeks
to uphold. Moreover the actual and possible consequences of the
application of the wealth-maximising test are often morally un-
persuasive, and are so in a way which runs counter to precisely
those moral considerations which are specifically the domain of
justice.

Thus, with apparently breathtaking callousness, Posner allows
that in the case of a feeble-minded person and others whose 'net
social product is negative' there is 'no right to the means of
support even though there was nothing blameworthy in his inability to support himself. This result grates on modern susceptibili-
ties, yet I see no escape from it that is consistent with any of the
major ethical systems' (p.76). This means that the interests of
those who cannot support themselves are on a par with the
interest of animals if these are thought to have significance only
in so far as they are valued as producers. The reverse side of this
particular implication is that he is able to draw on quasi-meritorian
considerations by pointing out that, although wealth-maximisation
has nothing to say on the initial distribution of wealth, his system
does see to the reward of talent and skill. However this nod in
the direction of desert is not developed, perhaps because of the
serious limitations which any extensive cognisance of desert would
impose on permissible inequalities of wealth and the fact that he
would have to define desert in terms of wealth productivity,
thereby introducing further circularity into the theory.

Conceptually, a difficulty with Posner's account of justice is
that it makes no effort to distinguish between justice and other
political ideals, a weakness which can be traced in part to his
acceptance of the Rawlsian catch-all definition of justice as en-
compassing whatever relates to the assessment of the basic structure of a society. Morally, the shortcomings of 'justice as

efficiency' is its inability to provide anything more than contingent justifications for any idea of real equality of satisfactions. Even the classical utilitarian principle that each is to count for one and no more than one is swept aside by the fact that suffering, unless accompanied by the capacity to pay, is irrelevant to economic 'justice'. The appeal to the satisfaction and liberty-promoting tendencies of wealth-maximisation might have more force if it were tied to something like Ackerman's notion of an initial situation of adult resource equality or Dworkin's idea of equality of resources, but Posner is not prepared to countenance the degree of redistribution that such principles would require.

Posner's own proposal – that resources be distributed where they are most productive of wealth – is methodologically as well as morally flawed. Wealth is a matter of the individual's ability to pay and cannot, therefore, without circularity, be used as the standard for determining the proper distribution of wealth. Because the distribution of wealth determines whose preferences are to be used to measure a society's wealth, Posner can, at most, proffer a theory of corrective justice. Given that the existing distribution of resources affects which laws are economically efficient, Posner is not able to provide the clear and objective test for evaluating law reforms which is promised as one of the improvements on the alleged 'sponginess' of the principle of utility. Moreover, as we shall see when considering the application of EAL to criminal behaviour, these theoretical difficulties are compounded when non-economic activities are taken into account. The general thesis that people are wealth-maximisers lacks substance when persons who choose to put such factors as leisure or status above an increase in their wealth are then said to be 'purchasing' them by foregoing actual wealth-producing activities, rather than admitting that they are acting for non-economic reasons. In non-economic areas EAL analysis makes the 'economic' analysis of human behaviour a vacuous and unverifiable hypothesis compatible with any consistent pattern of actual choices.

The economic analysis of criminal law

Although EAL has made its most striking contributions to legal theory through its application to the civil law of negligence and contract, Posner follows in the tradition of Bentham in deploying it in relation to the criminal law for which he regards it as particularly well suited. The Benthamite approach is to define crime in terms of acts which cause sufficient harm or suffering to others to justify the enactment of rules backed by sanctions which prohibit such behaviour. The efficacy of such rules depends on the assumption that the potential criminal will refrain from socially harmful activities which would benefit him if there is a sufficiently high risk of his incurring an unacceptably high level of pain, by way of the infliction of an official sanction, were he to be caught and convicted. In other words citizens are regarded as rational and prudent maximisers who will be deterred from 'criminal' activities if the 'price' is too high. Criminal legislation is justified if the end result is a maximal positive balance of pain prevented by the deterrence or prevention of harmful acts over the pain inflicted by way of punishment, together with the costs of administering the criminal justice system, including its penal institutions.

Bentham himself has wider consequential considerations in mind than simply deterrence since, believing as he did in the malleability of human nature and the efficacy of a rigorous system of negative and positive sanctions, he believed that a properly organised and designed prison could reform the criminal, deter potential criminals and even pay for itself.

Posner follows the Benthamite mode of analysis, but with more emphasis on costs than on suffering and a greater attention to the financial efficiency of the criminal process. For Posner 'a "crime" is simply an act that subjects the perpetrator to a distinctive form of punishment that is meted out in a distinctive kind of proceeding' (1979, p.163), and 'the purpose of the criminal law is to increase the costs of unlawful conduct where conventional damage remedies are insufficient' (p.164). He is careful to include in these costs not only the expected punishment but also the price of the equipment required to perpetrate a crime and the opportunity costs of the criminal's time. Similarly the benefits to the criminal include not only any material gains resulting from successful crime but also the 'intangible satisfactions' of non-pecuniary crime, such as rape. Consequently crime levels can be varied by altering levels of unemployment, which affects the opportunity costs of crime, as well as by varying the severity of penalties and the incidence of detection.

It is, however, on punishment that Posner concentrates his analysis. His model for 'optimal criminal sanctions' is worked out in the first place in monetary terms with the example of theft. Taking the 'expected punishment cost' to be a combination of 'the probability that the punishment will be imposed and the cost to the criminal if it is imposed', and assuming that the offender is 'risk-neutral', he argues that the expected punishment cost should be 'at least equal to the damage to the victim of the criminal act'. If the benefit to the criminal was higher than the social cost of the crime then its perpetration would be a contribution to welfare, and therefore, presumably justified. In fact he is prepared to concede that on occasions theft is indeed value-maximising, as when a hungry person steals food from an unoccupied cabin in the woods. This follows from his general assumption that social welfare is increased when resources are in the hands of those willing to spend available cash to buy them, which means that he has to allow that theft may be a justifiable activity when transaction costs are so high that they make the transfer of goods impracticable.

Such cases must be regarded as exceptional in a system whose wealth-creating power depends on flourishing voluntary transactions in conditions of low transaction costs, and it is this fact that makes theft a crime, for it undermines the normal incentives of the market system. With this in mind, punishment is inflicted to encourage the potential thief to enter rather than bypass the market. To do this we must set the expected punishment cost higher than the social cost of the object. In this case, assuming that the thief knows he will be caught and punished, purchasing an object will always be more rational than stealing it. Adding the costs of administering coercive sanctions to the social costs of the violation gives the appropriate level of fine, at least for those situations where it is thought desirable to encourage market transactions. In the extraordinary cases in which theft is 'justified' because of inordinate transaction costs, the criminal law may not deter but it may still exact the full cost of the thief using the legal system as a surrogate for the market.

The level of fine will of course have to increase as the probability of detection and enforcement decreases, although it is not clear why this should apply in the same way to 'justified' theft – which it is presumably not desirable to deter – as well as to genuinely harmful cases of theft. However, Posner often seems more concerned with recovering the costs of the administration of justice than with the calculation of efficient levels of deterrence, two aims that are clearly not always compatible.

Given the poverty of the average criminal, the obvious inadequacy of fines for recouping the costs of the criminal justice system is countered by the argument that imprisonment is an alternative way of imposing economic costs on violators. 'Imprisonment imposes pecuniary costs on the violator by reducing his income during the period of confinement and, in many cases, by reducing his earning capacity after release as well (the "criminal record" effect). It also imposes non-pecuniary benefits as well' (p.167). However, imprisonment is costly and these costs are not offset by any benefits which accrue to victims. Moreover imprisonment decreases the opportunity costs of future crime, for ex-prisoners are usually unable to find work because of their criminal record. Imprisonment can, therefore, hardly be efficient unless it acts as an effective sanction.

Posner does no more than sketch the tortuous calculations required to reckon the social cost of acts which are thereby defined as criminal as weighed against the social costs of effective enforcement of the criminal law. Nor does he make it clear how this method can be applied to non-pecuniary crimes like assault and homicide. He is clearly in difficulties when he moves from crimes and penalties to which measurable financial costs can be ascribed. As soon as it comes to questions about what value to place on a human life, or what a term of imprisonment 'costs' an unemployed man in terms of shame and suffering, or the degree of 'satisfaction' gained by those who perpetrate crimes of sexual passion, then the economic model of crime becomes nebulous and speculative. It can even be extended to include the 'satisfaction' felt by the vengeful citizen who likes to see offenders punished even if this does not reduce crime.

There is undoubtedly something of importance in calculating the cost of genuinely economic crimes such as theft, fraud and the destruction of property and weighing these against the cost of the administration of a criminal justice system which is aimed at reducing these offences, but the attempt to incorporate into this scheme the web of complex social judgements that go into the criminalisation of non-pecuniary offences and the determination of appropriate penalties even for pecuniary crimes is not successful at the level of sociological analysis and, in general, blurs the distinction between punishment and taxation.

The economic analysis of criminal law opens up the whole debate about the purpose and function of the criminal law and in particular the dispute between consequentialist theories of punishment (whether deterrent, preventative or remedial) and those which incorporate an element of retributive reasoning according to which punishment, whatever its consequences, is an appropriate response to harmful and wicked conduct. The strength of consequentialist theories is that they seem to justify existing practices without drawing on the morally questionable idea that the infliction of pain on an offender is a good thing in itself, but their weakness is that they license acts and institutions which are even less acceptable than pure retributivism. Whether it be the Benthamite objective of minimising the pains resulting from harmful and therefore criminal acts, or the Posnerian goal of minimising the wealth-reducing effects of 'crime', the efficient way of going about this – assuming the rational maximising hypothesis of human behaviour – must involve the unfairness of imposing penalties out of all proportion to the wickedness of those criminals who get caught, the possible victimisation of innocent persons in order to obtain strong deterrent effects and the discriminatory injustice of varying penalties according to such morally irrelevant factors as the possibility of deterrence and the cost of criminal law administration, thereby perpetrating systematic inequities between equally 'guilty' groups of people.

Posner attempts to deal with a number of such difficulties. Noting the apparent unfairness of imprisoning those who are unable to pay fines, which will in practice discriminate against the poor, he suggests that the 'rate of exchange' should be varied according to the wealth of the offender. If this meant that a wealthy person has to pay a larger fine to equate with the same period in prison than a poor man, this solution could be more efficient as well as fairer than flat-rate fines for specific offences, but Posner's requirement that the social cost of crimes be recouped means that the actual result would be quite different. The fines for rich and poor would have to be the same, with the variable rate of exchange affecting only the lengths of the equivalent prison sentences for rich and poor, for the poor will pay less than the rich to avoid imprisonment. And so, whichever way the trade-off between liberty and ability to pay is taken, it illustrates the inegalitarian implications of the economic analysis of law that the liberty of the poor man is of less value than that of the rich.

Even less attractive is Posner's response to the objection that low detection rates require high penalties, thereby imposing heavy sanctions on those few who are caught while the vast majority escape altogether. This he compares to a lottery which is fair as long as the *ex ante* costs and benefits are equal, whatever the eventual outcome. If all have an equal chance of getting caught, high deterrent penalties are said to be fair. One does not have to be a retributivist to be disturbed by the analogy between criminal law and a lottery.

The problem of keeping penalties proportional to the serious-ness of the offence, especially where there are maximum penalties, is simply noted as 'another factor to be considered' (1979, p.170). Scarcely more consideration is given to the absence of an efficiency rationale for harsh treatment of persistent offenders or the punish-ment of attempted crimes.

In dealing with the standard requirement of civilised legal systems that a person can commit a crime only when he acts intentionally, Posner ignores entirely the possibility that this may be explained by the relevance of intentionality to the assessment of moral guilt. Instead he gives three reasons for the importance of *mens rea* in the criminal law. First, he mentions its role in helping us distinguish between coercive transfers and mere acci-dents, to which different cost-benefits analyses are appropriate. Second, he notes the fact that calculating behaviour is less detectable than impulsive actions and therefore requires a higher expectation cost for deterrence purposes. Third, he indicates that only intentional behaviour can be controlled by criminal sanctions, so that there is nothing to be gained, for instance, from threaten-ing the insane who, by definition, are unable to calculate ration-ally. He does not take up the standard counter to this last point, namely that strict criminal liability may be efficient for the purpose of general deterrence even though the particular persons punished may not have been able to respond rationally to the threatened punishment.

The familiar problems to which utilitarian theories of punish-ment give rise have been dealt with much more extensively and sensitively by others, but Posner's relatively simplistic wealth-maximising version of the Benthamite method is a useful exemplar of the practical effects of translating questions of justice into arguments about efficiency. Even when it can be demonstrated that the efficiency approach to criminal law would not be quite so inegalitarian and morally offensive in its disregard for the moral merits of those caught up in its operations, it systematically fails to capture the real reasons why it is unacceptable, for instance, to punish the insane or incarcerate the morally and legally innocent. The sphere of the criminal law is thus peculiarly suited to bringing out the moral indecency of EAL, thus drawing attention to the need for a conception of justice that will hold in check the dominance of purely economic modes of thought.

6   Justice as Desert: Sadurski and Remuneration

In historical terms the idea that justice is a matter of people getting what they deserve is perhaps the most common and tenacious conception of justice. Indeed the connection between justice and desert has been frequently cited as part of the very concept of justice itself. In recent times, however, desert has had to take its place as, at best, only one amongst many competing criteria of justice and sometimes it is excluded altogether from the list of relevant justicising considerations.

For many, desert carries the flavour of a past age characterised by over-individualised forms of social relationships, dominated by a combination of moral book-keeping and the glorification of unfettered economic competition. For others, the idea of desert is associated with discredited 'intuitionist' accounts of ethics according to which we are alleged to have direct knowledge of self-evident moral 'truths', such as the unqualified duty to tell the truth or to execute murderers. Further, the belief in desert – the very idea that anybody ultimately deserves anything – seems to run counter to the common contemporary assumption that individual behaviour is, in the end, almost entirely the outcome of heredity and environment, with little if any significance being attributable to people's individual choices. The 'free will' assumptions behind traditional ideas of desert are certainly hard to fit into a scientific and determinist world view according to which human decisions are simply one part of a continuous causal chain. For all these reasons, it is tempting, therefore, to regard desert-based theories of justice as no more than historical curiosities.

Nevertheless the conviction that people should be treated in accordance with their deserts is not readily abandoned in practice and remains as an unstated assumption in many theories which purport to exclude it. Presuppositions about desert lie at the root of many of the central moral 'fixed points', to which appeal is made to determine whether situations are to be called 'fair' or 'just', and it is the strength of our instinctive feeling about the evil of inflicting unmerited suffering that lies at the core of our doubts about the reduction of justice to utility. Moreover any argument which brings in the intrinsic importance of rewarding people according to their labours has strong meritorian overtones.

It is unsurprising, therefore, that, given the acknowledged moral limitations of utilitarianism, there has recently been a return to the idea that desert is a central feature of justice, a return which is fostered by a growing recognition of the substantive emptiness of theories based on nothing more than the concepts of equality or impartiality and the perceived need to provide an underpinning for fundamental rights, particularly in the sphere of criminal law. While desert may never be re-established as the sole relevant moral criterion for the distribution of benefits and burdens in society, the contention that desert is the most distinctive criterion of justice remains a powerful one, particularly if justice itself is seen to be only one of many types of moral factors which bear on issues of social, political and economic equality.

It is not difficult to document historically an authoritative line of desert theorists from Adam Smith and Immanuel Kant to John Stuart Mill and Henry Sidgwick, but, although there has been a general resurgence of retributivism in the philosophy of punishment, there is perhaps no one recent theorist who is well known for championing a desert-based theory of justice in general. Despite many careful analyses of the nature of desert we do not have a recognised contemporary exemplar of a desert-based theory of justice. However, an impressive recent work by Wojciech Sadurski – a Polish philosopher now living in Australia – develops a largely desert-based analysis of justice which covers both legal and social justice. Sadurski's 'equilibrium' theory makes desert central to the idea of a hypothetical balance of benefits and burdens which justice in all its forms seeks to establish. While his is not a pure desert theory, Sadurski makes important

moves towards rendering the idea of desert intelligible and realis-
able, thus overcoming two of the major drawbacks of traditional
meritorian theories of justice. His important book, *Giving Desert
its Due: Social Justice and Legal Theory*, serves as the reference
point for the issues raised in this chapter.

The attractions of desert

The basic contention of what I will call the meritorian theory of
justice is that justice requires us to treat people as responsible for
their actions and therefore to praise or blame, reward or punish
them, in accordance with their conduct and character in so far as
these are the outcome of their own efforts and choices. Thus if
someone chooses to perform socially useful actions, particularly if
these involve the expenditure of time, effort or personal resources,
then he is deserving of praise and/or reward. If a person chooses
or is willing to perform socially harmful actions, particularly if
they produce benefits for himself, then he is deserving of blame
and/or deprivation of benefits, or punishment. Meritorian theorists hold that a society is just when the distribution of benefits and
burdens is in accordance with the distribution of good (that is
'positive') and ill (that is 'negative') desert. Just actions are those
which seek to maintain, achieve or restore this proportionality,
particularly through the administration of appropriate rewards,
punishments and compensations. Justice requires that, other
things being equal, people ought to get (or be given) what they
deserve.

The term 'desert' can be used very widely to cover, for
instance, the use of the term in the evaluation of such things as
works of art when they are said to be 'deservedly' famous, or in
the opinion that smoking 'deserves' its reputation as being dangerous to health. In the analysis of justice, however, 'desert' is
normally taken to mean moral desert in two senses of 'moral'.
Thus the meritorian conception of desert is of a 'moral' concept,
first because its preferred idea of desert is contrasted with conventional, or institutional 'desert', which is acquired merely by
satisfying established requirements. In contrast, the meritorian's
moral desert is 'natural' or 'raw' in that it does not presuppose
pre-existing social norms or distributional rules. We may say –

perhaps metaphorically – that a person 'deserves' a scholarship solely because he has met the criteria set for the award, whether or not this reflects his choices and efforts, but conventional or institutional 'desert' of this sort is more a matter of entitlement than desert. Certainly it is not the sort of desert with which the meritorian is principally concerned. In contrast to mere entitlement, moral, natural or raw desert features as a reason for establishing such conventional rules so as to ensure that scholarships and other benefits are distributed in accordance with what is antecedently thought of as deserving.

'Desert' may also be taken to be 'moral' in a second sense of that term in which it is now contrasted with 'natural' when this is equated with what happens 'naturally', that is, without human choice or intervention. Desert is then analytically tied to the notion of making choices and acting knowingly or intentionally, in contrast to 'natural' events which happen according to the normal processes of cause and effect. Thus responsibility, in the sense of accountability and liability to praise, blame, reward and punishment, is said to be attributable solely to agents, that is, to persons who can intentionally alter the course of 'natural' events through their own deliberate actions and according to their own purposes. Only the actions of such moral agents are said to be deserving or undeserving in the meritorian sense.

Sadurski's account of desert is moral in both these senses. Having distinguished desert from entitlement, he goes on to argue that the idea of desert is used 'to screen out all those features that are "unearned", that are beyond human control, that are dictated by dumb luck, and for which the person cannot claim any credit'. On this score, when considering desert in relationship to justice, 'what counts is conscientious effort which has socially beneficial effects' (Sadurski, 1985, p.116). For reasons which will become apparent when we consider his theory in more detail, Sadurski stresses that it is the effort to bring about socially beneficial consequences, rather than those consequences themselves, that is relevant to desert, a point which fits in with the idea that desert excludes 'dumb luck', since people cannot always be held responsible for the actual results of their conduct, which is often not completely in their control.

Sadurski points out that desert, so conceived, is (1) 'person-oriented', in that it is always attributed to persons on account of their conduct, (2) 'value-laden', in that it involves an assessment of this conduct as good or bad, and (3) 'past-oriented' in that 'when talking about desert, we are evaluating certain actions which have already happened' (ibid., p.118).

Many meritorian theorists would incorporate in their analysis of desert the requirement that desert has necessarily to do either with moral goodness or badness, or at most with some other morally praiseworthy or blameworthy motives. Sadurski, however, while accepting that desert covers only *intentionally* effortful activity directed towards socially valuable ends, emphasises that his 'theory of desert is not concerned with the "moral worth" of an individual, but with his socially valuable effort' (ibid., p.222). This means that desert takes in effortful behaviour which happens to benefit society even though that is not its motivation. We shall see that this broad conception of the concept of desert makes it easier for him to encompass all of justice within the ambit of desert, but it does tend to undermine the link between desert and morality, which looks beyond intentionality to motivation.

A further question relating to the analysis of 'moral' desert is whether or not it should incorporate the evaluation of prudential behaviour, that is the rationality of a person's actions in relation to his or her own interests and welfare. The failure of persons to take obvious precautions to protect their interests, when it is well within their knowledge and capacities so to do, is not immoral but it is imprudent, and yet we often say that such people deserve the ill consequences of their foolish conduct as well as the good consequences brought about by their own efforts. Meritorian theory can readily assimilate this use of the language of desert, since it accords with the common view that it is not unjust that people are left to enjoy the benefits of their prudence and suffer the burdens imposed by their own imprudence. On the other hand some meritorians regard this as an unacceptable dilution of the moral force of desert-based theories. Since Sadurski constantly stresses the importance of the social benefits of deserving behaviour, he would presumably exclude purely prudential conduct from the ambit of desert.

The most distinctive aspect of Sadurski's analysis of desert is his contention that desert, at least in so far as it relates to justice, always involves conduct which is in some way burdensome. Hence his emphasis on the effort involved in deserving conduct.

He also counts as burdensome anything which incorporates an element of 'sacrifice, work, risk, responsibility, inconvenience and so forth' (ibid., p.116). This, as we shall see, has advantages for his general theory, but it rather ignores the fact that we morally praise, and consider deserving of reward, conduct which is in no obvious sense effortful or burdensome as long as it exhibits morally admirable characteristics such as unselfishness or sensibility. The kind person who sends flowers to a sick friend or the rich person who employs a member of a socially deprived group are deserving of thanks and perhaps reward, even though their actions cause them literally 'no bother'.

Following some linguistic usages, Sadurski also restricts the concept of desert to behaviour which is 'deserving' in the sense that it manifests good rather than ill desert. When he comes to discuss the punishment of crime, for instance, he distinguishes this from rewarding desert, and so seems to deny the meritorian nature of his theory of punishment. However it is clear that no sharp conceptual distinction is intended here, since he views the function of punishment as balancing 'undeserved benefits', and presents himself as a retributivist in the theory of punishment and thus as someone who believes that 'criminal guilt is the sole reason for punishment' (ibid., p.223), going on to analyse criminal guilt in moral rather than purely legal terms. His thesis is, in fact, that socially useful conduct which is burdensome to the agent deserves reward, while socially harmful conduct which is beneficial to the agent deserves punishment. This is evidently a desert-based analysis of criminal law.

Whatever refinements we introduce into the analysis of desert, the idea that society should be organised so as to bring it about that valued and disvalued things like pleasure and pain, psychological satisfaction or material resources, are distributed in accordance with desert has many practical and theoretical difficulties which are discussed in the next section. It does, however, also have powerful justificatory and explanatory features.

In the first place, the idea of due deserts has the advantage of explaining the centrality of human agency in the idea of justice, and hence the close association of justice with such notions as respect for persons, autonomy, self-determination and human dignity. Justice is important in human society not simply because we care about who gets what, but also because we wish to be treated as human beings whose actions and choices are to be taken seriously and given respect. As Sadurski remarks, 'principles of justice are of fundamental, although not of absolute, moral importance. This importance stems from the links between the principle of desert and respect for persons' (ibid., p.251).

It may be this insight that provides the essence of the common belief that there is a sense in which human beings are equal, which is at the same time a basis for treating them differently. The fundamental equality involved here can be based on the idea that all persons are the source of choices which have equal worth, in that they should receive equal respect as the initiators of choices. This means that a concern for justice involves a commitment to the idea that people choosing for themselves is something worthwhile in itself and therefore to be valued and fostered for its own sake. Moreover, to accord proper respect to agents, it is not sufficient simply to foster their agency, although, other things being equal, that is what is required. Respect for agents also involves evaluating the choices and actions to which the exercise of agency capacities give rise. This means responding to persons in terms of the quality of their action choices and intended conduct. Respect for the equal worth of each individual is thus felicitously combined with attention to their unequal worthiness.

Also, meritorian theorists have no difficulty in accounting for the backward-looking nature of justice, in contrast with the forward-looking focus of utilitarian theorising, for, as Sadurski points out (ibid., pp.118f), desert is essentially a matter of evaluating past choices and conduct. In this respect meritorian justice is not, in Nozick's terminology, a pure patterned theory in which holdings are matched to present properties of individuals. Desert, like justice, has an essential 'historical' reference in that it is logically tied to past events and individual responsibility for them.

Viewing justice in terms of desert also enables us to explain the dual aspect of justice as involving both the maintenance of a pattern of distribution and the process of rectifying 'injustices'. All claims that situations are unjust imply that there is a baseline or presupposed balanced situation against which the background of judgements of injustice are made. They also imply that corrective action is in order. Desert fulfils this dual role, not by proposing a baseline of strict identity of situation, but by erecting an ideal of proportionality of desert, positive and negative, to experiences, good and bad, with the implication that, other things being equal, differential treatments should be instituted to achieve and restore that proportionality. In Sadurski's words: 'whenever an ideal, hypothetical balance of social benefits and burdens is upset, social justice calls for restoring it' (ibid., p.101).

Justice as desert can also account for the fact that, while not all actions which upset the baseline balance are unjust (the evil of torture, for instance, is not usually regarded as wrong because it is 'unjust'), nevertheless it is a matter of justice that the perpetrators of such acts be punished and the victims compensated by the offender. This is explained by the fact that intentionally harmful acts are wrong and hence merit punishment and the associated idea that the perpetrators of unjustified wrongdoings ought to compensate their innocent victims. The idea of rectificatory justice, both punitive and compensatory, covers such individual treatments and balances. However justice is more than taking account of the negative desert of wrongful actions. Justice takes in the pursuit of the general objective of matching benefits and burdens to appropriate degrees of positive and negative desert, even when no one can be identified as responsible for existing imbalances. Justice may require the compensation of undeserved suffering brought about through natural causes as well as recompense for suffering deliberately and unjustifiably inflicted by others. Indeed, it is this 'intuition' about the appropriateness of compensation from which Sadurski extrapolates to formulate his entire theory of justice.

The defence of the thesis that justice is essentially a matter of desert requires us to give an account of how other suggested criteria, such as need or choice, can be so readily, if erroneously, taken to be the bases for conceptions of justice. Sadurski does this by demonstrating first that, in general, where such criteria have to do with justice they are crucially related to desert and, second, that where those criteria are not related to desert they are not criteria of justice.

Thus utility, which, it is universally agreed, may often properly be allowed to affect the distribution of benefits and burdens, is excluded from justice when it is not the product of intentional and effortful contribution to the social welfare. Sadurski could take the same line with need and argue that 'need is a criterion of justice only where it happens to be associated in some way with our ideas of merit and demerit' (Campbell, 1974, p.14). Distribution in accordance with need could then be regarded as a matter of humanity rather than justice, unless it is related to desert in some significant manner. Interestingly, Sadurski takes a different view and argues that the satisfaction of basic needs – defined as those needs which 'may be said to constitute obviously and inherently a burden such that their satisfaction is a necessary condition of a person being able to fulfil his or her other needs and desires' – is unconnected with desert but nevertheless is an essential ingredient of the hypothetical balance of benefits and burdens on which all judgements of justice depend.

A purer form of meritorian theory would distinguish between the satisfaction of basic needs *per se*, and the significance of taking account of those undeserved needs which contribute to making individuals worse off than they deserve to be. That we have good, perhaps overriding, moral reason to relieve need, particularly in its acute forms, is not in doubt. What may be doubted is whether this is a requirement of justice. The relief of basic need may be a matter of justice where the need is undeserved, in that it is not the result of the foolish or immoral choices of the persons in need. That is, a person's needs may be a measure of the extent to which he falls below that level of benefits which is appropriate to his degree of merit. The relief of need is also a matter of justice when the need is the result of the blameworthy actions of other persons, in which cases there is an initial supposition that those responsible for the need should see that it is met. This applies also where persons are in need because of the benefits they have bestowed on others who, in justice, ought to repay them. It can also be argued that the satisfaction of basic need is a prerequisite of acting autonomously, and thus of being a person who can rightly be praised or blamed for their behaviour. But where need is not connected in some way with the deserts of those involved, while its relief may be a matter of humanity or benevolence, it may be confusing to say that satisfying even basic needs is a matter of justice. Sadurski is unhappy with this thesis because it seems to downgrade the priority of basic needs, but this does not follow unless it is assumed that justice is always the overriding social value. Further, throughout his book he brings in reference to undeserved burdens as a justicising factor, a rubric into which he could readily fit sufferings and incapacities derived from the frustrations of basic need. It might, therefore, require a relatively minor shift of emphasis to render his theory more purely meritorian.

Justice as desert can also account for the important but limited role of choice in the determination of what is just. For instance, Nozick argues that a person owns his own body and natural abilities and is therefore entitled to do what he likes with the fruits of his labours, quite irrespective of whether or not he may be said to 'deserve' them. However, as Sadurski points out (Sadurski, 1985 pp.135f), while there is a natural sense in which a person's body and skills belong to him in that they are *his* rather than anyone else's, this is not itself a matter of right, but of natural fact. It is a separate question whether or not the product of 'my' capacities is 'owned' in a way which gives rise to property rights, since it is not itself a matter of logic that the product of 'my' capacities is 'mine'. This inference can be supported if we presuppose a principle of liberty which requires non-interference in the use of our bodies and the right to enter freely into agreements of others, but there is no reason to suppose that such principles are absolute and unlimited in their scope, or that they are to be equated with justice. Indeed it would seem to be a characteristic problem of social organisation that such liberties may conflict with justice.

Desert theory can explain this situation by pointing out that while a person, through the exercise of wise choice and effort, may often deserve the fruits of his labours, these fruits may greatly exceed the degree of his merit. In such cases we may wish to leave him in possession of his surplus gains on the basis, for instance, that liberty is a significant independent value, but it is also open to us to override considerations of liberty in favour of other objectives, including the redistribution of wealth on the basis of desert, for some choices can produce for the individual benefits far beyond that which is proportional to the effort or wisdom involved. In other words meritorian theorists can explain why free choice is often relevant to justice and yet justice may often be more important than liberty.

Meritorian theory also explains the ambivalent place of promise-keeping in relation to the concept of justice. For some people, to break a promise is considered to be unjust. To others promise-keeping seems to be a completely different form of wrong-doing. The desert theorist can accommodate aspects of both these views. He can agree that, at one level, promise-keeping is simply one of the many moral duties whose violation can result in ill-desert and is therefore justly blamed, adding that, when it results in actual harm to some other person, either in disappointed expectations or losses incurred through reliance on that promise, justice may require the payment of compensation, or even punishment, as a matter of rectificatory justice. This does not make promise-breaking in itself unjust. Indeed, as Sadurski argues, 'to say that a person is entitled to some contractual benefits is not the same thing as to say that he deserves them' (ibid., p.120), and 'the duty to fulfill promises is not really a matter of justice because promises themselves (or rather, the structure of distribution produced by their fulfilment) may be assessed by standards of justice' (ibid., p.28).

On the other hand, at a deeper level of analysis, since the idea of keeping one's word is so closely associated with responsible moral agency and entitlement to respect as an autonomous person, it is natural to look on promise-keeping as the mark of a just person in the sense of a person who invites us to treat him in accordance with justice, that is to hold him accountable for his actions. It is even possible to argue that breaking a promise is an undeserved injury to the promisee. Nevertheless, the reason that it seems odd to regard promise-breaking as such as a form of injustice is that the promisee is not normally thought of as 'deserving' what he has been promised.

Finally, it is an advantage of meritorian theory that it enables us to make sense of the ambivalent relationships between the formalities of rule application and the concept of justice. It might be thought that the connection between desert and formal justice is best explicated by making treatment in accordance with existing rules a matter of desert. But we have seen that this involves a conflation of desert and entitlement, which weakens moral force of the theory. In the light of the moral thinness of pure formal 'justice', Sadurski wisely does not seek to incorporate formal justice under the rubric of desert by using the truncated conception of institutional desert. This is in line with the general meritorian view that justice arises only where the substantive rules have some relationship to the natural or moral deserts of those to whom they apply.

However, we have already seen, in Chapter 1, that if we adopt a broader and more substantial ideal of the rule of law, the governance of rules does relate to desert, and so to justice, in that much of its content has to do with treating persons as responsible agents, answerable for their actions, who ought to be given fair warning of possible penalties (and indeed of possible rewards) so that they can adapt their behaviour accordingly. Hence the requirements of technical 'natural justice' or 'due process' and the more general insistence on public and prospective legislation. These ideals are rooted in the same set of ideas as treatment in accordance with desert, namely that people are to be treated as responsible beings. Hence the close connection between the sphere of justice and developed ideas of the rule of law and the connections, also emphasised by Sadurski, between justice and respect for persons.

Problems of desert

As is to be expected with such a basic notion, desert gives rise to many problems, some of which are frequently considered fatal to its proper use in the political arena. Most often the idea of desert, perhaps because of its close connections with personal morality, seems to many people to belong to that aspect of human conduct which is least amenable to political administration. Meritorian justice, if there is such a thing, is said to be a matter for the judgement and execution of God, not man.

For instance, it is argued that there are insuperable theoretical and practical difficulties in measuring desert. Not only are there conflicting beliefs about what sort of conduct is deserving, but all these beliefs seem to require that we have considerable knowledge of the inner workings of the minds and emotions of the persons involved. This is particularly so if we take a narrow motivational view of desert which incorporates the morality of the motives of conduct, but it is pertinent also to the evaluations required by Sadurski's analysis, which are dependent on knowledge of intentions.

As an argument against the possibility of attaining complete meritorian justice this seems invincible. However there is nothing in the concept of justice itself which entails that its fullest realisation is practicable in human society. On the contrary there seems good reason to hold that human justice will always be somewhat controversial in theory and radically imperfect in implementation. The criticism is serious only if it can demonstrate that we cannot even approximate either to a consensus as to what actions are deserving or to reliable knowledge of the nature of individual actions. Yet there is no doubt that in many of the affairs of everyday life we work with a fair measure of normative consensus and rely on rebuttable presumptions that we have a rough idea of what persons intend to do and even why they perform certain acts. In any case, the problem is certainly diminished if we follow Sadurski and base desert on the intentions rather than on the motives of acts.

Critics of desert-based theories of justice also contend, however, that they encourage unwarranted coercive intervention in the lives of citizens, thus eroding the important boundary between morality and law. However, there is no analytic connection between justice and justifiable enforcement, or between substantive justice and law. Justice need not be taken as either a necessary or a sufficient condition for creating mandatory requirements or making coercive interventions in the lives of citizens. No doubt it is an acceptable legislative philosophy that extensive and manifest injustices be corrected by process of legislation and that where state action is legitimated on other grounds it should be as far as possible in accordance with substantive justice and the rule of law. But the automatic and insistent enforcement of justice in all aspects and in all spheres is an unattractive and dangerous ideal if only because of the necessarily varied views which coexist in modern society regarding what counts as meritorious behaviour and the consequent imposition of distributive rules on unwilling subjects. On the other hand, it is correct to say that meritorian justice is logically related to a belief in the appropriateness of gratitude and reward for positive desert, and of condemnation and punishment for negative desert, so that raising considerations of justice necessarily brings up questions about how we are to respond to the behaviour of others in these respects. This response need not, however, involve the mandatory application of distributive rules and, in the light of the difficulties involved in determining desert, there are good reasons for caution in moving from praise and blame to reward and punishment.

There is, however, no way of avoiding the political necessity of dealing with the choices which have to be made about the permitted system of economic allocation, educational opportunity and various forms of advantage taking. Ideas of desert have relevance in all these areas and societies have to do the best they can to devise means of gathering information about the merits of its members and evolving a consensus as to the value-judgements involved. Institutionally this requires reliance on the assumption that certain external behaviours are standard manifestations of characteristic intentions and motives and that contribution is a sound, if defeasible, measure of effort. That this will lead to mistakes is inevitable and of major relevance to enforcement, but that the attainment of meritorian justice is utterly impractical and therefore morally unenforceable is unproven. Indeed it is clear that actual societies do operate to some extent on a consensus as to what sorts of actions are meritorious and that it is often possible to be reasonably accurate in identifying motivation of the actions of others.

The difficulties involved in assessing the merits of persons are compounded by the fact that every agent works within the framework of his inherited potentials and the limitations of his social environment so that it is not possible to make an accurate estimate of the extent to which a person can take genuine credit for any of his actions. Given the pervasive influences and effects of environment and heredity it is by no means clear that any aspect of human conduct is unaffected by factors which are beyond the control of the individual.

Carried to its logical extreme such an approach amounts to the espousal of determinism in that it implies that every action is the necessary product of the previous state of the universe, or some part of it. In other words, there is no such thing as 'free' or 'contra-causal' action. An all-pervasive scheme of cause and effect seems to negate the idea of moral responsibility and leave no more foothold for speaking of the desert of a person than of the deserts of a hurricane or a frog.

Sadurski accepts this implication of determinism but offers the pragmatic argument that, if determinism is true, we have no real choice as to whether or not we seek to treat people in accordance with their deserts, so that there is no point in worrying about the issue. While this is hardly an entirely intellectually satisfying way of side-stepping the problems which determinism sets up for the desert theorist, there is no agreement amongst philosophers of action that determinism is true or even that a distinctive sense of agent-responsibility and determinism are mutually exclusive postulates. Certainly most of those who adhere to determinism still retain working conceptions of what distinguishes actions from movements and what sort of phenomena can sensibly be praised or blamed. As long as some notion of self-determination can be retained in practical situations, such as, for instance, when we are seeking to influence the conduct of others by praising and blaming them, then there is no clear impropriety in speaking of desert in a determinist world, although, in the view of many philosophers, the metaphysical significance of the concept may be unacceptably diminished if determinism is in fact true.

Even so, we are left with the difficult practical problem of unscrambling the different contributions of heredity, society and the individual, something which must be done if we are to make sense of the idea of individual merit as having to do with that which is in the agent's control and so can be credited to him. We have to be able to separate out the non-creditable from the creditable in the behaviour of persons if we are to determine deserts. By and large this can only be done by seeking to measure the impact of the various 'external' factors and then discounting their influence, leaving the individual's personal contribution as a residual category consisting of what remains after these deductions have been made.

In some instances the non-creditables that we are concerned with are the necessary prerequisites of action, such as the possession of a body, sound mental capacities and the absence of external obstacles to movement. These are relatively straightforward in contrast to the more complex matter of the extent in which more specific factors, like temperament or family background, make the performance of certain activities easier or more difficult for the individuals concerned. The nature of the development of human personality is such that it is often not possible to identify features of adult behaviour which are clearly creditable since all action is enmeshed in a continuing 'use' of inherited and environmental non-creditables.

Desert theory is also plagued by incommensurables. It is hard, some say impossible, to make the necessary interpersonal comparisons, not only of the relative deserts of individuals, but also of what would count as an equal reward or punishment, since individual preferences and tastes affect the way in which different treatments are actually experienced by different people. Moreover, even if it is possible to establish a scale of merit and a scale of punishments and rewards, there is no single way in which the degree of negative or positive desert can be matched to an obviously appropriate level of blame or praise, and reward or punishment. It seems arbitrary, for instance, to think of zero merit (neither negative nor positive desert) equating with zero allocation. A more realistic possibility might be to equate average merit with average benefits and average burdens, the baseline being that which would result from an equal division of the benefit and burdens or, in other words, a quantity equal to the average distribution. Even if this is possible, awkward choices have to be made about the degree of negative and positive desert which matches the various levels of reward and punishment. Thus if 'effort' is what counts, and can be measured in an objective manner, we still have to decide the extent to which differences in effort are to be reflected in differential rewards.

Sadurski's main contribution to desert theory is to propose a scheme which avoids these baseline difficulties by incorporating all justice-relevant considerations in the general idea of a balance of benefits and burdens. His contention is that 'whenever an ideal, hypothetical balance of benefits and burdens is upset, social justice calls for restoring it' (ibid., p.107). Generalising Feinberg's idea of 'compensatory benefits' (Feinberg, 1970, p.59), according to which many onerous jobs 'deserve' economic rewards so as to bring those who perform them back to a position of equality of burdens with those who do not have such strenuous occupations, Sadurski takes as his moral fixed point the intuition that certain burdens 'deserve' compensation to the point where a presupposed equilibrium of benefits and burdens is attained. This is then applied to all types of justice. The thesis is not simply that justice is about the distribution of benefits and burdens, but rather that it is always about striving for a balance of the burdens borne by each person and the benefits enjoyed by that same person, so that the benefits and burdens are 'equal' or 'equivalent'.

Sadurski accepts that talk of 'bringing someone back to a position of equality' is metaphorical in that the idea of balancing benefits and burdens cannot be taken literally since no actual scales are available to 'weigh' and therefore equalise the two elements. 'Burdens' – another metaphorical term – carries an image of weight not shared by the concept of a benefit, unless burdens are regarded as the absence of benefits, which is a rather artificial way to look at such benefits as social status or job satisfaction. The plausibility of Sadurski's theory depends, therefore, on giving a convincing cash value to the language of weights and balances.

The idea is not, I think, that one individual's burdens should always exactly match that same person's rewards, although there is an idea of the proper proportionality of burdens and rewards, as of benefits and punishments. Rather it is that the balance of benefits and burdens in each person's life should be equivalent to the balance in the lives of other members of the same society. Thus the person born with gross handicaps must be compensated with benefits which make his position as equivalent as possible to the balance of benefits and burdens in the lives of the non-handicapped. This has a similar form to the idea that the efforts of the socially useful worker be rewarded to bring him back to the position he had occupied before he performed the work, which is assumed to be the measure of equivalence which puts him in the same (no doubt hypothetical) position as everyone else. Similarly the criminal who steals something reaps the benefit of breaking the law and is punished to the extent that takes away this benefit and restores him to the same position as the non-criminal. In each case some type of compensation is at work. Because of this equivalence of form these are all different aspects of justice, hence the idea of 'justice as equilibrium' (ibid., p.3).

Sadurski does not attempt to develop an idea of an all-encompassing balance of benefits and burdens of all types in all spheres of life. Instead he concentrates on only three characteristics of the particular balance of benefits and burdens which he incorporates into his analysis of justice. The first is 'a social condition characterized by a state of mutual abstention from harm, that is to say, by a mutual respect for liberties. It is an equilibrium, in the sense that, in the situation of full respect for each person's sphere of autonomy, all enjoy equally the benefits of autonomy and the burdens of self-restraint' (ibid., p.104). This equilibrium presupposes rules which lay down what constitutes harm to others and hence an area of individual negative rights to be left alone. If this balance is upset by illegitimate intrusions into the sphere of autonomy of another person, then the balance may be restored by punishing the offender, and perhaps by compensating the victim. This gives substance to the idea of retribution in punishment and explains the renewed significance attributed to compensating victims through criminal as well as civil law.

'Secondly, equilibrium is characterized by equal satisfaction for all persons of basic material conditions of a meaningful life: no-one suffers burdens which make his subsistence, or participation in community life, impossible' (ibid., p.105). This is the area of basic human needs, the 'means of meaningful life', or 'the conditions of self-realization', whose satisfaction Sadurski considers an element of social justice. These burdens, but not burdens in general, call for compensation.

'Thirdly, social equilibrium means that everyone's work, effort, action and sacrifice, yield a benefit equivalent to the contribution; in other words, that a person's "outcomes" are equal to his "inputs"' (ibid.). Thus persons who do more for others than they take from them should be compensated by the amount of this imbalance. Extra benefits restore the equilibrium which has been upset by socially beneficial effort.

Clearly this scheme has the advantage of limiting the range of benefits and burdens which are of relevance to justice and aids comparability by distinguishing between three distinct spheres of justice, each with its own equivalent balances. On the other hand, from the theoretical point of view, it has the appearance of arbitrariness in what it excludes and includes. This is particularly so with the inclusion of only basic needs as requiring compensation rather than a more egalitarian position which takes as relevant all needs which affect a person's quality of life. In fact it would appear that, in this sphere, Sadurski is concerned to include only basic needs because these are the needs which he believes ought to be met by government action. It is, perhaps, for this reason also that he includes the compensation of basic needs in his account of justice at all, instead of bringing need into the sphere of justice only where it is related in some way to desert.

In general the assessment of Sadurski's innovative equilibrium theory requires detailed investigation of the sense which he can give to the ideas of benefits and burdens in each sphere, and the meaningfulness of the notions that these can be balanced and that these balances can be seen to be equivalent to each other. Thus, in the criminal sphere, he is less than convincing in categorising all crime as a form of illicit benefit-taking which can be measured and then balanced by appropriate punishment. Since not all crimes benefit the criminal, the 'benefits' which criminal acts confer have to be conceptualised in terms of avoiding the burdens of self-restraint imposed by the criminal law when it establishes that persons have rights to life, liberty, security and property. All these rights confer benefits, but the enjoyment of rights depends on the exercise of restraint by others. 'This self-restraint which is a precondition for the effective enforcement of rights, can be perceived as a burden. Indeed it is a limitation on the freedom to do as one wishes. If such freedom is a benefit, its limitation is obviously a burden' (ibid., p.226). In some such way, Sadurski has to maintain that conformity to the criminal law is always a burden, even if it is not felt to be so.

Despite these qualms about the general applicability of the idea of balancing benefits and burdens to all situations which are judged in terms of justice, the idea of 'justice as equilibrium' does help to give content to the often persuasive but too often obscure idea that there is a profound moral connection between moral deserts and just distribution.

Just remuneration

An important criticism of the analysis of justice as desert is that it is incoherent in practice because institutionalising the requital of desert undermines the basis on which desert is acquired. This argument assumes that, if a reward is offered for a naturally good form of behaviour, then this behaviour will thereafter be done in order to gain the reward, thus negating the putative moral deserts of its performers, whose motives are now purely self-interested. Similarly a person who refrains from naturally criminal acts because of the threat of sanctions is not said to be deserving in the same way as a spontaneously good person.

This critique is at its strongest where positive desert is taken to be moral desert in the narrow sense in which this involves either moral goodness (duty for duty's sake) or the desire to perform the action in question for the reasons that make it a good action, rather than for some ulterior self-interested motive (spontaneous goodness). On this moral interpretation of desert, it is a powerful critique of any organised system of rewards and punishments that it tends to undermine the scope for those forms of moral desert which are maximised by permitting the widest scope for alternative possibilities of action so as to bring out the best and the worst in people. Distribution by moral desert is best served by the minimisation of externally imposed rewards and punishments which muddy moral choices and mask moral goodness. On the other hand, since the whole point of a theory of justice is to provide a basis for justifying differential benefits and burdens, it seems incoherent to use the theory to argue against carrying out such distributions in a systematic and predictable manner.

The problem is reduced if we take in prudential conduct as a type of desert base, since the avoidance of sanctions and the pursuit of proffered rewards may be regarded as standard examples of prudential behaviour. These manifestations of prudence, however, are parasitic upon the prior existence of a system of rewards and deprivations and give no guidance as to the nature of the system that ought to be established. As far as natural or 'raw' desert goes, we have to consider what constitutes admirable prudence prior to the artificially contrived prizes and punishments. This can take in, however, the endorsement of such distributions as arise from the self-interested actions of individuals as they seek to fulfil their own desires, as long as these distributions are the outcome of their own efforts and skill. The pursuit of justice on this basis would require, in addition to the general legitimation of prudential behaviour, that individuals be not permitted to harm each other in the course of their self-interested activities. In other words, prudential deserts may be diminished or outweighed by moral demerits.

This approach takes us somewhere near the classical liberal scheme of free competition within a framework of restraints on harming others, as exemplified, for instance, by Nozick's entitlement theory of justice. In contrast to Nozick's relative free-for-all society, a more scrupulous, but still basically prudential meritorian theory, will require that the resultant differential benefits and burdens are indeed related to different prudential achievements rather than to other circumstances, such as luck, or the altruistic actions of others. Where rewards outstrip prudential merits, or deprivations are in excess of prudential demerits, reallocation is called for. On this basis, a scheme of rewards can be seen as an effort to adjust the consequences of self-interested behaviour in such a way as to approximate to a distribution which matches the levels of prudential desert. Thus gross incomes, which emerge from the self-interested rational conduct of individuals, may be subject to taxation in such a way that the net result is one in which people are rewarded according to the achievements for which they can take the credit.

Liberal philosophies standardly attach some, albeit variable, weight to self-directed individual achievement of this sort, at least in relation to the distribution of material benefits. The prudential frame of reference is not so evident, however, with respect to the systems of punishment, where demerit is more a matter of the harm caused to others than peoples' failure to look after their own interests. Moreover, even in the spheres of benefit distribution, most liberals extend their concept of desert to include rewards for conduct which benefits others. This approval of limited benevolence is sometimes masked by the assumption that, in order to encourage individuals to benefit others, it is normally necessary to offer them inducements, and hence to reward socially valuable work for utilitarian rather than meritorian reasons. It can be argued, however, that a system of just – as opposed to merely efficient – rewards, requires that these inducements should not be higher than a level which would match the deserts of those involved if they had been acting without regard to such inducements. A hypothetical desert scheme which makes inducements and penalties equivalent to those which are appropriate for useful behaviour when it is undertaken for morally, as opposed to prudentially, good reasons, offers a possible way round the paradox that rewarding virtue undermines virtue. At least it does not penalise the naturally benevolent whose actions are not affected by inducements. It is a scheme which gains further point to the extent that it is believed that individuals are not purely self-interested in their conduct and often do undertake socially valuable work for partially altruistic reasons.

Sadurski's analysis side-steps some of these problems by excluding the significance of motives and requiring only that deserving behaviour be intentional. He does not overtly apply his concept of desert directly to prudential behaviour, for he limits justice-relevant desert to intentional conduct which is socially useful. He is, however, able to take into account behaviour which is socially useful but is undertaken for prudential motives. Indeed, according to his scheme, which excludes motivation, this type of conduct must be viewed as just as deserving as altruistic conduct. Indeed it turns out that he does take into consideration effortful conduct which benefits the agent for, in measuring appropriate rewards, he proposes taking account of all productive labour:

> 'Social equilibrium means that everyone's work, effort, action and sacrifice yields a benefit equivalent to the contribution: in other words, that a person's "outcomes" are equal to his "inputs". A paradigm example of this aspect of equilibrium is that of a peasant who actually consumes the entirety of what he produces. At the initial, hypothetical stage of social equilibrium there is no exchange and no exploitation: everyone does everything for himself.' (Ibid., p.105)

Without going into whether or not there are any limits to the quantity of holdings that a person can accumulate by his own efforts, Sadurski points out that in normal economic systems people do make a contribution to the well-being of others. In general, Sadurski's model is similar to Rawls's in that he views modern society as a co-operative enterprise which produces an aggregate of benefits which fall to be distributed according to principles of justice. He differs from Rawls in holding that, in any situation where the individual's contribution is such that he creates a surplus beyond his own appropriations, then justice calls for compensatory rewards. More specifically, in the terms of his theory of equilibrium, one aspect, at least, of justice 'is achieved when the overall level is equal for all people, that is, when the ratio of one person's outcomes to inputs is equal to other persons' outcome/input ratio' (ibid., p.106).

It is a further feature of Sadurski's account of just remuneration that the measurement of input is in terms of effort rather than results. It is required that such effort does produce socially beneficial results but the relevant measure of input is not the quantity of the benefit but the extent of the burden undertaken in producing the benefit. Sadurski takes this position 'mainly because "contribution" or "success" reflect, among other things, factors which are beyond our control and thus for which we cannot claim any credit' (ibid., p.134). He does not specify exhaustively which features of a job performance are relevant inputs, but he mentions, as examples, the expenditure of energy, both physical and intellectual, and the degree of unpleasantness involved, whether this is due to physical conditions or mental stress. He is also prepared to take note of risks and opportunity-costs in the form of sacrifices incurred in order to undertake a task and the general inconvenience of making the contribution in question. In principle, however, almost anything can be regarded as a burden and therefore as part of the creditable input in any particular task. All that the theory requires is a reasonable degree of consensus as to what is burdensome and what is not. Here Sadurski has an interesting discussion of how to take into account the fact that some tasks have their own intrinsic rewards. Most people enjoy a degree of responsibility, or the opportunity to perform a useful task, so that not all aspects of employment are burdensome. The attractive features of work have to be set against the unattractive ones in order to establish those aspects of a job that require compensatory rewards.

Sadurski can deal with the problems which emerge in relation to individual differences of taste, which mean that the same task is more burdensome for one person than for another, by pointing out that any system of remuneration has to operate in a rough-and-ready way on the basis of average tastes and typical situations. A more intractable difficulty for his theory is that effort itself is not always a burden, but may be welcomed and enjoyed. Since it is effort that is the principal link between his idea of justice and the notion of what is in the control of the individual, and therefore deserving of reward, the prospect of effort being a benefit rather than a burden undermines his model of due deserts as a proper balance of benefits and burdens. In the end, when arguing for the practicability of his conception of desert in relation to just rewards, his appeal is to the choices which the average person would make when presented with a range of employment, each with its own bundle of attractive and unattractive features. The evidence is, he claims, that roughly the same choices would be made by the vast majority of individuals in the same society. It is assumed that, for the majority, effort is, on balance, a burden.

A similar approach is appropriate to the determination of what is to count as remuneration, a concept which must take in not only the level of wages and salaries and associated material benefits, but also any pleasant features which particular employments may have. The appeal to a consensus of public values may also be required if we are to measure what is to count as socially beneficial effort. Sadurski is unwilling to leave this matter to the choice of the market, if only because it is not possible to put market values on all socially valuable work. Moreover, as we have seen in the discussion of Posner (p.135), even in relation to consumer goods, it can be argued that the market gives disproportionate weight to the preferences of the already wealthy and is thus an inefficient measure of actual social value.

An important implication of justice as desert in relation to remuneration is that it encourages lower extrinsic rewards for intrinsically less burdensome jobs, thus running counter to the tendency for desirable high status jobs also to be the better remunerated ones. Noting the sociological prevalence of 'status consistency', that is, the tendency of high prestige to go with high income, he accepts that his theory may be out of line with contemporary moral views but nevertheless takes the line, reminiscent of Walzer's notion of undominated inequality, that material rewards need not be highly correlated with the distribution of other desired benefits, such as prestige and education.

These are important issues with which any theory of just remuneration must deal. It is to the credit of meritorian theory that it both reflects the complexity of the choices that have to be made and locates them in the need to reach agreed value-judgements as to what is burdensome and beneficial, both in the performance and in the products of different employments. In this respect desert theory outstrips its more simplistic rivals in its grasp of the nature of the questions to be asked in relation to just remuneration. On the other hand, the problem of establishing proper meritorian rewards for labour is even greater than is allowed for by Sadurski's division of justice into three relatively independent aspects, for, if we take taxation systems into account as part of what is involved in the determination of net rewards, there seems no reason not to use this in respect to the merits and demerits of individuals outside their employment and so seek an overall balance of benefits and burdens in all aspects of distribution. Meritorian theories lack other than purely pragmatic grounds for not taking all desert-relevant factors into one comprehensive assessment of the individuals merits, whether these relate to economic, criminal or social circumstances.

Another major and distinctive problem for a meritorian theory of remunerative justice is in the determination of what it is that individuals can claim credit for. The particular difficulty with which Sadurski deals in some detail is that individuals cannot take credit for their natural endowments, or for their developed potential in so far as this is due to the environment and support provided by others. Natural ability is no more deserved than are wealthy parents or good schoolteachers, and yet such things are central determinants of what it is that individuals are able to contribute to society.

Sadurski, and other meritorians, must, at this point fall back on seeking to isolate those ingredients of an individual's conduct that are the outcome of his own choices and efforts and see that these, rather than raw natural abilities, are rewarded. This is to reject Nozick's position that individuals own their capacities and are entitled to all the fruits of their use. Sadurski goes along with Rawls's idea of natural talents as common assets as 'there is nothing incompatible with the autonomy of individuals in the idea that the fruits of people's natural talents should be shared by all, since those natural talents are not deserved in any way' (ibid., p.127), but does not accept that what individuals make of these natural talents should be submerged in the same 'common pool'. The problem is that, not only may these ingredients turn out to be relatively minor, but, as Rawls argues, they themselves may be the outcome of a combination of heredity and environment not chosen or worked for by the individual. Even if we reject the total determinism of all aspects of human conduct, it seems clear that, once natural talents are discounted, the capacity to make an effortful contribution to the common good is not dependent solely on the exercise of the individual's will, in isolation from the social environment which nurtures it.

There are meritorian answers to these problems, some of which are answers which are exceedingly radical in their implications. We can, for instance, propose that the social arrangements for education and upbringing be such as to provide an equal chance for all individuals to exhibit the choices and efforts which are considered meritorious in a society. This entails not simply providing the same provisions for all children but in arranging superior circumstances and education for the less gifted children. Sadurski is willing to contemplate such a sweeping system of equal opportunity, particularly through the preferential treatment of disadvantaged groups in order to equalise their chances of meeting the criteria of desert applied in their society: 'it is not correct to classify as "equality of opportunity" a situation in which some people are excluded from obtaining a certain good on "appropriate" grounds when the possibilities of satisfying them were clearly unequal' (ibid., p.201). This requires, for instance, massive compensation for those born with such handicaps that they are deficient in basic need, but it presumably has similar, if lesser, implications for less severe incapacities which do not feature as fundamental deficiencies but nevertheless affect the individual's chances of obtaining higher rewards.

Even when this is achieved, however, natural differences will still come through and the inequitable results of employment in adult life have to be countered with other remedies, such as a tax system which disfavours individuals in proportion to their higher inherited capacities for choice and effort. Sadurski gives sympathetic consideration to the notion of a 'capability tax' which is 'based on the innate capabilities of individuals rather than their incomes, so that we do not tax the marginal efforts of persons' (ibid., p.128). This device has the effect of pressuring people to enter employments which maximise their incomes, but Sadurski takes this to be in line with other standard uses of taxation systems and believes that it is in itself an intrinsically fair distributional mechanism.

When contemplating these radical implications of justice as desert, it is important to remind ourselves that the meritorian theory of justice does not commit us to the view that justice is the sole or even the most important objective of political organisation and legal intervention. Just as the principal object of the criminal law may be to reduce harmful actions rather than mete out justice for its own sake, so in the allocation of many jobs, competence and promise may be more important than justice with its past-oriented response to praiseworthy efforts. Indeed the more pervasive ground for state action is the general welfare of citizens. Most rewards and punishments, and most strategies for the allocations of benefits and burdens, have been initiated with general utility rather than individual justice in mind.

The insistence that, for instance, whatever compulsory measures are introduced should be compatible with justice in general often serves the function of placing limits on the way in which the general good may be sought, rather than featuring as an overall justificatory reason for the measure in question. The distinct and sometimes competing values of the general welfare and the liberty and privacy of the individual may override the significance of due deserts in many circumstances. In relation to the justice of remunerating in proportion to past efforts Sadurski need not be committed to giving this dimension overriding force, certainly in the allocation of jobs. Further, in this context his commitment to the central role of desert within justice is weakest, for, as he notes, 'it often happens that distributive criteria other than desert (such as formal entitlements or basic human needs) override those of desert' (ibid., p.156).

When all this has been taken into account, however, it seems less than satisfactory to say that justice is a factor of major significance in relation to the level of remuneration, but of scarcely any importance in job allocation. Sadurski argues that, in most cases, we rightly follow utilitarian consideration in making appointments according to capacity and potential contribution: 'no reasonable person could claim that in a well-ordered society the allocation of jobs and positions should be based on compensatory criteria and that, for instance, the least able people should be hired for the most responsible jobs in order to have a general balance of benefits and burdens restored' (ibid., p.153). This fails to take sufficient account of the fact that, without a job, the individual has no chance to make the effortful contribution which merits reward. Equality of opportunity in the preparation for a job is inadequate if there are no tasks available through which the individuals can manifest the socially beneficial conduct that he is able and willing to undertake.

There is, in fact, no reason why a meritorian theory cannot use its major premise – namely that people are to be treated in accordance with their deserts – to argue that employment opportunities must be provided which enable individuals to display as well as develop their potential deserts. If, as has been argued, the moral basis of a meritorian theory is that it is right to treat people as responsible agents who are accountable for their behaviour, then it must be right so to arrange society that what happens to individuals depends on how they conduct themselves in conditions where they have a chance to demonstrate their responsibility. This must mean that all have a real chance to meet the preferred criteria of desert, which must include the availability of work appropriate to the individual's talents. This is a matter beyond the equal opportunity to compete for work. It is equality of opportunity to manifest desert in work. In other words, the 'equal worth' premise of meritorian theory requires that everyone have the same opportunity to exhibit their unequal worthiness.

While this is a perfectly coherent position for the meritorian to adopt, and may indeed be a model for a just employment system, it does bring justice into such practical conflict with economic realities that it may have the effect of displacing the pursuit of justice into radically utopian circumstances. Moreover it could be argued that rewarding in accordance with desert is not such an important moral goal that it justifies the reorganising of social and economic life in such a wholesale manner. On the other hand, if justice is only allowed to make a marginal difference to the level of remuneration and has little or no impact on employment distribution, then it becomes impossible to contend that existing social systems begin to approximate to what is just, a conclusion that most meritorian theorists have sought to avoid.

In the end Sadurski is left with an uneasy compromise whereby the lot of those unsuccessful in the employment stakes is taken care of by the aspect of justice which deals with the satisfaction of basic needs. Although the blamelessly unemployed may not have the opportunity to earn through contributing to the social good, their undeserved needs will be met in so far as these qualify as 'basic'. Interestingly such basic needs, while including that which is necessary for the individual to participate in society, do not appear to include the need to participate in the economic system as a worker. This possibility, however, constitutes another avenue through which we might arrive at a moral basis for full employment policies. Whether the provision of appropriate employment as a basic need would be regarded as a matter of humanity or justice will depend on the theory of justice deployed. For Sadurski, employment needs, if there be such, would be part of justice because of their status as basic needs rather than because of their connection with desert. An alternative view is that employment needs are grounds for claims of justice because their fulfilment is a necessary condition for the display of desert and thus a prerequisite for being treated with the respect due to a responsible being.

7 Marx and the Socialist Critique of Justice

The fact that the bulk of innovative analytical philosophising about justice in recent years has originated in the United States of America explains, but may not excuse, the imbalance of attention given in this book to 'liberal' over 'socialist' theorists. While Rawls considers his contract theory to be compatible with both free market and centralised economic systems, and at least some of the implications of both Ackerman's method of Neutral dialogue and Dworkin's rights approach are sufficiently egalitarian to count as radical liberal – in contrast to the rampant libertarianism of Nozick – to have only one chapter devoted to explicitly socialist theories of justice appears politically unbalanced.

On the other hand, the preponderance of liberal capitalist ideas within current theories of justice is in line with Marx's contention that rights and justice are essentially bourgeois ideas which impress the ideology of capitalist economic organisation. If justice is indeed an intrinsically capitalist concept, then it is predictable that those who propound a normative theory of justice will express the values of bourgeois individualism. If, as is stated in the *Manifesto of the Communist Party* (1872) 'communism abolishes eternal truths, it abolishes all religion, and all morality, instead of constituting them on a new basis' (Marx and Engels, 1958, vol. 1, p.52), then it is mistaken to look for a communist ethic or to expect a normative theory of socialist justice. Within the Marxian tradition, the whole mode of theorising typified by traditional political philosophy is politically and intellectually suspect.

According to this view, a socialist theorising about justice consists principally of a critique of the idea that justice represents a trans-historical ideal applicable to all types of economic system, the assumption being that talk of 'eternal justice', like the rhetoric of natural and human rights, is essentially an ideological device for presenting bourgeois interests under the guise of allegedly universal values. The battle-cries of Liberty, Justice and Equality are seen as purely ideological concepts which express and further the position of the dominant economic class within capitalism, 'justice' itself being no more than 'the ideologised, glorified expression of the existing economic relationships' (Marx and Engels, 1958, vol. 2, p.128).

There is a good deal of textual evidence for Marx's theoretical amoralism and his anti-justice and anti-rights stances. Certainly Marx did not think that juridical concepts like justice have any significant role to play in the explanation of social structure and social change. However recent debate on Marx and justice takes up the question of whether there might be – at a deeper level of analysis – distinctively socialist normative conceptions of rights and justice which capture at least some of the values which can be realised only in a socialist society. This approach draws on Marx's clear abhorrence of the miseries engendered by capitalism and his allegations that capitalism, as a form of theft perpetrated against the workers, fails to match up to even its own moral ideals.

More particularly, it is argued that socialist societies will at least approximate to, if not directly aim at, the genuinely socialist principle of distribution 'from each according to their ability, to each according to their needs', a maxim which Marx himself endorses. The communal egalitarianism implied by such a principle could be said to embody an aspect of socialism's moral superiority over other forms of political philosophy which is particularly relevant to justice. In brief, the socialist conception of justice can be regarded as distribution according to need. The fact that there will be no scarcity of resources in an actual communist society may render justice less problematic than it is in other societies, but this does not mean that socialist societies are not, in their own distinctive sense, just. Nor does it negate the claim that socialist justice is – in its proper historical context – to be preferred to other conceptions of justice.

Marx's strictures on justice and his failure to denounce capitalism as 'unjust' can be interpreted as a manifestation of his criticism of 'Utopian' socialists, whose primary failure was to assume that historical progress could be brought about by drawing up imaginary blueprints of an ideal form of society, and then exhorting people to set about transforming actual societies into the preferred Utopia. The Utopians were alleged to have ignored the fundamental historical realities which make it impossible to realise a socialist society until the existing or emerging material conditions are appropriate to it. Imaginative thinking, moral insight, and appeals to people's better natures are powerless before the underlying determinants of historical development.

However it is possible to share Marx's sense of history and acknowledge the futility of ahistorical moralising, while seeking to specify the values which are relevant to the assessment of the moral superiority of one form of society over another. Doubtless this was not Marx's prime concern, but there is sufficient indication of the values which are presupposed in his critique of capitalism and in his clear preference for the fulfilments and freedoms of socialist societies over against the barbarities and degradations of capitalism, to make it reasonable to develop a socialist set of values which may well turn out to include a conception of justice.

Nevertheless Marx's radically different starting-point implies that a socialist theory of justice must differ from liberal theories not only in the content of its principles but also in the function which it allots to justice discourse. It cannot be assumed, for instance, that justice necessarily embodies the priority principles of socialism, or that, in a socialist society, such principles of justice as obtain have to be consciously followed and applied in the face of hostile vested interests. Other standard liberal assumptions, such as the centrality of money as the prime value to be distributed, the fundamental fairness of the market and the associated individualistic modes of thought will not feature in the socialist account of justice. Nor is it likely that 'justice' would be seen as a rallying cry against exploitation and unfairness, since these would not be features of a socialist society. Rather, the import of justice talk in a socialist context would be seen as a way of identifying the moral benefits of socialism and in particular of drawing attention to the deficiencies of other forms of society. Education and evaluation, not prescription and protest, is the residual function of socialist normative political philosophy. Within this parameter the issues to be debated relate to the form and content of socialist justice, its superiority to other conceptions of justice and its relationship to other, perhaps more important, socialist values.

By raising in this way the question of the uses and significance of the language of justice, socialist theory takes us back to the topics of the first chapter, where we asked what justice is about. In particular the socialist critique of justice requires us to raise again the issue of whether justice has a distinctive meaning beyond conformity to established rules and practices and, if so, if this can be distinguished from and related to other social and political ideals. Consideration of the Marxian approach to justice is therefore an appropriate entrée to the summation of our survey of issues in recent political philosophy of justice.

Marx and formal justice

Opinions vary as to the extent of Marx's rejection of morality and moralising. On a strict interpretation of the doctrine of historical materialism all ideas, including moral ideas, are part of the 'superstructure', the effects rather than the causes of social phenomena, and hence utterly dependent on the material basis of the forces of production which are constituted by what a society produces and the manner of its production and distribution. It follows that moralising is not only futile but also baseless since there would seem to be no way of deciding that one moral opinion is better or worse than any other, all ethical systems being equally the products of non-rational economic forces. This reductionist assumption seems to undermine the purely evaluative as well as the prescriptive or exhortatory function of moral language and therefore renders nugatory the strongly normative aspects of the theories of justice which we have been considering. On such a strict interpretation of Marxian orthodoxy there is no way of demonstrating the moral superiority of the Rawlsian maximin principle over the wealth-maximising ideal of Posner or the Dworkinian conception of treatment as equals. Neither utilitarian calculation, nor contractarian imagination nor the procedures of Neutral dialogue can serve as anything more than the vehicle for pre-existing political prejudice.

On a looser interpretation of historical materialism, in which the superstructure of ideas may be allowed some causal efficacy, at least on the pace of historical development, there may be a place for timely moral persuasion, and there is also the possibility that an element of rational judgement may enter into the formation of political opinion, particularly as the necessities of capitalist society give way to the emerging freedoms of socialism. It is unlikely, however, that there can be any Marxian indulgence for the pretensions of those theories of justice which present themselves as the embodiment of universal truths which have application to any and every stage of historical development. Particularly vulnerable to the Marxian historical sensitivity are theories, like Nozick's, which are founded on unchallengeable natural rights and presuppose a form of individualism that ignores the interdependent and socially variable nature of man. Less vulnerable are the more modest objectives of Rawlsian reflective equilibrium which seeks only to express and render consistent the political outlook of a particular historical form of social organisation.

A characteristic socialist critique of all liberal theories of justice is that they oversell themselves in so far as they purport to provide an impartial analysis which is neutral as between the interested groups which coexist even within a particular society. In our consideration of, for instance, Dworkin's practical applications of the idea that we should treat people as equals, or Ackerman's attempts to generate specific social arrangements from the procedures of Neutral dialogue, we have noted that they cannot provide sufficient reasons for the conclusions they reach, in that the same principles can generate widely different practical recommendations for essentially similar circumstances. The same is true of all theories which posit the emergence of a rational consensus as to what is just, once partiality has been excluded by one device or another. The hidden selectivity involved in all potentially universalistic theories results in systematic bias in favour of certain social groups in a way which Marx predicts will occur with all aspiringly consensual political theories.

The most evident example of this covert (or, in this case, not so covert) ideological slant must be the wealth-maximising model of Posner, which can readily be seen as a rationalisation of capitalist accumulation, but similar critiques can be mounted of Rawls's lexical priority of liberty and his apparent neglect of the unemployable, and there is more than a hint of ideology in Ackerman's indifference towards those with below-average talents

and above-average needs. Similarly Sadurski's tendency to con-
clude that desert converges on socially valuable contribution is
readily presented as a modern variant of the recurrent liberal
thesis that those who come out on top in an equal opportunity
competitive society somehow 'deserve' to do so. In general,
however they are deployed, impartiality and neutrality have an
uncanny knack of coming up with ideals which do not pose any
real threat to the established economic inequalities of the liberal
societies from which they routinely emerge.

Faced with such swingeing critiques of liberal theories of
justice, socialists may think it wise to develop other terminology
to express their counter values, but, given the rhetorical force of
the language of justice and its constant re-emergence as the
expression of specific types of social criticism, it is hardly surprising that efforts are made to establish the credentials of a socialist
conception of justice through which to communicate at least part
of the vision of the socialist ideal. Even if justice is ultimately
dismissed as a purely ideological concept of mere transitory
significance we can still seek to discover what Marx considered
justice to be. And if, additionally, justice is to be allotted even a
marginal function within socialism, then its meaning requires
analysis and some analytical connection has to be established
between the justice of socialism and the justice of other forms of
social organisation.

The differing analyses of the Marxian concept of justice which
have been put forward can usefully be approached in terms of the
contrast between formal and material justice, the justice of adherence to rules as distinct from the justice of the rules themselves.
Marx himself often appears to move between the idea of justice
as conformity to the established practices of a social institution
and the more substantial idea of justice as it applies to the
assessment of these practices. It is clear that some of his observa-
tions on justice are directed at the idea of formal justice while
others have more to do with material justice.

Thus it is when Marx is thinking of formal justice that he treats
justice as a juridical concept which has to do with conformity to
established rules and hence the administration of law or 'justice'
within a particular system. From this point of view justice is
always 'internal' to a particular form of social organisation, since
it refers to no more than the efficient implementation of the

norms of the system in question. This means that the language of justice cannot be used as the basis for an external critique of the organisation as a whole or to condemn its constituent rules. Societies can be unjust in so far as they fail to apply their own rules consistently, but the rules themselves are never properly described as just or unjust. For instance, the capitalist judge who applies the property laws of capitalist society is acting justly, as the feudal courts are just when they uphold the different rights and duties which constitute feudal ownership. Justice is therefore relative to, and can be no higher than, the existing system of economic relationships.

According to this interpretation of Marx, it follows that societies are unjust only in so far as they do not consistently enforce their societal norms and laws. Marx does not appear to attach any moral significance to such inconsistencies, except perhaps to note as one of the contradictions of capitalism that its laws are often selectively enforced to the benefit of the bourgeois class. It might appear, therefore, that justice, for Marx, is a morally neutral and entirely relative concept, equally at home in all societies and in principle applicable to socialist societies in relation to the consistent application of socialist rules and standards.

However this conclusion misses Marx's contention that law is an intrinsically capitalist phenomenon, and one which will play no significant part within a truly socialist or communist society. Law, along with the State, will wither away with the demise of class differences and economic exploitation, to be replaced by a spontaneous order of mutual co-operation untramelled by the coercive apparatus of law and the restrictions of rigid social norms. In a society in which men are genuinely free to make their own relationships within uncoerced social groupings there will be no role for law and hence no place for justice.

There is no avoiding this conclusion if a strict juridical interpretation of justice is combined with a classical positivistic analysis of law which makes law, by definition, a coercive apparatus of the state. No Marxist could accept that a truly socialist society would have coercive laws backed by state sanctions. And yet, if justice is taken to include the quasi-juridical form of conformity to the non-legal rules or mandatory societal norms which lack the backing of formal sanctions, socialist communities would require a conception of justice to cover adherence to their non-coercive

societal rules. Alternatively, by revising the crude sanctions version of positivism to allow for the possibility of there being laws
which, while mandatory within a given territory, require no
sanctions to attract adequate conformity, justice can be freed
from its necessary connection with force and formal justice given
an acceptable role in socialist society. Either way, there is no
difficulty in making conceptual room for the idea of socialist
formal justice, or socialist legality. As long as there are socially
recognised rules which are authoritative within a territory and
which are applied by specialist bodies with responsibility for their
interpretation and adjudication in relation to particular cases,
then there is law in a sense which is sufficient for the language of
formal justice to gain a foothold.

Similar considerations pertain in relation to rights. If, following
the discussion in Chapter 2, we bypass the idea of moral rights,
and define rights in terms of the existing normative entitlements
to which appeal may be made to protect the interests of the
individual, all that is required for there to be rights is for there to
be a set of needs-based binding rules according to which individuals regulate their interactions. In a socialist society the binding
force of the rules rests on willing acceptance rather than the
threat of sanctions or the inducements of reward, but there is no
contradiction in the notions of continuing consent to obligations
and free acquiescence in a body of shared rules. If part of formal
justice involves treating individuals according to their rights, then
we can have a working tie-up between quasi-juridical conceptions
of rights and justice which have potential application to socialist
societies.

It is true that some forms of Marxian anarchism have no place
for rules of any sort and envisage all social co-operation as being
purely spontaneous and transient, thus requiring no basis in
expectations arising from an authoritative set of rights and duties.
However this model lacks plausibility in a society involving
modern production methods and large-scale social organisation.
Moreover, what little Marx himself has to say on the nature of
the ultimate form of communist society is compatible with the
continued existence of non-coercive and, in this sense, largely
'administrative' rules, and hence with the idea of formal justice.

Difficulties over the assumed coerciveness of law are not the
only ones, however, which prompt Marxist suspicions of formal

justice, particularly when it is assumed that formal justice involves treating individuals in accordance with their positive rights. There are a number of other question marks which hang over the compatibility of rights and socialism. Some of these concern the alleged universality and overriding inalienability of rights as expressed in connection with conceptions of natural or human rights. Not only did Marx castigate bourgeois moralists for presenting their class interests as universal interests, his sense of history led him also to reject the idea that there could be any paramount rights applicable to all persons in all ages.

We have already noted, in Chapter 2, that it is not necessary to invoke the concept of human rights to explicate the thesis that justice involves treating people in accordance with their rights, but other socialist objections to rights apply equally to rights in general, rather than to human rights specifically. For instance, it is argued that rights are essentially individualistic in that they are the 'property' of individuals and have the function of protecting the interests of their possessors against the perhaps otherwise justified claims of other individuals and groups. The idea is that rights are devices for legitimising possibly anti-social and certainly self-interested behaviour and hence get in the way of the organisation of a polity for the welfare of the society as a whole. This is given backing by the common jurisprudential analysis of positive rights in terms of the legal power to control the behaviour of others in specified ways, a power whose use is left to the discretion of the right-holder to use as he or she thinks fit. This device is alleged to be a reflection of the idea that a society is a collection of independent individuals whose interests are protected through the institution of rights which enables them to pursue their 'legitimate' self-interest.

The Marxian critique of rights in general can point to the increasing significance of rights in the legal systems of capitalist countries and the affinity between the idea of rights and the belief that obligations normally arise from the agreement of autonomous individuals in commercial-like transactions. The standard model is economic man acting in accordance with his own judgements as to his economic interests, a hypothesis which is given varying degrees of endorsement by all the theories of justice which we have considered. Clearly a large-scale commercial society requires laws which are framed in terms of rights and these rights dominantly assume a context in which individuals are acting in accordance with their own conception of their interests. Further, there is in historical terms a powerful correlation between rights and the exercise of individual autonomy in a manner which avoids the need to justify itself in community terms. This is most evident in the work of libertarians, such as Nozick and Posner, although, as we have seen, the latter does, at least in principle, subordinate individual rights to the social goal of wealth-maximisation.

This historical picture does not in itself demonstrate that other forms of society would not require and endorse a system of rights which serves other purposes. There is nothing in the concept of a right which requires that it goes along with the assumption that obligations, and hence their correlative rights, are primarily the outcome of voluntary agreement, let alone that this agreement is always made by essentially self-interested individuals. Nor is it necessary to analyse rights, as liberal theorists so often do, in terms of discretionary powers of rights-holders, whereby they may call on others to fulfil their obligations or may waive the obligations in question. We also speak of rights where there exist obligations to further the interests of another, as in the case of children's rights, whether or not the right-holder is required to initiate any claims and even where the right-holder is not able to waive the obligations which correlate with rights, as with the right of an unconscious person to medical treatment. It is not even necessary to assume that a system of rights requires that violations of rights be dealt with only on the complaint and initiative of the right-holder, although this may normally be an efficient way to organise the protection of interests.

It is possible, therefore, that socialist doubt about a legal system involving rights is a result of the failure to realise that not only the content of rights but their *modus operandi* and justificatory rationales can be quite different from that which typically pertains in capitalist societies. Even within the assumption that rights are often discretionary powers wielded by individuals, it is unproblematic to envisage a function for such rights in societies in which individuals are not selfish and whose self-interest is not rigidly separated from the interests of others. As long as individuals have desires (however altruistic) on which they wish to act and as long as such actions are facilitated in a socially beneficial way by allowing the individual a range of legal powers with which to pursue his interests, then there is reason to have a rights-based system of rules. It is only the assumption that individuals are inherently and irredeemable self-interested that renders the idea of rights anti-socialist. And so, while the significance of formal justice does not, of course, depend solely on the rules of the system being construed in terms of rights, establishing the coherence of the idea of socialist rights does clear the way for an open-minded assessment of formal justice within socialist theory.

Much discussion of this issue has had to do with how far, if at all, the rule of law can mitigate the evils of pre-socialist government by injecting an element of impartiality into the exercise of political power in non-socialist systems. There has been little direct discussion of the significance of formal justice once socialism has become a reality. Of course, if there is reason to have rules within socialism then there must be reason to have these rules effectively, and that must mean by and large accurately, administered. The issues which then arise concern the reasons that there might be for curtailing the discretion of officials to vary retrospectively the application of rules where this seems to them to be for the public interest. This question is addressed indirectly in the debate about the alleged utilitarianism of socialism and the tendency of socialists who, in their concern for the happiness of the mass of the people, adopt an act-utilitarian rather than a rule-utilitarian approach. Act-utilitarianism makes the commitment to government according to law provisional in that the system is open to the principle that the general interest can routinely be used to justify interventions in the normal processes of formal justice where this is clearly beneficial in utilitarian terms.

It is, however, by no means clear that Marx himself is a straightforward utilitarian either in his ultimate political values or in his attitude to rules. For instance, Marx is clearly committed to the importance of freedom within a communist society which requires that individuals and groups are able to pursue creative projects in co-operation with their fellows. His conception of the full development of a socialised human nature, which is manifested in the ideal of satisfying work in the service of genuine needs, leaves room for respecting the sort of individual and group autonomy that is furthered by giving the individuals and groups fixed sets of rules in the context of which they can plan and take responsibility for the outcome of their actions. Those aspects of the socialist ideal which stress the importance of creative endeavour, in addition to the simple pursuit of happiness, provide some basis for the view of man which relates respect for the individual to strict adherence to the rules which affect his or her welfare. Fixed rules provide a context within which socialists as much as capitalists can act responsibly in the light of the stability which such a system provides. Altruists, as much as egotists, are rule-dependent for the success of their projects.

There is nothing in Marx to suggest that he would give any weight to the value of the bare idea of treating like cases alike within a public set of rules, for this represents the sort of rule-fetichism which places abstract rationality above human interests, and frequently acts as an excuse for the perpetration of material injustice. However, since, as we have noted in Chapter 1, the independent value of formal justice is questionable, socialists may have no difficulty in dispensing with it. Further, much of Marx's critique of justice can be seen as directed to the unimportance of formal justice in situations where the substantive rules are exploitative. However, this does not rule out the possible instrumental significance of formal justice in situations where the rules are materially acceptable.

Marx and material justice

Exploring ways in which socialism might incorporate a conception of material justice requires us to have a reasonably clear idea what an actualised socialist society would be like. From Marx we can glean many negative descriptions of socialist or 'communist' society: there will be no classes, no exploitation, no conflict and no coercion. All this is due to the abolition of the private ownership of the means of production, in relation to which class membership is defined, through which exploitation occurs and because of which social conflict and coercion arise. The more positive aspects of socialist society are less clearly defined. The communal ownership of the means of production is said to achieve plenty, not in any crude materialistic sense, but in relation to the genuine needs of men and women in a society in which their social and creative natures can be expressed and fulfilled and true freedom experienced in the context of community life. This implies that there will be far less division of labour, and such as there is will be freely chosen. It also involves the end of market transactions as the prime determinant of production and distribution. It is also assumed that, once the various transitional stages have been gone through, there will be genuinely consensual democracy, so that all share in the direction of social organisation towards the satisfaction of needs and the expression of a freedom which involves the absence of practical as well as legal barriers to attaining the goals of human endeavours.

Interestingly this brief sketch of the *telos* of social evolution draws on the language of freedom and fulfilment and could readily have been couched in terms of equality, but the language of justice does not spring to mind as central or even essential to the exposition of the communist ideal, although there seems to be no awkwardness in asserting that a socialist society will not be unjust. The most straightforward explanation for the marginality of justice in socialist terminology is that, in communist society, the so-called 'conditions' of justice do not obtain: there is no scarcity of goods to be distributed, no conflict to be resolved, no systems of punishments and incentives to be administered. It can therefore be argued that there is no scope for the ideas of justice and injustice within communism because society has passed beyond the stage at which these ideas have anything on which to bite.

If, however, we take up a broad analysis of justice according to which it has to do with rightness in distribution, it is clear that abundance and harmony do not in themselves dispense with the role of justice. In situations of harmony and plenty distributive issues still require to be dealt with, if only to ensure that the needs and welfare of all members of a society receive attention. Abundance of goods does not necessarily entail their proper distribution and it seems likely that proper distribution even of what is plentiful is a condition of the continuing absence of conflict. Indeed there is no suggestion that in a communist society abundance and harmony are achieved without conscious effort and good organisation which involve decisions about production and distribution being made in relation to the chosen objectives of that society.

It may well be, however, that the reluctance of Marxian

theorists to articulate the distributive principles of communist society in the language of justice is rooted in their awareness of the conceptual tie-up between justice and desert and their instinctive hostility to the notion of desert and its alleged moral significance within capitalism. Bourgeois ideology attempts to justify the inequalities of capitalist society by appeals to the notion of the value of the contribution made by those involved in production and its financing, and behind this there are the assertions that those who succeed in a free enterprise private ownership system 'deserve' to do so through their wise choices, hard work, acquired skills and honest dealings. To Marxists this meritorian ideology is, of course, complete humbug, hence their scorn for appeals to justice in the context of capitalism. But the basis for their rejection of capitalist pretensions to justice vary and do not always carry the implication that the underlying ideas of meritorian justice are always without foundation.

Sometimes the denial of meritorian justice is based on the determinism of historical materialism according to which all human actions are the products of inevitable historical processes rather than the free actions of the participants. As we noted in Chapter 6, taking a 'hard' determinist line undermines all talk of human responsibility and accountability in the standard moral sense in which people are praised and blamed for their behaviour because it is their choice, effort or character which are at least important elements in the circumstances under scrutiny. If in a narrow sense people cannot control or act against their desires in the light of moral principles and are causally bound to do what they in fact do, then it makes no sense to blame or praise them for their conduct. For such reasons Marx seems no more inclined to blame capitalists than to praise proletarians: both are slaves to a process which rules their lives with an iron necessity. This may mean that when Marx denies that capitalist distribution is 'unjust' he intends to say not only that it is formally just within the system of capitalism, in that it is in accordance with the rules of the capitalist system, but also that it is meaningless to criticise this arrangement as materially unjust because it is an inevitable and historically necessary stage in human evolution.

Nevertheless this critique presupposes the labour theory of value according to which the value of a product is the quantity of labour that has gone into the making of it. This may involve the covert assertion that those who work to produce something are deserving of possessing, enjoying or disposing of it. There is a running assumption in the fierce rhetorical Marxian critique of capitalism that the exploitation of proletarians is wrong because they are the real creators of wealth. In the end, capitalists are seen to be superfluous parasites, even thieves, who contribute nothing of their own to the productive process and hence may be said to be undeserving of the rewards which they 'steal' from the workers. This fits easily enough into a critique of capitalism as unjust by the meritorian standards to which it makes ideological appeal but fails to achieve in practice. Since it makes perfect sense to say, in this context, that the proletariat deserve more and the bourgeoisie deserve less, we may see a meritorian view at work in the exposition of the shortcomings of capitalism.

Moreover, while Marxists agree that history is in the main a causally determined process, this is a matter which is admitted to be – to an extent – a matter of degree, particularly in relation to the historical period in question. Specifically it is alleged that, with the demise of capitalism, which culminates in a highly determined series of cataclysms, the developing forms of socialist and then communist society are marked by the growing emergence of the freedom of men and women to control their own destiny and make the institutions of society fit their genuine needs and hence achieve real fulfilment. The determinist veto on meritorian justice would not therefore apply once communism is achieved.

There are further reasons why justice is not to the fore in the Marxian picture of the communist millenium, particularly the assumption that the achievements of communist society will be communal, not individual. It is assumed that production methods will be social in that they involve a large number of people working together with the tools of modern industry. In this situation, since no one can claim to be the sole producer, it becomes increasingly difficult to identify the contribution of each individual to the final product and so the idea of rewards being commensurate with input of particular persons seems inapplicable. The results of communal effort may seem, by definition, to exclude the possibility of distribution in accordance with individual merit.

Yet it is normal to conceive of the deserts of groups as well as individuals, particularly where there are democratic processes at work, and the complete rejection of the individualisation of production in socialist accounting is too sweeping to be compatible with other elements of Marxist theory. It cannot take in, for instance, Marx's endorsement of reward according to contribution which pertains in the transitional stages of socialist society, nor does it accord with the degree of individualism implied by the communist slogan, 'from each according to his ability, to each according to his needs', a principle which calls for the identification of what it is that the individual contributes as well as individualised assessment of the needs which have to be met by communist production and distribution. This putative principle of communist distribution requires further analysis if we are to see how it might relate to the tradition of meritorian justice on which Marx depends in making many of his assessments of the different types of society.

The centrality of 'need' in the normative theory of communism is open to many different interpretations. To emphasise needs can be seen as a form of ethical utilitarianism, primarily 'negative' utilitarianism, in that it may indicate the material lacks which cause suffering and suggest that resources be directed towards eliminating the sort of human suffering which Marx saw as reaching their climax in the last days of capitalism, but also 'positive' utilitarianism, in that the object of communist society could be to maximise human happiness. This approach does not fit easily, however, with Marx's denunciations of utilitarians like Jeremy Bentham. Marx criticises both the individualistic theory of human nature espoused by the classical utilitarians and the ethical view that the satisfaction of any and all human desires is morally good.

Some compromise is possible here if we hold, in contrast to Benthamite utilitarians, that it is genuine happiness which results from real human fulfilment, and not simply the satisfaction on any desires, that Marx adopts as the criterion of value, his quarrel with Bentham being the latter's view that satisfying the wishes of men as they are in non-communist societies is productive of happiness. This line of thought leads into a more clearly non-utilitarian interpretation of Marx's concentration on need according to which it represents a teleological view of human nature of an almost Aristotelian type. *Homo sapiens*, as a species, exhibits its full potential only when it achieves a certain way of life which expresses its inner nature, an end which requires a development in the material conditions of life and corresponding social organisation that makes it possible for men and women to live together in harmony as creative and social beings. This teleological interpretation of the language of need in Marx's political philosophy draws heavily on his early writings with their themes of man as a 'species being' who is alienated from his own nature under the capitalist system. However, as an overall interpretation of Marxian ideas, this position rides rather uneasily with many of the things that Marx has to say about the plasticity of human nature and its derivative status in relation to the variable economic base of society.

Such issues cannot be settled by any evaluatively neutral analysis of 'need'. Certainly needs are often contrasted with wants, and to this extent appear non-utilitarian since utilitarians have characteristically sought maximum satisfaction of all wants, but the concept of need is in itself so open-ended that it admits of almost any practical deployment. Anything which can be said to be required to achieve any objective can be regarded as a need, so that any 'want' can thereby be the basis for a need. There is no necessary assumption that the objective for the attainment of which something is needed is morally good rather than evaluatively indifferent or even bad. In consequence, those who use 'need' as a political concept require to state and defend the goals which they covertly espouse by the use of this logically incomplete terminology. Some such goals – such as human survival – can, perhaps, be taken for granted, and it is often 'basic' needs, that is, the requirements for continued material existence, that are invoked by the political discourse of needs. Marx himself is clearly concerned with such basic needs not only because their neglect generates great suffering but also because it is the basis of his empirical theory of historical materialism that the manner in which a society goes about satisfying the material needs of its members determines everything else about it.

Once we go beyond the idea of basic needs it is possible to construct some hierarchy of needs which relate to the pursuit of an infinite variety of possible human objectives. It is at this point that it is possible to introduce a 'naturalistic' or natural law postulate to pick out certain goals as best suited to expressing human nature. Plausible contenders for this status have included rationality, autonomy and moral capacity. In Marx's case the most likely combination of 'natural' goals is a blend of creativity and sociability. It seems misleading to present these values, however, as a form of natural law theory, since Marx makes none of the characteristic natural law epistemological claims to the effect that the ends of man can be ascertained by rational insight or deduction from observation of normal human behaviour. Indeed the idea that communist society is directed towards the satisfaction of human needs is an open-ended principle that may well be compatible with a wide variety of ideas about fulfilling human activities.

It can therefore be argued that the Marxian approach to justice is essentially a Rawlsian one in that it concentrates on the alleviation of basic needs. This, it is said, is in effect to benefit the least advantaged section of the society. Certainly in his reaction to the suffering caused by capitalism Marx is moved primarily by the plight of those experiencing the greatest material deprivations. While such extreme suffering could not arise within the plenty of communist society, the analogous priority would be those whose personal characteristics make it most difficult to achieve a satisfying way of life.

It is doubtful, however, if the improvements which communism offers over capitalism with respect to the effective satisfaction of basic needs would be regarded by Marx as a matter of justice as distinct from liberty, community, self-realisation or plain humanity. In so far as prioritising basic needs implies an acceptance of the equal worth of all human beings. In that the suffering of each person counts equally, regardless of class or wealth, it has the ring of justice discourse about it, but such equality of worth could be said to underline other prescriptive principles, such as equal beneficence, or the equal maximisation of human potential.

At this stage in the analysis of socialist justice it is perhaps pointless to speculate on the extent to which Marx himself would regard the need principle as expressive of justice rather than some other ideal, but it is important to note that there is no built-in antithesis between need-satisfaction and meritorian justice. If, following Sadurski, we say that need satisfaction is reserved for basic needs, then this leaves plenty of scope for meritorian distributions in non-basic matters. Justice is then relevant to the surplus that remains once scarcity has taken care of basic needs.

What, presumably, is not allowed is to make the satisfaction of basic needs conditional on desert.

On the other hand, if the need principle is interpreted in a broad manner, so that it takes in what is required for a particular life-style, then this life-style can be delineated in such a way as to include the idea of treating people in accordance with their deserts. This is something which – it could be argued – is necessary for maintaining mutual respect and individual dignity within a society of responsible agents. A neo-Marxian account of justice may be unlikely to give such meritorian considerations the dominant role in the distribution of material goods, but its relevance to the distribution of more socialist values, such as creative opportunities and socially responsible tasks, to say nothing of the allocation of those important ingredients of social life – praise and blame – might well be deemed appropriate. It is not only a coherent but also in principle an attractive idea that human beings need to be treated as autonomous agents who are responsible for their actions and answerable for their conduct. Moreover, even basic needs are relevant to meritorian justice in that their satisfaction is often a necessary prerequisite for engaging in the sort of conduct which is the subject of meritorian assessment. We cannot live well unless we have the wherewithal to sustain our lives.

The issues here are not merely conceptual. Problems also arise from the difficulty we have in imagining what it would be like to live in an affluent and egalitarian society which does not depend on the positive sanctions of economic incentives or the negative sanctions of punishment to attain its objectives. In liberal theories of justice much effort goes into seeking to demonstrate that such sanctions are 'just' in that they are not only instrumentally necessary but also in some way 'deserved'. People must be bribed to work hard, but they also deserve rewards if they do work hard. In fully developed communism the incentive element drops out, but this does not imply that no recognition would be given to those who devote themselves to socially productive tasks. In the changed conditions of communist society rewards may be unnecessary and those of high ability, who are required to give more to the communal effort, may not in any important sense 'deserve' their higher abilities, but in a society which has escaped from the domination of historical forces and is able freely to explore the fulfilment of human nature it is likely that evaluations of behaviour in terms of its moral worth would be not only better founded, but of continuing significance.

The psychological barriers in the way of introducing an element of desert into the socialist account of human needs are formidable, given the entrenched misuse of meritorian ideas in the history of liberal political philosophy. There are, however, grounds for holding that the differing degrees of good and ill desert which would emerge in a socialist society are not so substantial as to warrant major differences in treatment once the basic needs of material subsistence have been adequately met. Nor does the endorsement of meritorianism have inegalitarian implications in its application to non-socialist societies in which the general absence of freedom of action makes meritorian assessment of conduct inappropriate. Where human behaviour is largely determined by economic forces the conditions of meritorian justice do not obtain, for no one can be held substantially accountable for their actions.

Further, due to the general absence of injurious and harmful behaviour there could be little role for rectificatory justice outside the educational sphere. The function of justice in socialist society will not be a matter of distributing the spoils of the division of labour in an incentive-based market economy. Socialist justice has to do with non-monetary ways of recognising the worth of the different efforts made by individuals and groups towards the realisation of a socialist society in which the full satisfaction of genuine human needs is the corporate *telos*.

Such speculations are of more than purely theoretical interest. It is important for the evaluation of the socialist ideal to know whether a communist society would be organised around the maximisation of pleasure or devoted to the development of a form of life which emphasises responsible choice and critical evaluation of conduct in terms of values other than pleasure. Moreover, coming to terms with the significance of (meritorian) justice for communist society has implications for the way in which socialists react to the language of justice within non-socialist societies. There is a major difference between totally dismissing all justice talk as an intellectually confused form of ideology, on the one hand, and using it to undermine the particular claims that are made about justice under capitalism, on the other. If the latter approach is adopted it becomes possible to argue the shortcomings of capitalism without endorsing the nihilistic view that justice is inevitably a chimera and to go on to use the terminology which has been developed in pre-socialist societies to commend a possible future in which at least some aspects of the unrealised ideal of liberal ideology would come to fruition.

It is widely assumed that there is an epistemological weakness in the Marxian tradition in that it provides us with no way of coming to reliable judgements as to the correct social and political values. There appears to be no Marxian equivalent to Rawlsian relective equilibrium or Posner's model of rational economic choice. Instead we are asked to wait and see how things turn out in the socialist millenium, when the nature and relevance of justice, along with so much else, will be made clear.

There is, however, an almost Aristotelian style of approach in Marx's naturalistic materialism which encourages us to look for answers to such major questions as the nature of the ideal society, not in the realm of value dispute, but by paying more careful attention to the facts about human nature and the conditions under which human beings flourish. True, this cannot be done simply by examining human nature as it now is, for such nature is in large part the result of economic and social circumstances, and will change as these circumstances change. Nevertheless there are intimations to be found in existing societies as to what is ultimately satisfying and fulfilling in human life, and it can be argued that we know enough already about the human *telos* to say that this must include the active realisation of the potential capacities of men and women as autonomous creators of their own way of life, who should be treated with the respect that is due to those who are capable of making their own history and natures. It is therefore a matter for investigation which social arrangements are most beneficial to human beings. In other words, the central questions about justice and other social values, are factual rather than evaluative. This, along with more overtly naturalistic types of argument, is a method which is clearly vulnerable to the criticism that it illicitly draws prescriptive conclusions from purely factual premises, but it is a form of moral realism which has some backing in contemporary philosophy.

The relative truth about justice

The intellectual contortions which must be performed in order to bring out a meaningful contrast between liberal and socialist theories of justice have much to do with the fact that basic social and political concepts are closely intertwined with the complex sets of ideas and practices which constitute different social structures. Where radically dissimilar types of society are under consideration there can be no neat way of identifying the major contrasts in their political concepts. Thus simply to feed in 'needs' to the formula 'to each according to their Xs' cannot focus adequately on the move from liberal to socialist assumptions. Such a formula, particularly when 'X'='need', conjures up the picture of a vast allocative mechanism externally attached to an economic system which produces the goods to be distributed and imposes the burdens which the system and its political supports demand. According to this model, the role of justice is to superimpose a reallocation of benefits and burdens on an essentially aggregative productive system which is directed towards the efficient output of material goods.

This approach cannot adequately encapsulate the socialists' shift of emphasis towards the idea that all social enterprises be directed towards an existence 'in which the free development of each is the condition for the free development of all' (Marx and Engels, 1958, vol. 2, p.54). This vision of communal endeavour directed towards the realisation of a fulfilling way of life for all members of society is claimed to transcend the sort of formula which is appropriate to the allocation of scarce benefits and oppressive burdens between competitive and self-interested individuals. Bringing about varied and fulfilling creative activities for all is not primarily a matter of distributing money, 'manna', or even education and employment, according to some mechanical equation. If justice has a role in this model of society, then it will be at once less evident and more central. Socialist justice has to do with more than the rectification of injurious interpersonal behaviour, the struggle to make competitive economic systems more 'fair', and the provision of a safety net for the sick, the old and the disabled. Rather it enters into the organising principles of all social activities, which will be directed at the satisfaction of 'needs' in a sense broad enough to take in all the creative and community aspirations of the fully developed individual.

Within the liberal tradition from which socialist theory has emerged it is more natural to present such a goal in terms of liberty than in the language of justice or equality, for liberty, when conceived of in positive terms as involving the power to realise capacities as well as the absence of the constraints of oppressive laws and social conventions, more readily captures the flavour of the contrast between socialism and capitalism. Yet it is misleading to present this as a contrast between liberty and justice, for it is assumed that the genuine interests of all members of a socialist society will have equal weight and it is denied that the tensions between these two norms, which is manifested in liberal societies, will be a feature of socialist ones.

There are clearly conceptual problems arising from the breakdown of the neat distinctions between aggregation and distribution, and between liberty and justice. What we are left with is too diffuse and speculative to withstand detailed analytical criticism. And yet, if we accept a version of the meritorian analysis of justice which traces the roots of the liberal concern with justice to the idea of treating individuals as responsible agents, and if we can free this notion from the accompanying individualistic assumptions that people are responsible only to the extent that they act by themselves rather than in concert with others, then it is possible to point to this meritorian element in the model of socialist society as the essence of socialist as well as liberal justice. It is because a socialist society will be, amongst other things, a community which encourages the fulfilment of the human capacities for choice, autonomous action and purposeful creativity, so that people are not only in command of their own environment but are in fact responsible for their social and individual existences, that it is illuminating to talk of a socialist society as a just society, although this may not be the principal thing that we might wish to say about it.

Are there, however, good reasons for accepting such a meritorian theory of justice? Indeed, are there grounds for preferring one analysis of justice over any other? It would seem that, in practice, what happens in the political philosophy of justice, as in the other spheres of the theory of practice, is that analyses depend primarily on the explication of the concepts at work in the conceptual schemes of specific historical groups, with an attempt to give these systems of thought a nudge in a direction preferred by the theorist in question. Understandably, the study of the actual language of justice throws up a host of variations and anomalies in our normative discourse and, given that conceptual schemes are in part at least devised to render the political world more intelligible and present us with manageable practical choices, some attempt at simplifying and rendering more coherent the confusion of the real world of political discourse is inevitable. Hence theorists are bound to invite us to see justice their way because they believe themselves to have worked out an approach which provides clarity and guidance in a confusing and disorienting world of contested ideological concepts.

In the end the acceptability of the alternative viewpoints put forward by different political theorists largely depends on how far they tune in with our existing understanding of the society and how far they help to clarify the political choices which confront us. If a theory can point up the value-laden choices with which we are presented and set them out with clarity and precision, then it has probably done as much as any philosophical theory can do. To be successful in this role a theory has to be relevant to the social and political system which is familiar to its audience and enable its readers to identify the fundamental value choices that call to be made. In highlighting the distinctive element of desert in those examples of contemporary justice discourse which utilise a reasonably specific and particular sense of 'justice' the meritorian approach brings a coherence to the variety of distinctive uses of the language of justice in a way which identifies its peculiar contribution to the range of social and political values. In doing so it is illuminating and clarificatory, but it cannot be claimed that it reflects all specific uses of justice discourse or clarifies all evaluative issues involving the dimension of justice. Indeed there can be no one correct or 'true' analysis or theory of justice of timeless relevance and acceptability. In the end utility rather than truth is the measure or criterion of a theory of justice. On so much could Rawls and Marx agree.

This is not to say that theories of justice are purely relative in that they can do no more than reflect the existing conceptual frameworks of particular societies. In so far as theories of justice transcend reporting conceptual schemes and propose refinements

and developments within and beyond them, some have more
utility than others in particular social and political settings. This is
particularly so when we move from the formal analysis of basic
terms to the methods that are suggested for decision-making
about the value of formal justice or the contents of material
justice. It is in this respect that recent theories of justice have
made their most important contribution. In Walzer's recognition
that different spheres throw up different distributive criteria,
Dworking's model of legal/moral reasoning, Rawls's method of
reflective equilibrium, Ackerman's device of Neutral conversations and Posner's use of hypothetical market transactions, we
have epistemological recommendations which may have more
lasting impact and importance than their background analyses of
'justice'. On the other hand, it can be argued that careful
conceptual analysis has not been a feature of much recent theoretical work on justice and that this has had a detrimental effect on
its coherence and utility.

It is clear, however, that such epistemologies of justice, when
conceived in the abstract, do not produce the substantive agreement which they promise. This may mean that their utility is
limited to clarifying the consensus which holds in specific cultures
at specific historical periods. Sometimes, however, we are confronted with a more malignant form of relativism whereby the
decision-making methods are seen to be no more than vehicles
for the users, pre-established and discriminatory value preferences.

In the absence of any confidence that we have access to a realm
of moral truth to settle the residual political disagreements it may
seem sensible to fall back on the assertion that justice, and virtue
in general, can only be concretised in the context of a particular
society with its set roles and traditions which shape its members'
values and expectations. Thus, in the writings of MacIntyre
(1981), Sandel (1982) and Walzer (1983), we see the development
of theories which are 'communitarian' in the sense that they
stress the social-determined meanings of value-laden terminology
to an extent that casts doubt on the utility of methods which
attempt to abstract decisions about what is just from the context
of specific communities of meaning. For the epistemological
communitarian the enemy is the very abstract theorising which
tries to rescue us from the burden of particularities and makes us

restless with uncritical acceptance of the consensus ideas of our own political setting.

For myself, it is a welcome aspect of contemporary theories of justice that in general they do strive to formulate ways of thinking which may enable us to stand outside our own inherited notions of the good society and help us to think creatively and purposefully about how we might move towards a better, perhaps a more just, form of social life.

Guide to Further Reading

For a general introduction to the topic of justice it is best to begin with Rawls's masterly *A Theory of Justice* (1971), which is dealt with in Chapter 3 of this work. This may be supplemented by David Miller, *Social Justice* (1976). Other excellent introductions include Arthur and Shaw (1978), Pettit (1980), Sterba (1986), Walzer (1983), Kamenka and Tay (1979), Benditt (1985) and Honore (1970). For a wider context see Raphael (1970), Sen (1970), Weale (1983) and Barry (1965).

For the discussion of rights in Chapter 2, see Waldron (1984), Feinberg (1970b) and Campbell (1983). Cohen (1984) contains a range of commentaries on the work of Dworkin and deals with the issue of discrimination, for which see also Goldman (1979).

Commentaries on Rawls are legion, but see particularly Barry (1973), Daniels (1975), Wolff (1977), Blocker and Smith (1980), Lessnoff (1986) and Raz (1982). For welfare issues consult Weale (1983) and Plant *et al.* (1980).

The best discussion of Ackerman's approach is to be found in Barry *et al.* (1983). For the debate on contract law see Fried (1981), Kronman (1980) and Waddams (1976).

The background to the economic analysis of law is well covered in Burrows and Veljanovski (1981). Posner's own works are very readable. See particularly Posner (1977). General critiques of Posner are to be found in Baker (1975) and Coleman (1984). For the application of EAL to criminal law see Becker (1968).

'Desert' is analysed in Kleinig (1971), Feinberg (1970a) and Garcia (1980). The justice as desert approach is criticised in Goodin (1985). For Rawls on desert, see Slote (1973). Issues of remuneration are considered in Dick (1975) and Sher (1979). The balancing theory of justice occurs in Ake (1975) and there is a similar thesis on the reciprocity theory of criminal law in Murphy (1979).

The dispute about Marxian justice is dealt with in Cohen *et al.* (1980), Buchanan (1982) and Wood (1983). For a more general discussion of socialism and justice, see Campbell (1983), Lukes (1985) and Elster (1985).

Not everyone will agree with the emphases of this book. More attention could have been given to Nozick and his critics, for which see Jeffrey (1981), and to traditional natural law theory, for which see Finnis (1980). Contemporary 'communitarian' approaches, which are dealt with in Chapter 1 and mentioned in Chapter 7 of this work, are exemplified by Sandel (1982), Walzer (1983) and MacIntyre (1981). A recent and important book which was published too late to be considered in the text is Heller (1986).

Bibliography

Ackerman, B. A. (1971) 'Regulating Slum Housing Markets', in *Yale Law Journal*, vol. 80.

—— (1980) *Social Justice in the Liberal State* (New Haven: Yale University Press).

—— (1984) *Reconstructing American Law* (Cambridge, Mass.: Harvard University Press).

Acton, H. B. (1973) (ed.) *The Philosophy of Punishment* (London: Macmillan).

Ake, C. (1975) 'Justice as Equality', in *Philosophy and Public Affairs*, vol. 5.

Arrow, K. (1984) *Social Choice and Justice* (Oxford: Blackwell).

Arthur, J. and W. H. Shaw (1978) (eds) *Justice and Economic Distribution* (Englewood Cliffs: Prentice-Hall).

Baker, C. E. (1975) 'The Ideology of the Economic Analysis of Law', in *Philosophy and Public Affairs*, vol. 5.

Barry, B. (1965) *Political Argument* (London: Routledge & Kegan Paul).

—— (1973) *The Liberal Theory of Justice* (Oxford: Clarendon Press).

——, B. R. Barber, J. S. Fishkin and R. C. Flathman (1983) 'Symposium on Justice', in *Ethics*, vol. 93.

Becker, G. S. (1968) 'Crime and Punishment: An Economic Approach', in *The Journal of Political Economy*, vol. 76.

Benditt, T. M. (1985) 'The Demands of Justice', in *Ethics*, vol. 95.

Blocker, H. G. and E. H. Smith (1980) (eds), *John Rawls' Theory of Social Justice* (Athens: Ohio University Press).

Buchanan, A. E. (1982) *Marx and Justice* (London: Methuen).

Burrows, P. and C. G. Veljanovski (1981) *The Economic Approach to Law* (London: Butterworths).

Campbell, T. D. (1973) 'Formal Justice and Rule Change', in *Analysis*, vol. 33.

—— (1974) 'Humanity before Justice', in *British Journal of Political Science*, vol. 4.

—— (1983) *The Left and Rights* (London: Routledge & Kegan Paul).

——, D. Goldberg, S. McLean and T. Mullen (1986) *Human Rights: From Rhetoric to Reality* (Oxford: Blackwell).

Carr, C. L. (1981) 'The Concept of Formal Justice', in *Philosophical Studies*, vol. 39.

Coase, R. H. (1960) 'The Problem of Social Cost', in *Journal of Legal Studies*, vol. 3.

Cohen, M. (1984) *Ronald Dworkin and Contemporary Jurisprudence* (London: Gerald Duckworth).

——, T. Nagel and T. Scanlon (1980) (eds) *Marx, Justice and History* (Princeton University Press).

Coleman, I. (1984) 'Economics and the Law: A Critical Review of the Foundations of the Economic Approach to Law', in *Ethics*, vol. 94.

Daniels, N. (1975) *Reading Rawls* (Oxford: Blackwell).

Dick, J. C. (1975) 'How to Justify a Distribution of Earnings', in *Philosophy and Public Affairs*, vol. 4.

Duff, R. A. (1986) *Trials and Punishments* (Cambridge University Press).

Dworkin, R. M. (1978) *Taking Rights Seriously* (2nd impression) (London: Gerald Duckworth),

—— (1981) 'What is Equality?', in *Philosophy and Public Affairs*, vol. 10.

—— (1985) *A Matter of Principle* (Cambridge, Mass.: Harvard University Press).

—— (1986) *Law's Empire* (London: Fontana).

Eckhoff, T. (1974) *Justice* (Rotterdam University Press).

Elster, J. (1985) *Making Sense of Marx* (Cambridge University Press).

Feinberg, J. (1970a) *Doing and Deserving* (Princeton University Press).

—— (1970b) 'The Nature and Value of Rights', in *Journal of Value Inquiry*, vol. 4.

—— (1973) *Social Philosophy* (Englewood Cliffs, N.J.: Prentice-Hall).

Finnis, J. (1980) *Natural Law and Natural Rights* (Oxford: Clarendon Press).

Fishkin, J. (1983) *Justice, Equal Opportunity and the Family* (New Haven: Yale University Press).

Fried, C. (1981) *Contract as Promise* (Cambridge, Mass.: Harvard University Press).

—— (1985) 'Distributive Justice', in *Social Philosophy and Policy*, vol. 1.

Friedrich, C. J. and J. W. Chapman (1983) (eds) *Justice: Nomos VI* (New York: Atherton Press).

Fuller, L. L. (1969) *The Morality of Law* (revised ed) (New Haven: Yale University Press).

Galston, W. A. (1980) *Justice and The Human Good* (University of Chicago Press).

Garcia, L. A. (1980) 'Two Concepts of Desert', in *Law and Philosophy*, vol. 5.

Gauthier, D. (1974) 'Justice and Natural Endowments', *Social Theory and Practice*, vol. 3.

Gewirth, A. (1978) *Reason and Morality* (Chicago University Press).

Gilbert, A. (1982) 'An Ambiguity in Marx's and Engels' Account of Justice and Equality', in *The American Political Science Review*, vol. 76.

Goldman, A. H. (1979) *Justice and Reverse Discrimination* (Princeton University Press).

Goodin, R. E. (1985) 'Negating Positive Desert Claims', in *Political Theory*, vol. 13.

Hare, R. M. (1952) *The Language of Morals* (Oxford: Clarendon Press).

—— (1962) *Freedom and Reason*, (Oxford: Clarendon Press).

—— (1973) 'Rawls's Theory of Justice', in *Philosophical Quarterly*, vol. 23.

Hart, H. L. A. (1961) *The Concept of Law* (Oxford University Press).

—— (1973) 'Bentham on Legal Rights', in A. W. B. Simpson (ed.) *Oxford Essays in Jurisprudence* (Oxford: Clarendon Press).

Hayek, F. A. (1976) *The Mirage of Justice* (London: Routledge & Kegan Paul).

Heller, A. (1986) *Beyond Justice* (Oxford: Blackwell).

Honore, A. M. (1970) 'Social Justice', in R. S. Summers (ed.) *Essays in Legal Philosophy* (Oxford: Basil Blackwell).

Hume, D. (1739) *A Treatise of Human Nature* (London: John Noon).

Jackson, M. W. (1986) *Matters of Justice* (London: Croom Helm).

Jeffrey, P. (1981) *Reading Nozick* (Totowa: Rowan and Littlefield).

Kamenka, E. and A. E. Tay (1979) (eds) *Justice* (London: Edward Arnold).

Katzner, L. I. (1971) 'Presumptive and Non-Presumptive Principles of Formal Justice', in *Ethics*, vol. 81.

Kleinig, J. (1971) 'The Concept of Desert', in *American Philosophical Quarterly*, vol. 8.

Kronman, A. T. (1980) 'Contract Law and Distributive Justice', in *Yale Law Journal*, vol. 89.

Lessnoff, M. (1986) *Social Contract* (London: Macmillan).

Lucas, J. R. (1980) *On Justice* (Oxford: Clarendon Press).

Lukes, S. (1985) *Marxism and Morality* (Oxford University Press).

Lyons, D. (1965) *Forms and Limits of Utilitarianism* (Oxford: Clarendon Press).

MacCormick, D. N. (1977) 'Rights in Legislation', in P. M. S. Hacker and J. Raz (eds) *Law, Morality and Society* (Oxford: Clarendon Press).

MacIntyre, A. (1981) *After Virtue* (Notre Dame University Press).

Macpherson, C. B. (1977) *The Life and Times of Liberal Democracy* (Oxford University Press).

Marx, K. and F. Engels (1958) *Selected Works* (2 volume ed) (London: Lawrence and Wishart).

Mill, J. S. (1863) 'Utilitarianism', in J. S. Mill (1910) *Utilitarianism, Liberty, Representative Government* (London: J. M. Dent).

Miller, D. (1976) *Social Justice* (Oxford: Clarendon Press).

Murphy, J. (1979) *Retribution, Justice and Therapy* (Boston, Mass.: D. Reidel).

Nielsen, K. (1979) 'Radical Egalitarian Justice: Justice as Equality', in *Social Theory and Practice*, vol. 5.

Nozick, R. (1974) *Anarchy, State and Utopia* (Oxford: Blackwell).

O'Connor, F. (1977) 'Justice, Desert and Rawls', in *Philosophical Studies*, vol. 25.

Pennock, J. R. and J. W. Chapman (1982) *Ethics, Economics and the Law: Nomos XXIV* (New York University Press).

Perelman, C. (1963) *The Idea of Justice and the Problem of Argument* (London: Routledge & Kegan Paul).

Pettit, P. (1980) *Judging Justice* (London: Routledge & Kegan Paul).

Plant, R., H. Lesser and P. Taylor-Gooby (1980) *Political Philosophy and Social Welfare* (London: Routledge & Kegan Paul).

Posner, R. A. (1977) *Economic Analysis of Law*, (2nd ed) (Boston, Mass.: Little, Brown).

—— (1979) 'Utilitarianism, Economics and Legal Theory', in *Journal of Legal Studies*, vol. 8.

—— (1981) *The Economics of Justice* (Cambridge Mass.: Harvard University Press).

Raphael, D. D. (1970) *Problems of Political Philosophy* (London: Pall Mall).

—— (1980) *Justice and Liberty* (London: The Athlone Press).

Rawls, J. (1971) *A Theory of Justice* (Oxford University Press).

—— (1980) 'Kantian Constructivism in Moral Theory', in *Journal of Philosophy*, vol. 77.

Raz, J. (1975) *Practical Reason and Norms* (London: Hutchinson).

—— (1982) 'The Claims of Reflective Equilibrium', in *Inquiry*, vol. 25.

Rescher, N. (1966) *Distributive Justice* (Indianapolis: Bobbs–Merrill).

Runciman, W. G. (1966) *Relative Deprivation and Social Justice* (London: Routledge & Kegan Paul).

Sadurski, W. (1985) *Giving Desert its Due: Social Justice and Legal Theory* (Dordrecht: Reidel).

Sandel, M. J. (1982) *Liberalism and the Limits of Justice* (New York: Cambridge University Press).

Sen, A. K. (1970) *Collective Choice and Social Welfare* (San Francisco: Holden–Day).

Sher, G. (1979) 'Effort, Ability and Personal Desert', in *Philosophy and Public Affairs*, vol. 8.

Sidgwick, H. (1901) *The Methods of Ethics* (6th ed) (London: Macmillan).

Slote, M. A. (1973) 'Desert, Consent and Justice', in *Philosophy and Public Affairs*, vol. 2.

Sterba, J. P. (1974) 'Justice as Desert', in *Social Theory and Practice*, vol. 3.

—— (1986) 'Recent Work on Alternative Conceptions of Justice', in *American Philosophical Quarterly*, vol. 23.

Veljanovski, C. J. (1982) *The New Law and Economics* (Oxford: Centre for Socio-Legal Studies, Oxford).

Waddams, S. M. (1976) 'Unconscionability in Contracts', in *Modern Law Review*, vol. 39.

Waldron, J. (1984) *Theories of Rights* (Oxford University Press).

Walzer, M. (1983) *Spheres of Justice* (Oxford: Martin Robertson).

Weale, A. (1983) *Political Theory and Social Policy* (London: Macmillan).

Wolff, R. P. (1977) *Understanding Rawls* (Princeton University Press).

Wood, A. W. (1983) *Karl Marx* (London: Routledge & Kegan Paul).

Zaitchik, A. (1977) 'On Deserving to Deserve', in *Philosophy and Public Affairs*, vol. 6.

Index